A PICTURE HISTORY OF EASTERN EUROPE

EASTERN EUROPE

Present Boundaries

0   250   500

Tallinn
ESTONIA

LATVIA
Riga

LITHUANIA
Vilnius

EAST
Berlin
GERMANY

POLAND
Warsaw

Prague
CZECHOSLOVAKIA

UKRAINE
Kiev

Budapest
HUNGARY

ROMANIA

Belgrade
YUGOSLAVIA

Bucharest

Sofia   BULGARIA

Tiranë
ALBANIA

A PICTURE HISTORY OF EASTERN EUROPE

by ELLSWORTH RAYMOND

Head, Russian Area Studies · New York University

and JOHN STUART MARTIN

author of *A Picture History of Russia*

CROWN PUBLISHERS INC., NEW YORK

LIBRARY OF CONGRESS CATALOG CARD NUMBER: 76–93415
PRINTED IN THE UNITED STATES OF AMERICA

PUBLISHED SIMULTANEOUSLY IN CANADA BY GENERAL PUBLISHING COMPANY LIMITED

Contents

Acknowledgments

INVALUABLE ADVICE and assistance in preparing this book were generously given by many experts on East European countries. Various chapters were enriched with special information added by these thorough scholars: Alex Harsanyi; Leonhard Vahter, Chairman, Committee for a Free Estonia; Vilis Hazners, Chairman, Committee for a Free Latvia; Dr. Rexhep Krasniqi, former professor of history in Tiranë; Kestutis Ciziunas, doctoral candidate in Eastern European history at New York University; and the following professors of New York University: Dr. Gisbert Flanz and Colonel Roman Michalowski of the Department of Politics; Dr. J. Robert Wegs of the Department of History; and Bernard Koten, Director of the university's Russian Library.

Substantial help, in a number of important ways, was provided by: Dr. Paul Horecky, Library of Congress; Mrs. Yolanda Horan; Dr. Jaroslav Steyn; Mrs. Galia Zilionis, Donnell Library, New York City, and Committee for Free Lithuania; Peter Shumanoff, Bulgarian National Committee; Dr. Georgi Dimitrov, President, Bulgarian National Committee; John Lexa, Czechoslovakia Society of Arts and Sciences; Dr. Josef Korbel, Free Europe Committee; Uno Teemant, Library of Congress; Ernst Jaakson, Estonian Consul-General; A. Waldman, Estonian Education Society; Imre Kovacs, Free Europe Committee; Dr. Elmer Bako, Library of Congress; August Molnar, Rutgers The State University; Hon. Arnold Spekke, Minister-in-Exile from Latvia; Mrs. Victoria Checheta; Professor Ludwig Krzyzanowski, Polish Institute of Arts and Sciences; John Vardala, Romanian National Committee; Fric Frankl, Yugoslav Information Bureau; Nikola Vukicevic, Yugoslav Embassy, Washington, D.C.

The difficult task of procuring appropriate pictures was greatly eased by Professor Ludwig Krzyzanowski, Secretary-General of the Polish Institute of Arts and Sciences in America, who placed the entire facilities of his institute at our disposal. Mrs. Anna Lipski, the institute's librarian, personally unearthed many rare books containing equally rare paintings, photographs, and portraits. Karlis Balodis, Curator of the American Latvian Association Exhibition, allowed unrestricted use of his exhibit pictures and charts. Reproduction photography of both book and exhibit pictures was performed by Alan Raymond.

Very helpful was Alfreds Berzins, former Latvian Minister for Public Works and Social Affairs, who loaned us his private collection of political pictures. Both the Bulgarian Tourist Office and Albanian Mission to the United Nations donated many official photographs of scenes in their home countries.

The immense task of seeking, selecting, and assembling the thousand photographs in this book was primarily performed by Mrs. Sandra Norre, Patricia Appel, and John Stuart Martin.

All maps are by Graphic 70.

Key to special picture-credit abbreviations:

BTO — Bulgarian Tourist Office
CTB — Czechoslovak Travel Bureau
ECG — Consulate General of Estonia
EPA — Editorial Photocolor Archives, Inc.
LC — Library of Congress
NYPL — New York Public Library
PIAS — Polish Institute of Arts and Sciences
PTB — Polish Tourist Bureau
SAM — Socialist Albania on the March
UDS — Ústav Dějin Socialismu

Preface

"I WILL SHAKE MY LITTLE FINGER—and there will be no more Tito," Stalin said. "He will fall."

"No matter how much or how little Stalin shook," said Khrushchev, "not only his little finger but everything else that he could shake, Tito did not fall. Why? . . . Tito was backed by a state and a people that had gone through a severe school of fighting for liberty and independence, a people who supported their leaders."

And Tito: "Just look how a barehanded and poorly armed people offers fierce resistance when it has one goal—to free itself and to be independent."

These bitter statements from both sides of the Soviet-Yugoslav dispute again confirm an age-old truth: no Great Power can permanently enslave Eastern Europe.

Many have tried. In antiquity the Romans, Huns, Avars, and Byzantines created great empires ruling large East European areas. Later came conquests by the Germans, Austrians, Tsarist Russians, and Ottoman Turks. Every East European nation has suffered for centuries under harsh alien rule. And each nation in some cruel era has lost half its population by being the hapless battleground for unwanted wars.

By iron will and immense persistence the East European nations have survived all alien tyranny, never losing their native languages, traditions, or culture. Often they rebelled against foreign oppression, and were proud to be rebels even if the revolt ended in bloody failure.

Both World Wars began in Eastern Europe, when small Slavic countries rejected harsh demands from Germanic Great Powers. World War I erupted after Serbia refused to accept all the terms of an Austrian ultimatum. Hitler unleashed World War II because Poland dared to defy him. Neither the Aus-

trian Empire nor Hitler survived the world wars that they started, but Poland and Serbia (now within Yugoslavia) are still energetically alive.

Into East Europe at the end of World War II came a new conqueror—Russia's Red Army. Ignoring East Europe's passion for freedom, Moscow tried to create a new oppressive Communist empire. The results were almost predictable: Balkan leader Tito soon quarreled with Stalin, who in 1948 angrily expelled Yugoslavia from the Soviet orbit of nations. Stalin's death in 1953 was celebrated throughout East Germany by widespread worker riots. Khrushchev's clumsy destalinization of 1956 created a bloodless Polish revolution, which freed Poland's internal affairs from Soviet control.

In the same fateful year all Hungary rose in a rebellion which only a huge Soviet army could suppress. Next to defy giant Russia was tiny Albania, which was driven out of the Soviet orbit in 1961. Meanwhile Romania began wooing the West and reducing Romanian-Russian cooperation. By 1968, 200,000 Soviet troops had to invade Czechoslovakia to block a Czech changeover from Communist dictatorship to socialist democracy. Like all previous empires, Russia is learning from bitter experience that East Europeans cannot be forever enserfed.

In words and pictures, this book relates the story of East Europe's centuries of struggle against alien tyranny. This story is incomplete, because more East European rebellions will occur in the future.

In compiling this book, place-names presented a major problem. Many regions, cities, rivers, lakes, and even countries possess two or more names, given by ruling nations in different eras. We have adopted the policy of using the names most familiar to the

West. Thus the book refers to "Albania" instead of the more correct "Shqiperi," Livonia rather than Vidzeme, and Stettin instead of Szczecin.

Many of the statistics cited in this book are approximate rather than real. Pre-World War II figures are generally accurate, but the postwar Communist statistics contain many distortions in an attempt to prove Marxist progress. Communist statisticians often count industrial waste and spoilage as part of production, list a field crop rather than the smaller actual harvest, or change methods of computation if the change makes Communism look better. With the exception of Lithuania, the countries described in this book refuse to reveal the enormity of damage wrought by World War II. Therefore many of the "post-World War II" statistics actually refer to 1948 or 1949, when some peacetime recovery had already occurred.

To be absolutely precise, prewar, postwar, and present statistics should deal with identical areas. But of our book's twelve countries, five (Czechoslovakia, Estonia, Hungary, Poland, and Romania) lost territory as a result of World War II. Four others (Bulgaria, Lithuania, the Ukraine, and Yugoslavia) made small territorial gains. East Germany did not exist before the Second World War, and prewar statistics were not compiled according to present boundaries. Thus the book's prewar and postwar statistics must compare nations rather than national areas.

Despite all these faults, the statistics reveal the great changes in East Europe between prewar, postwar, and present periods. Only too clear is the wartime massacre of millions of Jews, and the postwar expulsion of Germans from non-Teutonic East Europe into East Germany. In the Communist period, industry, education, and urbanization have vastly expanded everywhere in East Europe, while agriculture and transportation have progressed much less and sometimes even regressed. The prewar Uniate Church has simply vanished, with its worshipers forced to join the Orthodox faith. And as the statistics show, most East European nations still enjoy a higher standard of living than the mighty Russians.

ELLSWORTH RAYMOND

EAST EUROPEAN STANDARDS OF LIVING
(compared to West Germany and the USSR)

Country	% of West German level	% of USSR level
East Germany	66	183
Czechoslovakia	59	164
Estonia	52	144
Hungary	51	141
Latvia	50	139
Bulgaria	44	122
Poland	38	105
Lithuania	37	103
Ukraine	36	100
Romania	33	92

THE ARMED FORCES OF EASTERN EUROPE

Country	Manpower			Equipment		
	Army	Air Force	Navy	Tanks	Combat Planes	Largest Warships
(Independent Communist countries)						
Albania	35,000	2,500	4,000	110	70	4 submarines
Yugoslavia	200,000	20,000	18,000	650	340	{ 5 submarines 3 destroyers
(Warsaw Pact nations)						
Bulgaria	130,000	12,000	7,000	2,000	290	2 submarines
Czechoslovakia	150,000	18,000	—	3,400	620	—
East Germany	92,000	21,000	16,000	1,900	275	3 destroyers
Hungary	90,000	10,000	1,500	750	150	4 gunboats
Poland	195,000	25,000	22,000	2,950	800	{ 5 submarines 3 destroyers
Romania	165,000	8,000	8,000	1,450	250	3 escorts
East Europe Warsaw Pact totals	822,000	94,000	54,500	12,450	2,385	{ 7 submarines 6 destroyers 4 gunboats 3 escorts

RUSSIAN ARMIES STATIONED IN EAST EUROPE
Soviet Occupation Forces

Occupied country	Divisions Motorized	Divisions Armored	Troops	Tanks
Poland	—	2	16,500	650
Hungary	2	2	36,500	1,000
Czechoslovakia	5	—	50,000	775
East Germany	10	10	182,500	5,000
	17	14	285,500	7,425

PART 1

THE SOVIET SATELLITES

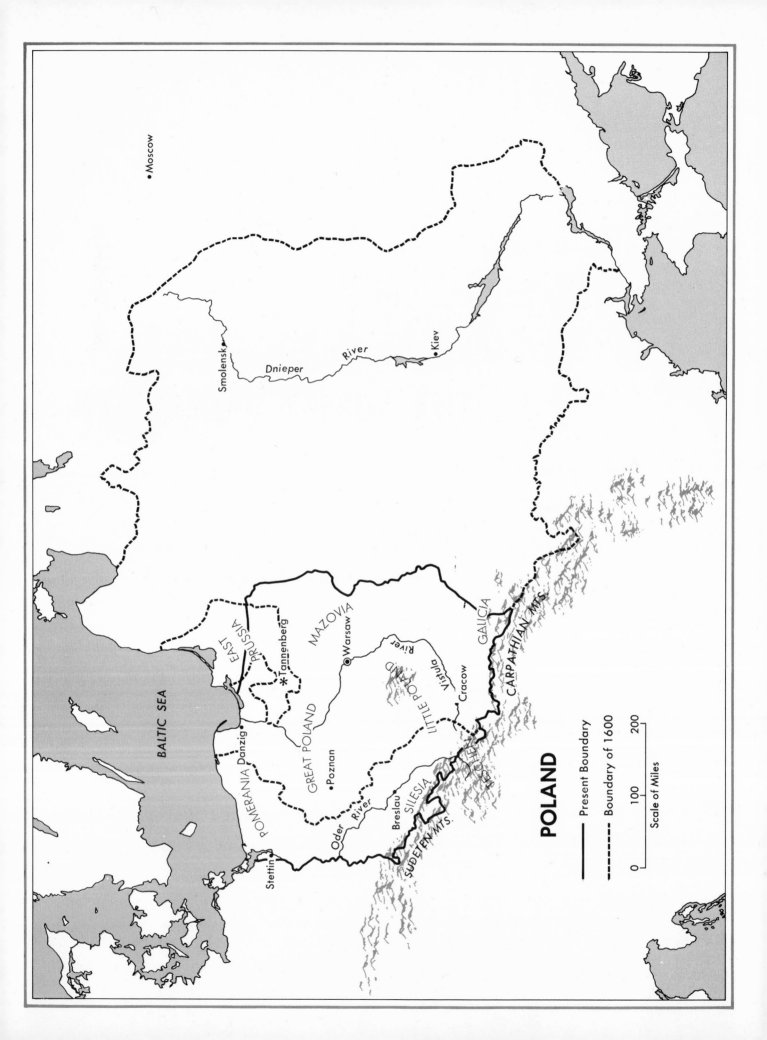

POLAND

— Present Boundary
---- Boundary of 1600

Scale of Miles
0   100   200

Moscow

Smolensk

Dnieper River

Kiev

BALTIC SEA

EAST PRUSSIA

Tannenberg

MAZOVIA

Warsaw

POMERANIA

Danzig

GREAT POLAND

Poznan

LITTLE POLAND

Vistula River

Cracow

GALICIA

CARPATHIAN MTS.

BOHEMIA

SILESIA

Breslau

Oder River

SUDETEN MTS.

Stettin

Poland

BRAVE, PROUD, freedom-loving Poland is the most dramatic of all East European countries. No other nation has reached such heights of glory only to sink into utter humiliation. Medieval Poland ruled a great empire extending from the Baltic to the Black Sea. Among East European countries the Polish kingdom was the first to curb autocracy, the first to tolerate all religions, and the only one welcoming large-scale immigration by the Jews.

But parliamentary anarchy finally paralyzed the Polish monarchy, which also sapped its strength fighting endless foreign wars. As modern history dawned, Poland began to lose its vast empire. Then the Polish kingdom simply disappeared from the map, gobbled up by its more powerful neighbors. For a century and a half there was no Poland. Instead, there were only Poles, struggling to keep their culture and identity alive under alien rule.

A brief period of freedom between the two World Wars ended in the terror of Nazi occupation, which was succeeded by the Communist dictatorship still ruling today.

One wonders how the Polish nation could survive such tragedies. Countless Poles perished in modern wars, while others emigrated to seek a safer life. The United States today has no less than six million citizens of Polish descent.

Yet tremendous endurance was displayed by the Poles who did not emigrate, for Poland not only survives, but has the largest population of any East European country. Though resenting dictatorial Communist rule, the tall, blondish Poles do not despair. They describe themselves as "hopeful romantics," waiting for another chance to regain real democratic freedom.

Besides being largest in population of all East European countries, Poland has the largest territory; its area of 121,000 square miles is as big as the state of New Mexico. Roughly rectangular in shape, Poland is bounded on the north by the Baltic Sea, on the east and northeast by the Soviet Union, on the west by Germany, and on the south by Czechoslovakia.

Only in the south does Poland have easily defensible frontiers in the Carpathian and Sudeten Mountains. The word "Poland" means "field country," a logical name since most of Poland is one vast plain. In ancient times this plain was covered by forests which gave the early Poles some protection from outside invasion. During medieval centuries, Polish peasants cleared the trees to create plowland, so four-fifths of present-day Poland is open fields. Huge crops of grain, potatoes, and sugar beets grow on these fertile fields, which also feed large herds of cattle, sheep, horses, and hogs. Poland is second only to the Soviet Union in harvests of potatoes and rye, and it exports fine ham to all parts of the world.

A view of the countryside in Little Poland, showing the broad fertile fields and small forests typical of almost all Polish territories. *EPA*

Since the "field country" can easily be invaded by land from either east or west, and even by boat from the Baltic Sea, Poland has a grave geographic weakness that has lured countless invaders. It has also been the historic highway for European attack on Russia and for Russian invasion of Europe. Along such a strategic highway there can be little peace. Poland has often been the first victim of someone else's war.

Traveling across Poland, one sees a flat plain with patches of woods. There appears to be little difference between one province and the next, but contrasts in history have given distinctive names to various areas. In the west is Great Poland, the homeland of the first Polish kings. Originally a land of marshes, Great Poland long ago was re-

claimed by drainage into very fertile soil. Here the largest city is Poznan, founded in the tenth century and the site of Poland's first Catholic bishopric. In modern times Poznan became a great center of armament industry, and since 1922 has held an annual international trade fair attended by businessmen from all corners of the world.

In the south of the field country is Little Poland, the birthplace of Polish culture. Its largest city is Cracow (Krakow), founded in the fourth century and capital of Poland from the twelfth to the sixteenth centuries; no other Polish city has so many historic buildings and monuments. Cracow is the site of Poland's first university and abounds in castles, churches, and scientific academies. Besides being the intellectual center of Poland, it has many

From prize pigs like these comes the tasty Polish ham, which is exported to stores and restaurants all over the world. *PIAS*

Poland has many open plains, providing lush pasture for large herds of cattle. *PIAS*

Mechanized grain harvesting on one of the few Polish collective farms. *PIAS*

For many centuries cavalry were the shock troops of the Polish army. Though cavalry has been outdated by tanks, large herds of pedigree horses are still raised and used as draft animals on private and collective farms. *PIAS*

Peasant huts and a flock of fat sheep in the south Polish highlands just north of the Carpathian Mountains. *PIAS*

Poland is a great grower of sugar beets, here being harvested by special machines which unearth the beet roots. *PIAS*

Poznan, the largest city in Great Poland, is still governed from this medieval city hall which was built in the late thirteenth century. *EPA*

The exhibition halls and grounds of Poznan's annual international trade fair, where Western businessmen bargain with Communist commercial bureaucrats. *PTB*

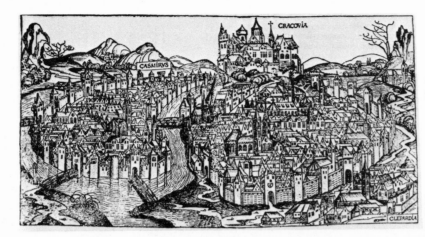

Cracow, Little Poland's largest city, as it looked in the Middle Ages. *PIAS*

Largely destroyed during World War II, the Polish capital city of Warsaw was rebuilt with something new added: broad modern expressways to speed automobile traffic. *PTB*

factories, including the largest steel plant in the country.

Central Poland is known as Mazovia, which from the twelfth to the sixteenth centuries was an autonomous princedom separate from the Polish state. The main city is Warsaw, the capital of the Polish nation since 1595. With its population of 1,300,000, Warsaw is the largest city in Poland. Almost totally destroyed during World War II, Warsaw was rebuilt to accommodate modern traffic; two expressways crisscross the city east-west and north-south. As reconstruction progressed, the Polish Communist government carefully restored Warsaw's palaces, churches, monuments, and medieval "old town" to look exactly the same as before. Most of Warsaw's buildings are low, so the skyline is dominated by the Soviet-built Palace of Culture—a lavishly ornamented skyscraper with the appearance of a gigantic wedding cake. Vividly reminding the Poles of Soviet overlordship, the palace was

Warsaw's medieval "Old Town," destroyed during World War II and carefully restored brick by brick to be preserved as a historic monument. *PTB*

Modern Warsaw's skyline is dominated by the skyscraper "Palace of Culture"—a gift from Stalin to appease the Polish people after his Red Army failed to save the city from destruction by Nazi German troops. *PTB*

a gift to the Polish people from Stalin. (He would probably turn in his grave if he heard today's jazz and rock-and-roll bands blasting wild music in the palace halls.)

Great Poland, Little Poland, and Mazovia are the Polish heartland. Around them are other areas, sometimes Polish in the past and now again within Polish frontiers. In the northwest along the Baltic coast lies Pomerania, which literally means "by the sea." With its yellow beaches flanked by green pine forests, this is one of the most scenic regions of Poland. Here the chief city is Stettin (Szczecin), a huge port where the Oder River flows into the Baltic Sea. Famous for two enormous churches, Stettin has a diversified industry including large shipbuilding yards.

In northeast Poland, also along the Baltic Sea, is East Prussia (now Masuria), which contains thousands of wooded lakes as well as beautiful beaches. In the forests live small herds of an almost extinct animal—the European bison. At the mouth of the Vistula River is Danzig (now Gdansk), Poland's largest port on the Baltic Sea.

A close-up of Warsaw's Soviet-built Palace of Culture, showing the tasteless stone ornaments so typical of Stalinist architecture. *PTB*

Stettin (now Szczecin), largest city and biggest seaport in Polish Pomerania. This view from the water shows massive buildings constructed by the former German rulers. *PTB*

THE POLISH NATION

	Pre- World War II	Post- World War II	Present
Area (square miles)	150,000	120,664	120,664
Population	35,300,000	23,900,000	32,300,000

	In percent of total population		
Rate of literacy	77%	77%	95%
Urban populace	39%	30%	50%

Major nationalities			
Poles	69%	98%	98%
Ukrainians	14%		
Jews	9%	2%	2%
Belorussians	6%		
Germans	2%		

Main religions			
Catholic	75%	94%	96%
Orthodox and Protestant	15%	4%	3%
Jewish	10%	2%	1%

THE POLISH ECONOMY

	Unit of Measurement	Pre- World War II	Post- World War II	Present
Industrial Production				
Electricity	(kilowatt-hours)	3,900,000,000	6,600,000,000	55,500,000,000
Steel	(metric tons)	1,400,000	1,600,000	11,000,000
Iron ore	" "	800,000	500,000	800,000
Coal	" "	38,000,000	70,000,000	129,000,000
Salt	" "	600,000	600,000	2,500,000
Cement	" "	1,700,000	1,500,000	11,600,000
Refined sugar	" "	500,000	900,000	1,800,000
Agricultural Production				
Wheat	" "	2,000,000	1,600,000	3,900,000
Rye	" "	6,500,000	6,300,000	7,800,000
Barley	" "	1,400,000	1,000,000	1,400,000
Oats	" "	2,600,000	2,400,000	2,800,000
Potatoes	" "	35,000,000	26,700,000	48,600,000
Length of railways	(miles)	11,200	8,000	17,000

With its narrow streets, gabled houses, old churches, city gates, and many towers, Danzig looks like a quaint medieval town. But it has large shipyards and many factories producing consumer goods.

Before World War II, Poland was an agrarian nation, though a small heavy industry operated in the Polish part of Silesia. After the war Poland inherited much more heavy industry by annexing German Silesia. Located along the Oder valley in southwest Poland, Silesia is rich in deposits of coal, iron, and other minerals. The east bank of the Oder is a fertile plain, while the west bank contains foothills of the Sudeten Mountains. Silesia's largest city and chief industrial center is Breslau (now Wroclaw), producing railway cars and various types of machinery. Late in World War II, Breslau was heavily bombed by a British-American mass air raid, then further destroyed when the Germans leveled the city center to build an airfield. Much of the city still lies in ruins.

A confusing geographic term is "Galicia,"

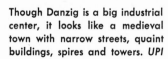

Danzig (now Gdansk) is Poland's largest port on the Baltic Sea. *UPI*

Though Danzig is a big industrial center, it looks like a medieval town with narrow streets, quaint buildings, spires and towers. *UPI*

In the forests of East Prussia (now Masuria) live small herds of European bison —wild animals that once roamed much of Europe but are now almost extinct.

Above right: By inheriting German Silesia after World War II, Poland gained a huge heavy industry it had never possessed before. Pictured above is one of the Silesian steel mills. *PIAS*

Center: Silesian coal ready for shipment. Poland earns much hard currency by selling coal and coke to Western Europe. *PIAS*

Below: Breslau (now Wroclaw) on the Oder River is the largest city and biggest industrial center in Silesia. Largely destroyed during World War II, the city is still repairing war damage. *PTB*

whose area has often changed. During medieval centuries, it included southeast Poland plus adjacent Russian lands. In more modern times, when Austria controlled much Polish territory, all southern Poland constituted the Austrian province of Galicia. Today, Galicia is simply a hilly wooded region in the Polish southeast.

All these regions are interconnected by an elaborate system of inland waterways. Poland has many rivers, the two largest being the Vistula and the Oder. The rivers are linked together by various canals. From Warsaw, on the Vistula River, one can sail by canalboat across Poland into either Germany or western Russia. Poland also has a good railway network and some long-distance highways. Warsaw is the main junction for all types of transportation.

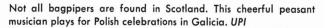

Floating timber on a fast-flowing river in the Galician hills. *PIAS*

Not all bagpipers are found in Scotland. This cheerful peasant musician plays for Polish celebrations in Galicia. *UPI*

East Poland and adjacent Russian territories were the original homeland of all Slavic peoples. Therefore, the Poles, who are West Slavs like the Czechs and Slovaks, inhabited Poland from ancient times. The early Poles were pagan tribes, slowly clearing the forests and protected from outside invasion by heavily wooded frontiers. No great ancient trade routes crossed Poland, whose northern location was also out of the path of the barbarian hordes attacking the Roman Empire. For centuries Poland slumbered in relative peace and isolation. Despite intensive historical research, scholars know very little about the ancient Poles.

In Greater Poland early in the ninth century, a forgotten dynasty of unknown name united the tribes of Polians—the "people of the fields," whose name, modified to "Poles," was later adopted by the entire Polish nation.

Much of Poland's bulk freight travels along rivers interconnected by canals. A view of barge traffic on the Vistula River. *EPA*

During the mid-ninth century, the first Polish dynasty was succeeded by a second, allegedly founded by a peasant named Piast. Modern Polish historians believe that "Piast" was probably the formal title of a court official of the first dynasty. The official overthrew his ruler and established a new dynasty named after his old title.

So poor are the records that we do not know the names of the first three Piast princes. But these unknown geniuses created the first Polish state by uniting Little Poland, Mazovia, and Silesia to Great Poland.

Polish recorded history begins in the year 963, when a minor German count invaded Poland with a small band of troops, who were easily defeated by Mieszko I—the fourth ruler of the Piast dynasty. But the brilliant Prince Mieszko realized that the Holy Roman Empire of Germany was a grave danger to the Polish realm, and that many more Teutonic invasions could be expected in the future. So he brought Poland out of isolation into the European community of nations. After marrying the Czech Princess Dubravka, who was Christian, Mieszko converted himself and the entire Polish na-

A fine highway and the Dunajec River wind through the rich farmlands and Carpathian foothills of southern Poland. *EPA*

Prince Mieszko I (960–92) was not the first Polish ruler but is the first whose name was ever recorded. He repulsed a German invasion of Poland. *PIAS*

Czech Princess Dubravka, who married Mieszko I in 965, was a Christian who induced her pagan husband to adopt Christianity both for himself and for his Polish nation. *PIAS*

tion to Catholicism. The Germans could still invade Poland, but nevermore could justify their aggression as a crusade to bring Christianity to Slavic heathens. Mieszko also paid tribute to the Holy Roman Emperor, and to safeguard his princedom put all Polish lands under the protection of the Pope of Rome.

Mieszko was succeeded by his son Boleslaw I the Mighty (992–1025), who conquered part of the Ukraine, including its capital city of Kiev. To free Poland from religious domination by German bishops, Prince Boleslaw convinced the Pope to establish a Polish archbishopric governing the Polish church. In 1024, shortly before his death, Boleslaw elevated his realm from a principality to a kingdom by being crowned King of Poland. During his reign, Poland's first literature appeared in the form of historical "annals," written in the church language of Latin.

Boleslaw the Mighty was succeeded by Mieszko II the Weak (1025–34), who lost considerable territory, some of which was regained by the next king—Casimir the Restorer (1038–58). After Casimir came another able ruler, Boleslaw II the Bold (1058–79). But Boleslaw finally disgraced himself by murdering Bishop Stanislas of Cracow on flimsy charges of treason. The entire Polish nation was shocked, and Stanislas was made Poland's patron saint. Boleslaw was dethroned by his brother and died in exile in a monastery, mourning his evil deed.

Happier years came during the reign of Boleslaw III (1102–38), called Wrymouth because of his crooked chin. An invasion of Silesia from the Holy Roman Empire was repulsed. Poland conquered and Christianized the Pomeranians, who were Slavs kindred to the Poles. From this period come the first Polish historical chronicles, still

Mass conversion of the Poles to Christianity in the year 966. *PIAS*

Boleslaw I the Mighty (992–1025), who in 1024 was crowned the first "King of Poland." *PIAS*

The coronation of King Boleslaw I. *PIAS*

King Mieszko II the Weak (1025–34), who lost much Polish territory to neighboring countries. *PIAS*

King Casimir the Restorer (1038–58) regained some of the lands lost by Mieszko II. *PIAS*

King Boleslaw II the Bold (1058–79) was overthrown after executing Bishop Stanislas of Cracow for alleged treason. *PIAS*

Bishop Stanislas, executed on false charges, was so revered that he was made the patron saint of Poland. *PIAS*

King Boleslaw III (1102–38) ended Polish unity by foolishly dividing his kingdom into five principalities for his five sons. *PIAS*

written in Latin but much more complete than the annals.

Wrymouth foolishly ended his kingdom by dividing Poland into several principalities so that, when he died, each of his sons would rule a separate territory. By doing so, he hoped to avoid quarrels among the sons for the kingship. But the sons quarreled anyway, and so did their successors. For two centuries Poland was a disunited nation of squabbling principalities. Benefiting from these regional feuds was the nobility, which gained privileges by supporting one prince against another.

The Germans also benefited from a divided Poland. During the thirteenth century, many German families settled in Silesia and Pomerania. The towns arising throughout all Poland were at first largely inhabited by Germans.

A grave error was made when the Prince of Mazovia in 1226 asked the Teutonic Knights to help him conquer the heathen Prussians, who were constantly invading Mazovia. The Prussians were not Slavs but an Indo-European people akin to the nearby Lithuanians. The Teutonic Knights were a German religious army originally formed to crusade against the Moslems in the Holy Land. When crusades in the Near East failed, the Knights began campaigns of conversion against various pagan tribes along the shores of the Baltic Sea.

So formidable were the Teutonic Knights that in five years they conquered all East Prussia and converted it into a German state. The original Prussians were massacred or assimilated, ceasing to exist as a nation. Today only their name remains, now meaning Germans of the Baltic coast. The Knights became a far greater danger to Poland than the Lithuanian Prussians.

Two leaders of the Teutonic knights in the fourteenth century. Considering themselves Crusaders, the Knights decorated their armor, cloaks, and shields with Christian crosses. LC

Castle built in Poland by the Teutonic Knights—the German religious army which conquered East Prussia in the thirteenth century. PTB

Another danger of the thirteenth century vanished as soon as it arose. The fierce Mongols, who had conquered giant Russia, overran Little Poland in 1241. But the Mongol generals went home to elect a new khan and their armies left Poland.

Polish unification began in 1314, when Wladyslaw I united Great and Little Poland. In 1320 he was crowned the Polish king—the first since 1138. But he was too weak to prevent the Teutonic Knights from seizing Pomerania, which became a German province.

Wladyslaw was succeeded by his son Casimir (1333–70), the only Polish king entitled "The Great." He enlarged his realm by annexing Mazovia and Galicia, and he brought peace to a Poland long troubled by war. To unite more firmly the formerly independent Polish princedoms, Casimir reformed the currency and codified the laws. In 1364 he created Poland's first university at Cracow. A great builder, he "found a country of wood, and left a country of stone." Wisely, he continued a century-old Polish policy of encouraging large-

Wladyslaw I (1305–33), the first Polish ruler to be crowned as "King of Poland" since 1138. This likeness is his statue on his tomb in Cracow cathedral. *PIAS*

King Casimir the Great (1333–70) who brought peace and unity to Poland, and enriched Polish civilization by many wise reforms. *PIAS*

King Wladyslaw I in 1321 breaking his friendship treaty with the Teutonic Knights, who then attacked Poland but were badly defeated. *PIAS*

An artist's idyllic portrayal of classes at Cracow Academy (Poland's first university), which was founded in 1364 by King Casimir the Great. *PIAS*

The Cracow Academy, as it appears today. *PIAS*

King Casimir the Great welcoming Jewish refugees from Western Europe, where they had been accused of causing an epidemic of cholera. Thousands of these refugees settled in Polish towns, contributing their skills to the growth of commerce. *PIAS*

Casimir the Great rebuilt so many cities that Poles said he "found a country of wood, and left a country of stone." So well did he build this Cracow palace, that it is still usable today. *EPA*

scale immigration by Jews, who were being expelled from many European nations. The Jewish immigrants usually settled in Polish towns, where they became a constructive middle class of tradesmen and artisans.

Casimir had no sons, so his death ended the Piast dynasty. He willed Poland to his nephew Louis I of Hungary, who was Polish king from 1370 till 1382, when he also died without male heirs. Louis had given the Polish nobility tax exemptions, in return for which he was to be succeeded by his daughter, Mary. But upon Louis's death, the nobles rejected Mary and chose his younger daughter Jadwiga to be the Polish queen. Twelve-year-old Jadwiga was delighted by her coronation ceremonies in 1384, without understanding the seriousness of the occasion.

When Jadwiga reached the ripe age of fourteen, the nobles made her marry Grand Duke Jagiello of Lithuania, who became king of Poland. Thus, peaceably, in 1386, Poland and Lithuania united into one nation.

Previously, Lithuania had been pagan. In order to gain the Polish throne, Jagiello had to adopt Christianity for both himself and his Lithuanian nation. Since Poland was Catholic, Lithuania accepted the spiritual leadership of the Pope and is still Catholic today.

The united Polish-Lithuanian kingdom was the largest empire in East Europe, for Lithuania already controlled the Western Ukraine and Belorussia (the Russian territory nearest Poland). The new kingdom soon showed its power when, in 1410, a combined Polish-Lithuanian army routed the Teutonic Knights at the Battle of Tannenberg in East Prussia. Though the Teutonic Knights continued to exist, never again were they a threat to Poland or Lithuania.

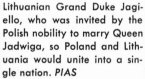

Jadwiga, a Hungarian princess who at the age of twelve became Queen of Poland in 1384.

Lithuanian Grand Duke Jagiello, who was invited by the Polish nobility to marry Queen Jadwiga, so Poland and Lithuania would unite into a single nation. *PIAS*

After the marriage in 1386, Jagiello was immediately crowned as King of Poland (1386–1434), and Poland and Lithuania combined to form Eastern Europe's largest empire. *PIAS*

The fateful Battle of Tannenberg, where in 1410 an international army led by King Jagiello routed the Teutonic Knights, who never again were a threat to Poland-Lithuania. *PIAS*

Monument in Cracow commemorating Poland's victory at Tannenberg. The knight on horseback is Jagiello. *PIAS*

King Casimir IV (1447–92) was a great military leader, conquering Moldavia, Pomerania, and East Prussia. *LC*

Nicolaus Copernicus (1473–1543), a Polish priest, the world's first astronomer to prove that the earth and planets circle the sun, not vice versa as believed before. *PIAS*

Mikolaj Rej (1505–69), "father of Polish literature," wrote both satires and Protestant religious works. More important, he wrote only in Polish, not in the previous literary language of Latin. *NYPL*

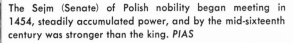

The Sejm (Senate) of Polish nobility began meeting in 1454, steadily accumulated power, and by the mid-sixteenth century was stronger than the king. *PIAS*

Jadwiga and Jagiello founded the Jagiellon dynasty, which brought Poland to the peak of its power. After Jagiello's death in 1434, there came a century of great kings and great victories. Particularly successful was Casimir IV (1447–92), whose son was also king of Bohemia and Hungary. Completely defeating the Teutonic Knights, Casimir in 1466 annexed Pomerania and forced East Prussia to become a vassal of Poland. Victory over the Turks added Moldavia to the Polish-Lithuanian Empire.

Meanwhile, under Jagiellon rule, Polish culture developed at a rapid pace. The Lithuanian nobility adopted the Polish language and customs. Nicolaus Copernicus (1473–1543), a learned Polish priest, was the world's first astronomer to discover that the earth revolves around the sun. Earlier scientists had believed the opposite. Copernicus knew his findings to be so heretical that he published them only while dying.

King Sigismund I (1506–48) crushed a revolt in Moldavia, and enlarged his empire by annexing Mazovia. *PIAS*

A contemporary of Copernicus was Mikolaj Rej (1505–69), the father of Polish literature. He was the first writer to abandon Latin entirely and write only in Polish.

In the meantime, Polish autocracy was curbed. The Jagiellon dynasty was put in power by the Polish nobility, who in return demanded more privileges. Jagiello himself gave the right of habeas corpus to the nobles and gentry. In 1454 an assembly of nobles called the "Sejm" began periodic meetings. The Sejm consistently gained power until by the mid-sixteenth century it was even stronger

Queen Bona Sforza, wife of Sigismund I, induced her husband to fortify the Ukrainian "savage steppe" for protection from the fierce Tatars. After his death she retired to her native Italy, where she was poisoned by a faithless lover. *PIAS*

than the king. Poland changed from an autocracy into a feeble monarchy dominated by the gentry.

Last of the Jagiellon kings was Sigismund II Augustus (1548–72), who annexed Livonia (Latvia and south Estonia) and in 1569 integrated Poland and Lithuania into a tighter union. During his reign, the Protestant Reformation spread into Poland, attracting a wide urban following. At one point the Sejm itself had a Protestant majority. In the Polish tradition of tolerance, Sigismund did not suppress Protestantism, except to banish Protestant extremists. But the Protestant movement slowly faded away, largely because of Polish patriotism. Confronted by hostile Protestant Germans on the west and aggressive Orthodox Russia to the east, the Poles clung to Catholicism as their own beloved national religion.

Sigismund Augustus died childless. Influenced by bribes from the French ambassador, Poland's nobles awarded the throne to Henry of Valois, son of the King of France. Henry's Polish reign set a record for brevity. After donning the Polish crown in 1573, he fled the country in 1574 to assume the more important position of King of France.

Yet Henry's brief reign produced two important edicts of lasting effect. The Warsaw Compact granted freedom of religion to all Polish Protestants. And the Henrician Articles (which Henry was forced to sign) proclaimed Poland a republic with an elected king, an elected queen, and Sejm permission required to send Polish troops abroad. Thus Poland became the most tolerant and least autocratic state in all East Europe.

After Henry ran away, the first elected king was Stephen Bathory of Transylvania (1575–86), who was a great warrior. Besides crushing a revolt in Danzig, he three times defeated the Russian armies of Tsar Ivan the Terrible. These victories partly resulted from Bathory's skillful use of infantry, which he introduced into the Polish army. Previously, the army had been limited to cavalry provided by the nobles and gentry.

But Bathory was more than a warrior. He created Poland's first supreme court, and established a university in the Lithuanian city of Vilno. To aid the Jews, he founded a Jewish assembly, which endured until 1764. Poland reveres Bathory as one of its greatest kings.

The next elected king was one of Poland's

King Sigismund II Augustus (1548–72) and his wife Barbara who was not of royal blood. He expanded his domains by annexing Latvia and southern Estonia. *PIAS*

The Grand Master of the Teutonic Knights kneels in allegiance to King Sigismund Augustus, who held German East Prussia as a vassal state. *PIAS*

Henry of Valois, son of the King of France, occupied the Polish throne 1573/74, then returned to his homeland to become French king. *PIAS*

King Stephen Bathory (1575—86) was a great innovator, founding Poland's supreme court, Vilno University, and a special parliament for Polish Jews. *PIAS*

Russian Tsar Ivan the Terrible, whose armies invaded Poland three times, only to be defeated by the military skill of Stephen Bathory. *NYPL*

King Sigismund III (1587—1632), "very silly and very obstinate," exhausted Poland by warring with Sweden, Russia, and Turkey. Early in his reign he was almost dethroned for treasonable dynastic intrigues. Yet Poles admire him for twice capturing Russia's capital city of Moscow. *PIAS*

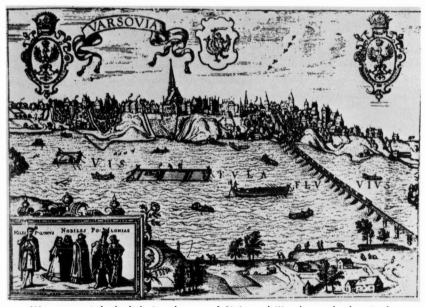

Warsaw, as it looked during the era of Sigismund III, who made the city his capital. *PIAS*

The man-of-war *Saint George* —flagship of the Polish navy built by Sigismund III. *PIAS*

worst. Sigismund III (1587–1632) was a Swede who specialized in hopeless adventures. He warred with Sweden in an attempt to regain the Swedish throne, which he had formerly occupied. He intrigued to place an Austrian on the Polish throne in order that he might return to Sweden to be king. When the plot was discovered, Sigismund was brought before a court of inquisition consisting of Polish nobles. He thus achieved the dubious distinction of being the first Polish king to be put on trial.

After the court permitted him to remain king, Sigismund ruled so harshly that the gentry revolted against him. The revolt was suppressed, but the gentry won the legal right to depose a bad monarch.

Meanwhile, in Russia, the Rurik dynasty had died out, and there was civil war over succession to the throne. Sigismund decided to profit from Russia's misfortune. He lent troops and moral support to two pretenders to the Russian crown, both named Dmitri and both claiming to be sons of the dead Tsar Ivan the Terrible. Then Sigismund himself invaded Russia, captured Moscow in 1610, and placed his fifteen-year-old son Wladyslaw on the Russian throne. When Sigismund announced that he himself might become tsar, Russia rebelled and drove the Polish army back into Poland. Sigismund's unhappy reign ended with wars against Turkey.

Within the Polish Empire, Sigismund had attempted two major improvements. He built Poland's first navy, and he founded the Uniate Church, which used the Orthodox ritual but paid allegiance to the Roman Pope. This religious organization was an attempt to bring Orthodox Ukrainians under papal control. But the Uniate Church became a hotbed of anti-Polish Ukrainian nationalism, and the Polish navy fell into permanent neglect.

Sigismund's reign was the start of more than a century of endless, exhausting wars. Sweden, Russia, Turkey, the Crimean Tatars, and rebellious Ukrainian Cossacks all attacked Poland, which was now on the defensive. Polish historians describe this unhappy period as the "deluge," during which Poland's empire began to shrink. Livonia was surrendered to Sweden in 1660, and Russia took much Belorussian and Ukrainian territory in 1667.

But the Polish Republic had developed a grave internal weakness: the "Liberum Veto," (free veto) in the Sejm. Any member of the Sejm could veto any bill, preventing it from becoming law. Also, any member could dissolve a meeting of the Sejm, stopping further deliberation. The theory behind this ultrademocracy was that each member of the Sejm was a gentleman whose attitude must be respected.

No other country has ever distorted parliamentary procedure into such absurdity. The Sejm had difficulty in handling even trivial affairs. Foreign ambassadors bribed Sejm members to veto measures disliked by the ambassadors' home countries. The liberum veto often paralyzed the Polish government in the very midst of war.

Still the Polish Republic produced one more great warrior-king: John III Sobieski (1674–96), a Pole who first achieved fame by halting a Turkish invasion of the western Ukraine. Then, in 1683, a huge Turkish army besieged Vienna, the capital of Austria and largest city in the Danubian basin. If Vienna fell, all south-central Europe would be in danger.

Austria asked Poland for help, and John Sobieski led his Polish army to the rescue. He defeated the Turks so badly that they never threatened Vienna again.

When John died, Prussia and Russia forced Poland to elect as king the ruler of Saxony, Augustus II (1697–1733). He started his Polish reign well by forcing the Turks to surrender a large Ukrainian territory. Then came the disaster of the Great Northern War (1700–1721), in which Poland, Russia, and Denmark fought Sweden. Poland

The Polish Sejm, a parliament consisting of upper nobility. By the mid-seventeenth century any member could veto any Sejm decree, stopping it from being put into force. PIAS

John Sobieski in 1683 at the Battle of Vienna, where he led an international army to victory against the Turks, ending forever the Turkish threat to the Austrian capital. *PIAS*

John III Sobieski (1674–96), the warrior king, who gained early fame by blocking a Turkish invasion of the Ukraine. *PIAS*

Palace built by John Sobieski near Warsaw, using Turkish prisoners of war as construction workers. *PTB*

was one of the war's main battlegrounds, invaded at various times by the Swedes, the Russians (pursuing the Swedes), and even the Saxons. To make matters worse, Lithuania sided with Sweden. At the war's end, Poland lay in ruins and its military strength had vanished.

After the death of Augustus, the Polish nobleman Stanislas Leszczynski (1733–35) was elected king with the hope that he might revive Polish strength. But an able king was not desired by Russia, whose troops immediately invaded Poland. This "War of the Polish Succession" lasted until 1735, when defeated Poland yielded the throne to Augustus III (1735–63), the son of Augustus II. The third Augustus was simply Moscow's puppet, letting Russian troops roam freely through the Polish lands.

When Augustus died, Russia forced the Sejm to give the crown to Stanislaw II Poniatowski (1764–95), former Polish ambassador to the tsarist court. Since Stanislaw had been a lover of the Russian empress Catherine the Great, he was expected to obey Russian orders. But he proved to be a Polish patriot rather than puppet.

In 1767, with support from Russian troops, Poland's Protestant and Orthodox minorities demanded and obtained religious equality with the Catholics. This blatant Russian interference in Polish internal affairs aroused a Polish Catholic revolt against Russian occupation troops.

The revolt failed, and in 1772, Austria, Prussia, and Russia seized and annexed one-third of Poland's territory. Belorussian lands went to Russia, Little Poland and Galicia to Austria, and Pomerania to Prussia.

Poland, now alarmed, introduced long overdue governmental reforms. To encourage Polish national culture, the king created a ministry of education—the first in all Europe. A new constitution of 1791 made the monarchy hereditary and abolished the liberum veto.

But the reforms came too late. In 1793 Prussia seized Great Poland, and Russia took more eastern Polish territory. Russian troops forced Poland to abandon the new constitution. Now the whole Polish nation, led by Tadeusz Kosciuszko, who had already displayed great military skill as one of George Washington's generals in the American Revolution, rose in revolt. However, Kosciuszko was defeated in 1794 by combined Prussian-Russian forces. And in 1795, Austria, Prussia, and Russia made a third partition of Poland, wiping the poor country off the map. Russia took Lithuania, western Belorussia, and the western Ukraine. Austria and Prussia divided Mazovia. After more than eight hundred years of independence, the Polish state ceased to exist.

Polish hopes then centered on Napoleon, who was fighting Poland's oppressors and who wished to weaken Austria and Prussia. Émigré Polish soldiers eagerly joined the French army, fighting in the Egyptian, Haitian, and various European cam-

1. King Augustus II (1697–1733), who was almost dethroned during the Great Northern War of 1700–1721 by Swedish invasions of Poland. *PIAS* 2. Charles XII, warrior king of Sweden, who during the Great Northern War led Swedish invasions of Poland and Russia. *NYPL* 3. Russian Tsar Peter the Great, ally of Augustus II, finally saved Poland from Sweden by defeating Charles XII. *NYPL*

1   2   3

1. Polish King Stanislas Leszczynski (1733–35), overthrown by a Russian invasion of Poland. *PIAS* 2. King Augustus III (1735–63), installed by Russian troops, was Moscow's Polish puppet ruler. *PIAS* 3. Stanislaw II Poniatowski (1764–95), last king of Poland, who tried and failed to stop Austria, Prussia, and Russia from seizing his country. *Eastfoto* 4. Empress Catherine the Great of Russia who placed Stanislaw Poniatowski on the Polish throne, then annexed most of his empire. *NYPL*

An eighteenth-century cartoon of the three Partitions of Poland (1772, 1793, 1795), which erased the Polish Empire from the map of Europe. *NYPL*

paigns. After defeating Austria, Prussia, and Russia, Napoleon in 1807 created the Duchy of Warsaw from territory Austria and Prussia had received in the partitions of Poland. The duchy consisted mainly of Great Poland, Little Poland, and Mazovia—the three original Polish lands. The Poles were delighted, even though their duchy was a mere puppet state of France.

When Napoleon invaded Russia in 1812, one of every six soldiers in his Grand Army was Polish. The whole Polish nation hoped that Napoleon would win; then Poland could recover areas it had

Street celebration for the new Polish constitution of 1791, which strengthened the Polish monarchy. Russia forced this constitution to be annulled. *PIAS*

Too little and too late, patriotic Poles made last-minute attempts to save their country from partition. This Sejm of 1788–92 surrendered some of its own privileges, in order to give Poland's king more power. *PIAS*

One of Poland's greatest heroes, Tadeusz Kosciuszko, who loved liberty so much that he volunteered to be one of George Washington's generals in the American Revolution. *Eastfoto*

Kosciuszko in America, fortifying Saratoga to repulse a British attack. *PIAS*

After distinguished service in the American Revolution, Kosciuszko returned to Poland to lead the revolt against Austro-Prussian-Russian tyranny. Here, in peasant costume, he arouses Polish farmers to fight for freedom. *Eastfoto*

Many Poles hoped that French Emperor Napoleon would restore Polish freedom. This painting shows a Warsaw crowd welcoming the French troops who captured the city in 1806. *PIAS*

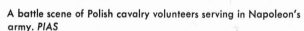

A battle scene of Polish cavalry volunteers serving in Napoleon's army. *PIAS*

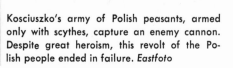

Kosciuszko's army of Polish peasants, armed only with scythes, capture an enemy cannon. Despite great heroism, this revolt of the Polish people ended in failure. *Eastfoto*

lost to Russia. But Napoleon was defeated by Russian sabotage, guerrilla warfare, and winter cold. In pursuit of the retreating remnants of the Grand Army, Russian troops in 1813 conquered and ended the short-lived Duchy of Warsaw.

While Napoleon met his final defeat at Waterloo in 1815, European leaders convened in Vienna to determine Europe's future. Tsar Alexander I of Russia demanded that Poland be reunited into a kingdom, with himself as king. Other European Powers feared such westward extension of Russia's frontiers. A compromise was worked out. Austria retained Galicia, and Prussia kept Pomerania and Great Poland. Cracow and its surrounding region became a tiny republic. Mazovia and most of Little Poland became a new kingdom of Poland, with the Tsar of Russia as its constitutional monarch. Thus

Poland remained divided among Austria, Prussia, and Russia, with most Polish lands now under the Russian tsar.

But the Poles did not accept foreign rule passively. Throughout the nineteenth century, every generation of Poles rebelled. Each revolt was suppressed, and usually induced reprisals. After the uprising of 1830/31 against Russia, the tsar abolished the Polish constitution and closed Vilno University. The 1846 and 1848 revolts against Austria resulted in Austrian annexation of the Cracow Republic. The 1846–48 rebellion against Prussia led to Germanization of Pomerania and Great Poland. Similarly, Russification of the Polish kingdom occurred after the 1863/64 revolt.

Meanwhile, Polish culture flourished, vividly expressing Polish aspirations for unity and freedom.

Death in battle of Prince Joseph Poniatowski, who commanded Napoleon's Polish troops. Before being killed in action, he was one of Napoleon's army marshals. *PIAS*

Tsar Alexander I, who in 1812 almost annihilated Napoleon's army in Russia, thus ending Polish hopes for immediate independence. *Photoworld*

The Congress of Vienna, which in 1815 made most of Poland a supposedly constitutional monarchy with Russia's tsar as Polish king. Other Polish territories remained under Austrian and Prussian rule. *NYPL*

1. Every generation of nineteenth-century Poles revolted against Austria, Prussia, or Russia. Rebel life was dangerous, as shown in the different fates of these three leaders of the anti-Russian uprising of 1863. Marian Langiewicz survived all revolutionary turmoil. 2. Ludwik Narbutt died in revolutionary battle. 3. Zygmunt Dolega-Sierakowski was executed by the Russians. *PIAS*

1. Russia imprisoned Adam Mickiewicz (1798–1855), Poland's greatest poet, for his anti-Tsarist writings. 2. Frédéric Chopin (1810–49), Poland's most renowned composer, dedicated most of his works to the cause of Polish freedom. The portrait below bears his autograph. *Eastfoto* 3. Chopin's constitution was weak, and he died of tuberculosis before the age of forty. This drawing shows him already in declining health. *NYPL*

Literature was romantic, often recalling the greatness of Poland's past. Artists painted scenes of former grandeur. Poland's greatest poet, Adam Mickiewicz (1798–1855), was imprisoned by Russia for preaching revolution. Frédéric Chopin (1810–1849), the world-famous Polish composer, dedicated most of his music to Poland's sorrows.

Émigré Poles often achieved brilliant careers abroad. Joseph Conrad (Teodor Józef Konrad Korzeniowski, 1857–1924) wrote ever popular tales of the sea. Marie (Sklodowska) Curie (1867–1934) won two Nobel prizes for her trailblazing research on radium.

As time passed, the Poles at home were less oppressed. When Russia abolished serfdom in 1864, the serfs of the Polish kingdom were freed. After Austria in 1867 granted equality to Hungary within the Austrian Empire, Galicia was given local autonomy and elected Polish representatives to the Austrian parliament. Austria encouraged Polish culture, and some Poles even held high positions in the Austrian governmental bureaucracy. Poles participated in the 1905 Russian Revolution, which forced the tsar to establish a Russian parliament called the "Duma." As part of the Russian Empire, the Polish kingdom elected deputies to the Duma, where they played an important role by joining the democratic opposition.

Then World War I (1914–18) erupted, with Poland as the main battleground of the eastern front. The Polish kingdom was conquered by the German and Austrian armies, which remained un-

til the war ended. Though causing death and destruction, the war suddenly made Poland important, since both sides sought support from the Poles. As early as 1914 the tsar promised to unite all Polish territories, which would then become autonomous within the Russian Empire. With Austro-German encouragement, Josef Pilsudski, a Polish socialist, organized a Polish legion to fight the Russian army. By 1916 Germany and Austria offered to free the Polish kingdom, but without Great Poland, which would remain a German province. Russia made a counteroffer to free all of Poland. In the meantime Germany arrested Pilsudski, who was becoming increasingly friendly toward the Western Allies.

1. Henryk Sienkiewicz (1846–1916), Polish author of the world-famous historical novel *Quo Vadis.* 2. Joseph Conrad (1857–1924) was born in Poland, but wrote his exciting tales of the sea while living abroad, mostly in England. *Photo by Craig Annan* 3. Marie Curie (1867–1934), Polish winner of two Nobel prizes in physics. When young (as in this picture), she was an assistant to her French scientist husband. *NYPL*

1   2   3

After her husband Pierre Curie died in an accident, Marie took his place and continued his vital research on radium. *NYPL*

Alexander II, Russia's "Tsar-Liberator," who in the 1860s freed all serfs in his empire, including Polish peasants. *Photoworld*

Liberation of serfs at a Russian-Polish estate. Since the great majority of Poles had been peasant serfs, most of the Polish nation was released from slavery. *NYPL*

Among other noted Poles at the dawn of the twentieth century was Dr. Lazar Ludwik Zamenhof —inventor of the international language of Esperanto. Above is the unveiling of a Warsaw monument to this genius. *Photoworld*

During World War I, Poland was the hapless battleground between Austro-German and Russian armies. Here are the ruins of a Polish village after Russian bombardment. *Photoworld*

A German military plane on a Polish plain during World War I. *Photoworld*

German troops parading in Warsaw after capturing the city in 1915. *Photoworld*

German and Austrian cavalry cross the Vistula River near Warsaw in 1915, chasing the retreating Russians. *Photoworld*

Jozef Pilsudski, who during World War I organized a Polish legion to fight for Poland's independence. The two charming girls are his daughters. *PIAS*

A Warsaw crowd celebrating the 1916 German offer to make Poland an independent nation. *Photoworld*

German and Austrian soldiers sharing lunch in a Polish village they captured during World War I. Meanwhile many Poles were suffering from hunger. *Photoworld*

During World War I the German invaders planned to stay permanently in Poland. Here German officers give school lessons to Polish peasant children. *Photoworld*

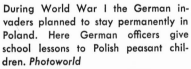

For the Western Allies were also interested in Polish independence. By 1917, Britain, France, Italy, and the United States recognized the Polish National Committee in Paris as the representative of the Polish people. Founded by Polish émigrés, this committee was headed by the moderate politician Roman Dmowski and the world-famous pianist Ignace Jan Paderewski (1860–1941). When U.S. President Woodrow Wilson issued his peace program of "Fourteen Points," the thirteenth was that Poland should be reunited and independent.

The Polish kingdom was supposedly freed in the spring of 1918 by the Treaty of Brest-Litovsk between the Central Powers and a defeated Russia now under Bolshevik rule. But Poland remained under Austro-German military occupation. Meanwhile, Britain, France, and Italy announced they would make Poland truly free.

When World War I ended in Austro-German defeat during the autumn of 1918, Poland declared its independence under the leadership of Pilsudski, who became president of the new Polish republic, with Paderewski as premier. After 150 years of enslavement, Poland was again a free nation.

Retreating Russians burned this ammunition depot in Poland to prevent the explosives from falling into the hands of the Germans. The wheels belong to Russian gun carriages which were also destroyed. *Photoworld*

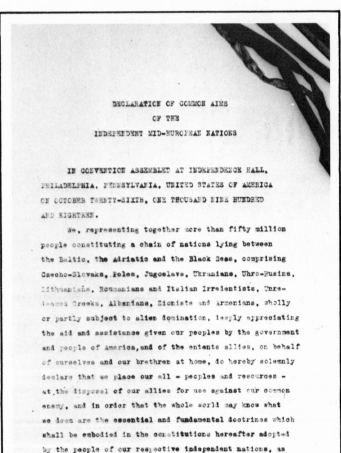

A 1918 declaration by East European exile leaders in America that after World War I their nations should be free. It was sent to President Woodrow Wilson, who advocated East European independence. *UPI*

Point 13 of President Wilson's "Fourteen Point" program for ◄ post-World War I peace demanded freedom for Poland. Here Paderewski, the world-famous Polish pianist, helps Wilson compose this Thirteenth Point. *PIAS*

In accord with the Wilsonian principle that state boundaries should be racial, the Paris Peace Conference after World War I awarded Great Poland, Little Poland, Mazovia, and part of Silesia to the new Polish state. To ensure Polish access to the Baltic Sea, a narrow corridor of land was given to Poland along the Vistula River to the seacoast. This "Polish Corridor" lay between Pomerania and East Prussia, both of which remained German provinces. The corridor's seaport of Danzig was inhabited mainly by Germans, so this city was internationalized under the control of the League of Nations.

Poland had unrestricted use of Danzig's port facilities. Since Soviet Russia was not invited to the Paris conference, no decision was made on Poland's eastern frontier. Britain's foreign minister Lord Curzon suggested the so-called Curzon Line—a racial border leaving western Belorussia and the west Ukraine under Russian rule.

Despite the conference decisions, every mile of the new Polish boundaries was contested by Poland's neighbors, and the Poles had to fight for their frontiers. Marshal Pilsudski expanded his legion into a powerful army, which he led with great

President Wilson boarding ship in 1918 en route to the Paris Peace Conference, which made Poland independent. PIAS

Roman Dmowski, Poland's able representative at the Paris Peace Conference. Photoworld

When Poland was freed in 1918, pianist Ignace Paderewski (1860–1941) served as its first premier. NYPL

A photo of Marshal Pilsudski, when he was Poland's first president after World War I. He was also commander in chief of armed forces. *UPI*

The Polish foreign legion in France during World War I, leaving for the front to battle the Germans. After hostilities ceased, they returned to Poland to join Pilsudski's army. *Photoworld*

Post-World War I Poland had to fight for every mile of its new frontiers. This rugged Polish machine gunner is on duty near the German border. *Photoworld*

German troops in 1920 evacuating Danzig, which went under League of Nations' control to serve as a Polish port. *Photoworld*

Marshal Pilsudski, dining with his staff, during Poland's frontier wars after World War I. *NYPL*

After World War I and the Soviet-Polish conflict of 1919–20, much of Poland lay in ruins. Below is a wrecked railway bridge near Warsaw. *Photoworld*

What was left of the east Polish city of Brest-Litovsk after Russian retreat. *Photoworld*

skill. During 1918/19, Poland won Galicia by victories over the Ukraine. Posen (Poznan) was wrested from Germany in 1919 by hard fighting. In the same year, Czech-Polish skirmishes erupted over the industrial border district of Teschen (Cieszyn). The Western Allies intervened, giving most of Teschen to Czechoslovakia.

Overshadowing all these campaigns was the Soviet-Polish War of 1919–20. Taking advantage of the civil war between Red and White Russians, Pilsudski invaded the Ukraine to regain Poland's historic eastern territories. After initial success, his forces were driven back by the Bolsheviks to the gates of Warsaw. But Russia's Red Army overextended itself, Warsaw was saved, and Poland again took the offensive. An armistice was declared, and by the 1921 Treaty of Riga, Soviet Russia ceded western Belorussia and the western Ukraine to Poland. A side action of this war was the Polish annexation of Vilno—a predominantly Polish city located in Lithuania.

Poland's hard-won frontiers were not racial, and one-third of the country's inhabitants were not Poles. Ukrainians composed 14 percent of the population; Jews, 9 percent; Belorussians, 6 percent; and Germans, 2 percent. Thus the new Poland had a grave minorities problem that was never solved. Polish businessmen resented the commercial prowess of the Jews. The Ukrainians were forever restless, demanding a free Ukraine. The Germans looked to Germany for protection, and the Belorussians were pro-Russian.

The Jewish hat and clothing market in Warsaw. Between World Wars I and II, Christian businessmen resented Jewish commercial competition. *Photoworld*

There were other Polish problems. World War I had damaged almost all factories and railways, besides destroying one of every seven peasant villages. Reconstruction of war damage was difficult and slow.

Since prewar Poland had belonged to three different countries, it had lived under three types of law: Austrian, German, and tsarist Russian. To avoid instability, Poland retained Austrian law in Galicia and Cracow, German law in Great Poland, and Russian law in Mazovia, Little Poland, west Belorussia, and the western Ukraine. Finally, in 1928, a new law code provided uniform laws for all Polish regions.

Marshal Pilsudski retired from politics in 1922, after Poland adopted a democratic constitu-

Tired of an inept democratic government, aged Marshal Pilsudski in 1926 returned from retirement to become Poland's dictator. *UPI*

tion. But free elections created thirteen political parties whose endless squabbles hampered governmental efficiency. Disgusted with democracy, Pilsudski seized power in 1926 by a military coup d'etat, appointed himself premier, and established a mild dictatorship. He remained dictator until his death in 1935, after which the dictatorship was led by his cronies called the "colonels."

Meanwhile, to safeguard itself from foreign aggression, Poland concluded alliances with France and Romania in the early 1920s, and nonaggression pacts with the Soviet Union and Nazi Germany in the early 1930s. Poland itself became aggressive in 1938, seizing Teschen from a Czechoslovakia already weakened by Nazi occupation of the Czech Sudetenland.

Yet the Poles sensed danger when, in the spring of 1939, Hitler annexed all western Czechoslovakia. He then demanded Danzig and German control of a railway and highway across the Polish Corridor. The Polish government refused, relying on its alliances with Britain and France.

In summer, while conducting negotiations with Britain and France, Russia asked whether Soviet troops could enter Poland to defend the Poles against Germany. The Polish government refused, fearing that Soviet troops might stay in Poland permanently. Then Stalin rejected the Anglo-French

The Polish cabinet that took power in 1935 after dictator Pilsudski's death. *Photoworld*

Polish President Ignatz Moscicki signing a 1939 law strengthening Poland's air force against expected German attack. *UPI*

Soviet dictator Joseph Stalin and German Foreign Minister Joachim von Ribbentrop smile and shake hands after signing the 1939 Nazi-Soviet Pact partitioning Poland. *PIAS*

Nazi Storm Troopers parading in Danzig on the eve of World War II. *UPI*

offer of alliance and signed a nonaggression pact with Hitler. This fateful Nazi-Soviet treaty of August 23, 1939, contained a secret protocol dividing Poland between Russia and Germany.

Hitler attacked Poland on September 1, 1939, and Britain and France responded by declaring war on Germany. Thus began World War II. Russia invaded east Poland on September 17, after most of the Polish army had been defeated by the Germans.

Again Poland disappeared from the map. Western Belorussia and the western Ukraine were incorporated into the USSR. Germany annexed the Polish Corridor, Great Poland, and Polish Silesia, converting Mazovia and Little Poland into a protectorate called the General Government.

The Nazi governor of Poland proclaimed: "Poland shall be treated as a colony; the Poles shall be the slaves of the Greater German world empire!" This was no empty threat. More than a million Poles were deported into Germany as slave labor. Most Polish schools and all universities were closed, because slaves required little education. Intellectuals were rounded up and executed. Polish industry and agriculture were bled white to supply the German army.

Suffering most were the Polish Jews, who were methodically exterminated in the gas chambers of Nazi death camps. About half a million Jews were herded into the Warsaw ghetto. In 1943, after executions, starvation, and disease had reduced their number to 70,000, the Jews began to fight back. Gestapo troops invaded the ghetto, burning down every house. But the Jews fought bravely for a month before being wiped out.

Today a large square has been laid out where the ghetto once stood. At the end of the square is a huge monument to the ghetto Jews. It is made of marble Hitler sent to Warsaw for a statue of himself.

Countless Poles also fought against the Nazi occupation. An underground army of 350,000 men and women harassed the German conquerors, even establishing a clandestine Polish government with its own local administration, schools, and courts. Meanwhile, Polish émigré political leaders formed an exile government located first in France and later in London. The government in exile also controlled an army in exile. As many as 300,000 Poles living or escaping abroad eagerly joined the Allied armed forces. One of every seven German planes destroyed in the Battle of Britain was shot down by a Polish pilot.

A machine gunner of the German army invading Poland during September 1939. *UPI*

Germany's conquest of Poland did not always go smoothly. Here captured German soldiers are paraded through Warsaw under heavy Polish guard. *UPI*

Hitler in Warsaw reviewing the German troops that had captured the Polish capital. *UPI*

During the Nazi occupation of Poland, Hitler's Gestapo slaughtered most Polish Jews. These Jewish women and children are being herded from the Warsaw ghetto for transportation to concentration camps for execution. *PIAS*

Jewish corpses being cremated at the notorious Nazi concentration camp in Auschwitz. *Eastfoto*

Decayed corpses of Polish army officers massacred by the Russians during 1940 in the Katyn Forest of Belorussia. These bodies were unearthed in 1943. *UPI*

In its 1939 invasion of east Poland, the Soviet army had captured about a million Poles. After Hitler invaded Russia in 1941, the Polish government in London resumed relations with the USSR and obtained Soviet permission for Polish women and children to leave Russia. Able-bodied Polish men in the USSR were organized into an army to fight the Germans on the Russian front. When this Polish army was unable to obtain equipment, it also left Russia and later distinguished itself in the Battle of Italy.

Then, in 1943, the Germans discovered mass

Ruins of Warsaw after the Nazis destroyed most of the city in 1944. *Eastfoto*

Jewish survivors of Nazi occupation marching in mourning through the rubble of the Warsaw ghetto. *Eastfoto*

graves containing several thousand Polish officers in the Katyn Forest of Belorussia. Evidence indicated they had been shot by the Soviet secret police. Emotionally, the London Polish government asked the International Red Cross to investigate. Russia, highly annoyed, broke diplomatic relations with the London Poles.

Driving back the Nazi army, Russia's Red Army in 1944 reached the outskirts of Warsaw. In response to a Soviet radio appeal for help, the Warsaw underground rose against the local German garrison and soon controlled half the city. But the Nazis began bombing and shelling Warsaw, block by block, while the Red Army sat motionless, not advancing to help. After two months of fighting, the underground surrendered to the Nazis, who had destroyed 85 percent of Warsaw and killed 200,000 of its people.

In the baggage train of the Red Army was a Polish Committee of National Liberation consisting of Communist agents. Russia installed this committee as the new Polish government, which recruited some London Poles to form a coalition regime. But from the very start, the coalition was dominated by Polish Communists.

Russia also kept the western Ukraine and western Belorussia. In compensation, Poland was given German Silesia, Pomerania, Danzig, and most of East Prussia. Germans living in these territories either fled or were expelled.

Of the prewar 3,400,000 Polish Jews, only 90,000 survived the Nazi death camps. Having lost its Ukrainians, Belorussians, Germans, and most Jews, the new Poland had no minority problems. Postwar Poland was 98 percent Polish in population.

War losses were so great that the Polish Communist government had to rebuild most of Poland. The population had shrunk from 35,000,000 to 24,000,000. Besides the Jews, 3,000,000 Poles had been killed. Warsaw and Breslau lay in ruins. Almost all motor trucks and railway freight cars had been destroyed. Two-fifths of the railway tracks and one-third of the highways were badly damaged. Sad for scholars was the loss of 85 percent of all library books. The one consolation was annexation of Silesia, which gave postwar Poland a larger industry than it had had before the war.

Though disliking communism, the Polish people worked hard to rebuild their beloved country.

Troops of the Polish legion of the Soviet army parading in Warsaw after the Nazis had been expelled. *Eastfoto*

The 1956 anti-Communist riot by workers in the city of Poznan. Here the rioters have captured a Polish army tank, which was trying to crush the uprising. *UPI*

After defying Russia, Polish Communist leader Wladyslaw Gomulka proudly announces his 1956 program liberalizing Poland's dictatorship. *UPI*

Meanwhile, the government converted Poland into a Soviet satellite. Industry was nationalized, and collective farms began forming in the villages. Heavy industry greatly expanded, and annual steel production rose from 1,400,000 tons to the present 11,000,000. The Catholic Church was continually harassed, with the government trying to appoint the clergy. Foreign trade, which had been mainly with the West, was diverted to the Soviet bloc. Poland allied with Russia, and refused U.S. Marshall Plan aid.

Still the Poles showed signs of independence. When Yugoslavia left the Soviet orbit in 1948, one-fourth of the Polish Communist Party was purged for sympathizing with Tito. The most famous purge victim was Wladyslaw Gomulka, the party secretary-general, who was imprisoned. After the purge, Marshal Konstantin Rokossovski of the USSR was made Polish Minister of Defense, so Russia could control the Polish army.

Poland was quiet until 1956, when Poznan workers rioted for better wages during the city's international trade fair. Troops suppressed the riot, whose ringleaders received surprisingly light punishment. All Poland became tense and demanded reforms. Virtually in panic, the Communist Party reappointed Gomulka its secretary-general. But his promises of liberalization alarmed Russia, whose troops in Poland began marching on Warsaw. Gomulka ordered the Polish police army to defend the capital, whose workers were also given guns. Then Soviet leader Khrushchev arrived to stop Polish reform.

After a tense meeting, Khrushchev called back the Soviet troops and agreed to Polish liberalization. In turn, Gomulka promised to support Soviet foreign policy. Poles call this event the bloodless 1956 October Revolution; it gave Poland control over its internal affairs for the first time in seventeen years.

Gomulka allowed collective farms to disband and private stores to reopen. He raised worker pay and eased state censorship over artists, scholars, and writers. Cardinal Stefan Wyszynski, the head of the Polish Catholic Church, was released from prison. Marshal Rokossovski was dismissed and sent home to Moscow. Poland obtained an American loan and forced Russia to pay higher prices for Polish coal.

But as time passed, Gomulka began undoing his reforms. Though collective farms almost van-

ished, peasants were pressured to join new state farms. Inflation undermined worker wages, while censorship tightened over literature and art.

By 1968 the Polish government was openly anti-Semitic, blaming Poland's unrest on the Jews, who now numbered only 65,000 in a total population of 32,000,000. Mild student demonstrations for intellectual freedom were suppressed by great police brutality; Poland even joined Russia in invading Czechoslovakia to stop Czech liberalization.

But the freedom-loving Poles always rebel against blind tyranny. A revolt had to come and did, in December 1970, when humble workers in several cities rioted against pay reductions and price rises. Communist party offices and secret police stations were wrecked and burned. The Com-

At the right is Cardinal Stefan Wyszynski, head of the Polish Catholic Church, after being released from prison by Gomulka. *UPI*

munist government ordered its police to "shoot to kill," so the riots subsided. Yet the leadership was badly shaken. Gomulka resigned, retiring into oblivion. Poland's president, premier, and several cabinet ministers were removed. Frantically, the new regime promised state aid to very poor families.

The heroic Poles can never be permanently enslaved; they will rebel again.

Polish troops aiding the 1968 Soviet invasion of Czechoslovakia. Once again Poland's Communist government slavishly obeyed Moscow orders. *UPI*

Czechoslovakia

SMALL IN AREA and population but huge in industry and engineering, Czechoslovakia is the most efficient of all East European nations. With its wooded mountains, green valleys, and hilltop castles, Czechoslovakia has the appearance of a medieval fairyland. But it is a dreamland filled with smokestacks. A common sight is the small farm village of stone cottages dwarfed by the nearby giant industrial plant. Since the winds blow gently and the air is often still, many a lush Czech valley is shadowed by clouds of factory smoke floating motionless in the quiet sky.

Czechoslovak industrial development is truly fabulous. When the nation was part of the Austro-Hungarian Empire, the Czech lands alone contained three-fourths of the empire's entire industry. On the eve of World War II, Czechoslovakia exported porcelain, glassware, shoes, and beer to all corners of the world, and the Czech armament industry was larger than that of Italy. Postwar Communist dictatorship eagerly increased the already great industrialization. Today, in production per capita, Czechoslovakia is ahead of France in electric power, coal mining, and the smelting of steel.

Nor do the Czechoslovaks live poorly. These gentle people have one of the highest standards of living of any Communist nation, much better than Marxist Mother Russia. Per person, Czechoslovaks consume more meat than Italians, more milk and sugar than the Italians, French, and West Germans. Amid a world haunted by ever increasing inflation, Czechoslovakia has reduced store prices year after year since the early 1950s.

Such phenomenal success has been created by the managerial ability of the 14,000,000 Czechoslovak people. Actually, there are two peoples—Czechs and Slovaks—who in the distant past were of similar nationality but were divided by history into slightly different languages and cultures. Both are West Slavs like the Poles, distantly related to the East Slavic Russians and Ukrainians and to the South Slavic Bulgarians and Yugoslavs.

Why are the Czechs and Slovaks better businessmen than other Slavs? Love of culture is one explanation. The three greatest leaders of Czech nationalism—Jan Hus, Thomas Masaryk, and Eduard Benes—were all college professors. Among East European nations, only Czechoslovakia had a school system rivaling West Europe during the years of independence between World Wars I and II. With its forty-three-letter alphabet, Czech is the most phonetic of all European languages. Among all Slavic tongues, Slovak is the most international—combining West, East, and South Slavic words.

A long tradition of democracy is another reason for Czech success. The medieval Czech king-

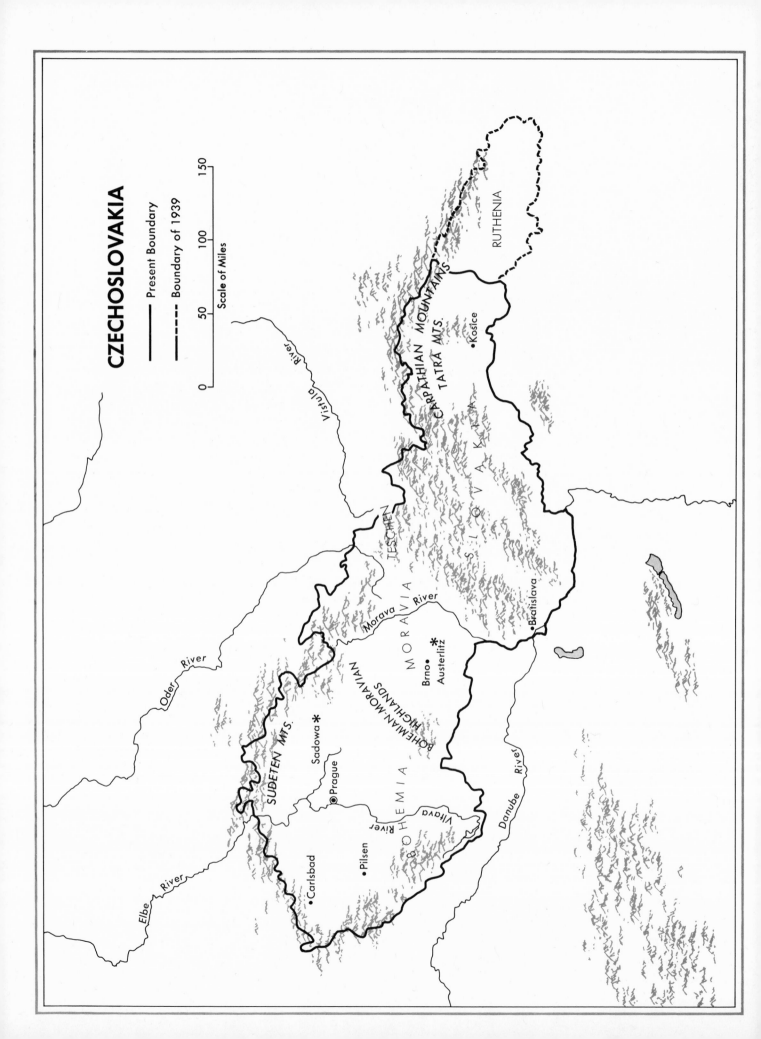

CZECHOSLOVAKIA

— Present Boundary

--- Boundary of 1939

Scale of Miles

0   50   100   150

Vistula River

Oder River

Elbe River

SUDETEN MTS.

Carlsbad

Sadowa *

Pilsen

Prague

BOHEMIA

BOHEMIAN-MORAVIAN HIGHLANDS

Vltava River

Danube River

MORAVIA

Morava River

Brno

Austerlitz *

TESCHEN

CARPATHIAN MOUNTAINS

TATRA MTS.

S L O V A K I A

Bratislava

Košice

RUTHENIA

Amid the wooded mountains of Czechoslovakia rise hundreds of hilltop castles. This thirteenth-century fortress is at Orava (Oravsky Podzamok) in central Slovakia. *Eastfoto*

A poultry market in Prague. Czechoslovaks eat well, consuming more food per person than some West European peoples. *UPI*

Czechoslovak industry has long been famous for high-quality steel. Here a huge casting is forged at a huge foundry. *CTB*

Jan Hus, one of the greatest Czech heroes, was an early Protestant leader burned at the stake in 1415 for criticizing Catholic Church doctrine. *NYPL*

The Czechoslovaks, a highly educated nation, revere their great writers. This Prague palace, formerly a monastery, is a museum entirely devoted to Czech literature. *Eastfoto*

Two professors, Thomas Masaryk (*left*) and Eduard Benes, who were elected as the first and second presidents of pre-Communist Czechoslovakia. *UPI*

The Good Soldier Schweik, a world-famous Czech novel, poked fun at the Austro-Hungarian army in which Czechs and Slovaks formerly had to serve. Here is a 1965 tableau of crippled Schweik being wheeled by his landlady on his way to join the armed forces. *Eastfoto*

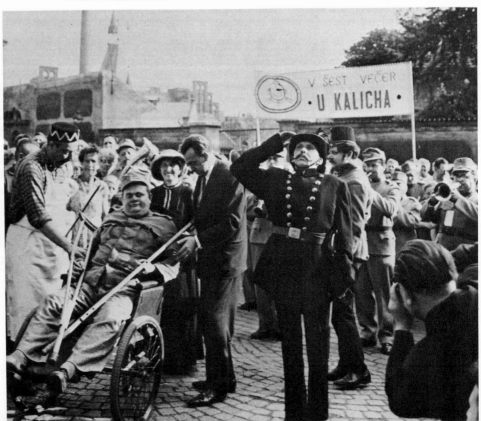

Tiny Schweik dolls are symbols of Czechoslovak passive resistance to alien tyranny. This little fellow performs in a puppet show. *CTB*

Soviet leader Khrushchev sometimes visited Czechoslovakia, trying to make himself popular. Here he pats two children dressed in Czech ceremonial costumes. *Stebou, Zemé*

The Elbe River amid the Carpathian Mountains. Riverboats ply its waters all the way from Czechoslovakia through Germany to the North Sea. *CTB*

The busy Danube River port at the Slovak city of Bratislava. *CTB*

dom of Bohemia was unique in Europe because it elected its rulers. At first the great nobles chose the future monarch. Later, when cities arose, town leaders shared the honor of selecting the noble to wear the crown. This love of democracy survived three centuries of Austrian rule. It is beautifully satirized in Jaroslav Hasek's world-famous novel, *The Good Soldier Schweik:* Schweik cheerfully sabotaged Austrian army commands by obeying them to absurdity. Today many Czech and Slovak homes display tiny Schweik dolls to show contempt for Communist dictatorship.

Fine sand is quarried in Bohemia and used for making the famed Czech glassware and porcelain. Here the sand is washed downhill to be loaded into trucks. *UPI*

Small porcelain statues like this shepherd have been made for centuries by skilled Czechoslovak craftsmen. *CTB*

Czech passive resistance to foreign oppressors was delightfully revealed in the late 1950s, when Soviet Premier Khrushchev visited Prague to speak to a mass audience in a park. Several thousand Czechs came to the meeting, bringing children and babies. Surveying the throng, Khrushchev was pleased that youngsters were there to adore him—the leader of the communist world. He did not realize that, if children were present, Czech adults were not seriously interested in his pronouncements.

Khrushchev began to orate. After two sentences the crowd burst into wild applause. He spoke another two sentences, only to be overwhelmed again by mass clapping of hands. So it continued.

For the first five minutes Khrushchev was pleased, believing the applause to be sincere. Then he realized that the Czech crowd would not let him speak. In helpless anger he stalked off the podium, unable to punish six thousand Czechs for phony applause.

Nature has been kind to Czechoslovakia. The country is small, its 49,370 square miles of territory being about the size of New York State. Furthermore, Czechoslovakia is peculiarly shaped: 600 miles long from west to east but only 174 to 45 miles wide from north to south. It is squeezed into the Sudeten and Carpathian Mountains with adjacent lowlands of Poland on the north, Germany on the northwest and west, Austria and Hungary to the south, and Russia in the east. Thus Czechoslovakia is the crossroads of East Europe, and even in medieval centuries was famous for lucrative trade.

Before the age of steam, Czech commerce traveled abroad via the great rivers which arise from Sudeten and Carpathian mountain springs, for Czechoslovakia is the East European watershed. Flowing northward to the North and Baltic seas are the Elbe, Oder, and Vistula, while the Morava and other streams go south into the Danube River, which eventually enters the Black Sea. Today the rivers have lost their importance, and most international commerce travels across Czechoslovakia by rail. Only the Danube, Elbe, and Morava are still used for river shipping; the railways haul ninetenths of all freight.

The Czechoslovak mountains are fortunately rich in minerals. In medieval times gold and silver mining brought wealth to the Czechs, whose silver coins were used as legal tender throughout West Europe. Czech industry arose in the nineteenth century on the basis of large deposits of iron, copper, uranium, black and brown coal, fine sands (for making glass), and equally fine clay (for molding

Typical rural scene in Bohemia: a castle, wooded hills, and fertile farmlands. *Eastfoto*

The "green gold"—hops to make the Pilsner beer exported to all parts of the world. *CTB*

Large herds of fine sheep graze in highland pastures of the Carpathian Mountains.

The winter wonderland of rural Czechoslovakia. *CTB*

Mechanized agriculture on a Czechoslovak collective farm. *Stebou, Zemé*

Villagers in the Tatra Mountains celebrate the spring thaw by burying "old man winter." *UPI*

Wild game like this huge deer is abundant in Czechoslovakia's mountain forests. *CTB*

A lakeside tourist resort in the Carpathian Mountains. *CTB*

porcelain). Today Czechoslovak industry is so large that native mining is inadequate for factory needs. Vast quantities of raw materials, especially iron ore from Russia, are imported.

Though Czechoslovakia is hilly and mountainous, there is a surprising amount of good farmland. About two-fifths of the country is sown to crops, and another sixth is used for pasture. Wheat, barley, rye, oats, sugar beets, and potatoes are the main crops. Grapes are grown for wine, and hops for the famous Czech beer. Large herds of sheep graze in the mountain pastures, providing high-quality wool for the well-developed textile industry. Czech horses are noted for their size and strength, and in past centuries were widely used in the Austrian imperial cavalry.

The Czechoslovak climate favors agriculture. Most rainfall comes in the spring and summer, which is ideal for growing crops. Winters are cold,

the average temperature being at the freezing point. Summers are pleasantly cool, average temperatures (Fahrenheit) being in the 60s.

Before World War II, private farming in Czechoslovakia was so well developed and well mechanized that the country was self-sufficient in food. Today, communist collective farming has reduced productivity, and many rural youths have left the villages to work in industry. So Czechoslovakia must now import some foodstuffs, particularly grain from Russia. One of every three loaves of Czechoslovak bread is baked today with flour milled from Soviet grain.

Czechoslovakia is a tourist paradise, and tourism is officially encouraged as an additional source of national income. Hunters trek into the mountain forests to stalk the numerous wildcats, foxes, wolves, deer, bears, and boars. The mountains are dotted with resorts and ski lodges for

THE CZECHOSLOVAK NATION

	Pre-World War II	Post-World War II	Present
Area (square miles)	54,244	49,370	49,370
Population	14,700,000	12,300,000	14,400,000

In percent of total population

	Pre-World War II	Post-World War II	Present
Rate of literacy	95%	95%	100%
Major Nationalities			
Czechs and Slovaks	66%	92%	93%
Magyars	5%	2%	4%
Germans	23%	4%	1%
Ruthenians	4%	1%	1%
Main Religions			
Catholic	74%	78%	77%
Czechoslovak (Protestant)	5%	7%	8%
Protestant	8%	7%	7%
Orthodox	4%	0.3%	0.5%
Jewish	2%	0.4%	0.5%

THE CZECHOSLOVAK ECONOMY

	Unit of Measurement	Pre-World War II	Post-World War II	Present
Industrial Production				
Steel	(Metric tons)	2,300,000	2,300,000	10,000,000
Black coal	" "	16,700,000	16,200,000	26,900,000
Brown coal	" "	17,900,000	22,400,000	74,100,000
Cement	" "	1,300,000	1,400,000	6,500,000
Processed meat	" "	400,000	300,000	900,000
Refined sugar	" "	600,000	600,000	1,000,000
Agricultural Production				
Wheat	" "	1,500,000	1,400,000	2,500,000
Rye	" "	1,600,000	1,100,000	800,000
Barley	" "	1,100,000	900,000	1,900,000
Oats	" "	1,200,000	900,000	1,000,000
Sugar beets	" "	4,700,000	4,500,000	7,700,000
Potatoes	" "	9,600,000	6,600,000	6,000,000
Length of Railways	(miles)	8,455	8,161	8,313

summer and winter sports. Invalids and the elderly come to Czechoslovakia from all countries of Europe to bathe in the soothing waters of hundreds of mineral springs. The most famous Czech spa is at Carlsbad (now Karlovy Vary), which in bygone days was the swank resort for European nobles, emperors, and kings.

Lovers of nature delight in touring the hundreds of huge mountain caves, some of which contain underground rivers, lakes, and even waterfalls. One cavern in south-central Czechoslovakia is so vast that explorers can find neither beginning nor end. But in frontier regions tourists are not welcome at some caves, where large stockpiles of Czech and Soviet arms are hidden, waiting for future European war.

For history-loving tourists all Czechoslovakia is one vast museum. Very striking are the medieval statues of saints at many bridges and crossroads—a vivid reminder that three-fourths of the Czechoslovak nation are still Roman Catholics. These statues are so artistic that the atheist Communist government has allowed most of them to remain with their stone hands and crucifixes blessing passers-by.

Then there are no less than two thousand medieval castles, some in cities but most scattered through the countryside on the crests of mountains and hills. Today they are often used as schools, hospitals, or government offices. Many are open to tourists, but some are off limits—especially the fortresses which are now communist prisons.

Since Czechoslovakia was a battleground in countless European wars, there are many famous battlefields. Some are national parks—for instance, Austerlitz, where Napoleon defeated a combined Austro-Russian army in 1805, or Sadowa where Prussia crushed the Austrian forces in 1866. Guides at such fields carefully explain the battle tactics and maneuvers.

Most interesting for erudite tourists are the old sections of Czechoslovak cities. Here one strolls along narrow crooked streets amid palaces, castles, cathedrals, town halls, and quaint medieval homes built anytime from the tenth century onward. The tourist can view every era and style of East European and German architecture, though Gothic predominates. Since these beautiful old buildings were constructed with stone, they are well preserved, and the Czech Communist government safeguards them as jewels of history. Some Czechoslovak towns are so old and picturesque that the government has declared their entire area to be a national monument.

With its warm mineral springs, Carlsbad (now Karlovy Vary) in Bohemia has long been a spa for the European rich. This 1840 Carlsbad crowd includes a Russian, Turks, and French dandies. *Eastfoto*

Only too often Czechoslovakia has been the battleground for other nations' wars. Shown above is the Battle of Austerlitz in Moravia, where Napoleon's army of 65,000 routed a combined Austro-Russian force of 80,000 men *NYPL*

Austerlitz today—a peaceful rural park. *Eastfoto*

Lively Slovak peasants dance in an upland pasture of the Carpathian Mountains. *CTB*

Czechoslovakia has existed only since 1918 as a unified country. Before then the Czechoslovak lands were the Austro-Hungarian imperial provinces of Bohemia, Moravia, and Slovakia. Each province differs in terrain, history, and development. Bohemia, the most westerly and most industrial, is a mosaic of hills and valleys ringed by mountains. In the north and northwest are the wooded Sudeten Mountains—the Sudetenland which in the past was largely German in population, and which Nazi Germany temporarily annexed. Other border heights are the Bohemian forest in the southwest and the Bohemian-Moravian highlands of the southeast.

The only large lowland in Bohemia is the Elbe River valley. Prague (Praha), the Czechoslovak capital, is on both banks of the Vltava River—a tributary of the Elbe. With a population of more than 1,000,000, Prague is the only large city in Czechoslovakia and is the nation's greatest industrial and cultural center. Called the city of a hundred towers because of its many castle turrets and church spires, Prague was founded as early as the ninth century but grew into a large city only during the industrialization of the last hundred years.

The second largest Bohemian city is Pilsen (Plzen), with about 120,000 people and the biggest breweries in Czechoslovakia. Tangy Pilsener beer is exported to all corners of the world. Here too is the giant Skoda (now Lenin) factory—one of the largest armament plants in Europe. Besides making munitions for the Czech and Soviet armies, Skoda builds a variety of machinery, locomotives, and automobiles.

Moravia, the central province of Czechoslovakia, is more agricultural than Bohemia. Like the Bohemians, the Moravians are Czechs. Again there are mountains: the Sudetens in the northwest and Carpathians in the northeast. But southern Moravia is a fertile plain, where so much fruit is grown that entire regions resemble vast orchards. In this plain is Brno, the Moravian capital with a population of 328,000. With its medieval streets and modern factories, Brno has the largest textile industry of any Czechoslovak city. Military guns are also a major manufacture.

High in the Tatra Mountains a skier kicks off some sticky snow. *CTB*

With its winding streets, quaint buildings, spires and towers, the "old town" section of Prague looks like a medieval city. *UPI*

Prague, Czechoslovakia's capital, is a city of contrasts. Here a modern bus station operates in front of a lofty medieval church. *Eastfoto*

The Czechoslovak National Theatre, near one of Prague's beautiful river bridges. *CTB*

Entrance to Prague's symphony hall. In the background rises Hradcany Castle—center of Czech government since the Middle Ages. *Sovfoto*

In the Bohemian city of Pilsen is the giant Skoda plant, mass-producing locomotives, automobiles, artillery, and automatic weapons. *UPI*

A huge Skoda assembly line, chromium-plating automobile parts. *UPI*

Kegs of Pilsner beer being unloaded from a freighter in New York harbor. *UPI*

Bratislava, the Slovak capital, a scenic city encircled by vineyards and parks. *Eastfoto*

Overlooking Bratislava is this medieval castle, which for 200 years was the palace of Hungarian kings. *Eastfoto*

This crude Venus, unearthed in Moravia, was carved during the Stone Age by ancient tribesmen who preceded the Slavs. *Orbis*

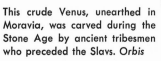

65

The most easterly province is Slovakia, inhabited by Slovaks and more rural than either Bohemia or Moravia. Most of Slovakia consists of the Carpathian Mountains, which rise to their greatest height in the High Tatra range near the Polish frontier. But even the Tatras are only half the height of the Alps and therefore lack the glaciers so common in Switzerland.

In the south along the Danube is a small plain where the Slovak capital city of Bratislava (formerly Pressburg) was founded about the year 1000.

Statue of a fierce pagan god worshiped by the ancient Slavs, who migrated into Czechoslovakia between the fifth and seventh centuries. CTB. Ruins of a well-planned ancient settlement discovered by Czech archaeologists. CTB

Surrounded by parks and vineyards, Bratislava with a population of 268,000 is Czechoslovakia's main railway junction and chief Danubian port. There are annual business fairs with much trading in grain and wine. For more than two hundred years (1541–1784), when most of Hungary was occupied by the Turks, Bratislava was the Hungarian capital.

Ancient history of the Czechoslovak provinces and peoples is shrouded in obscurity. From Roman chronicles we know that in the first century B.C. Bohemia and Moravia were inhabited by Celtic tribes called Boii, and Bohemia is named after them. About 15–10 B.C. these Celts were conquered in Bohemia by the Germanic Marcumanni and in Moravia by the Germanic Quadi.

The Marcumanni and Quadi held the area until the fifth century A.D. when they were defeated and dispersed by an overwhelming Hunnish invasion. But the nomadic Huns did not settle in the Carpathians, thus leaving an empty region which the Czechs and Slovaks quickly occupied.

Eastern Poland, the original homeland of all Slavic peoples, was probably the area from which the Czechs and Slovaks migrated into Bohemia, Moravia, and Slovakia. At the time they were disorganized and rather primitive tribes paying tribute to the Huns.

The Hunnish empire crumbled when its ruler died and its army was decimated by plague. The Avars, another Asian Mongoloid tribe, conquered the Huns and established a domain extending from central Europe to the Volga River. From the sixth

Czech Princess Libusa in 722 founds a settlement at Prague, dreaming how it will grow into a glorious city. LC

to the ninth centuries, the Czechs and Slovaks lived mostly under Avar rule.

Revolt against the Avars was the first Czech independence movement. Under the leadership of Samo, a Frankish merchant, Bohemia became a free nation about 623. Samo's Bohemian kingdom was the first Czech state and—more important—the first organized Slavic state anywhere in East Europe. But the tiny kingdom was too weak to survive, and in 659 it again fell under Avar control.

Samo and his kingdom actually existed, though we know few details. But from the Avar period also came a romantic legend:

In southern Poland of the eighth century there lived a nobleman named Cech (Czech) who committed a murder and had to flee for his life. With his followers, he found sanctuary in Bohemia. Cech had three daughters, of whom the third was the beautiful Libusa. Spurning the proposals of noblemen, she married a handsome but humble peasant named Premysl whom she truly loved. Thus began the Premyslide dynasty of Bohemian princes.

One day, while traveling along the Vltava River, Libusa was delighted to find a charming valley. She stopped and prophesied: "I see a city whose glory shall reach the stars!" On this site, in 722, Premysl and Libusa founded the city of Prague.

Not legendary but very real was Frankish King Charlemagne's defeat of the Avars in 796, freeing Bohemia, Moravia, and Slovakia from Asian rule. In the power vacuum arose the Great Moravian Empire, which at its height controlled Moravia, Bohemia, Slovakia, southern Poland, and part of Hungary. At the time, the Czechs and Slovaks were still pagans, but Moravian Prince Rastislav (846–70) desired his empire to become Christian. Fearing that German priests might spread Teutonic influence, the prince asked the Byzantine Empire to send him Slavic-speaking missionaries. In response came Saint Cyril and Saint Methodius—two renowned Greek monks who invented the Cyrillic alphabet used today in Russia, Bulgaria, and part of Yugoslavia. Methodius personally baptized Prince Borivoj of Bohemia in 873.

Had the work of the two saints been of lasting effect, Czechoslovakia today would use the Cyrillic alphabet and be mostly Greek Orthodox in religion. But after Cyril and Methodius died, German bishops gradually took control of the Czech and Slovak churches, establishing Roman Catholicism with its Latin alphabet.

The Great Moravian Empire lasted about a hundred years. At the close of the ninth century, costly wars were fought against German princes while a new threat arose from the east—the Asian Magyars (Hungarians) who were swarming into the Danubian basin. The last Moravian ruler, Mojmir II, died in 906 fighting the Magyars who conquered Slovakia, ravaged Moravia, and founded a Hungarian kingdom on the Danubian plain.

Defeat by the Magyars exerted grave, long-time influence on the Czech and Slovak future. Hungarian rule of Slovakia was to continue a thousand years, with the Slovaks being peasant serfs of the Magyar landlords who replaced the Slovak nobility. Hungarian overlordship was not only harsh but unprogressive, with little done to develop trade or handicrafts. So Slovakia stagnated for a millennium, but the Slovak peasants kept their language

Holy Roman Emperor Charlemagne, who by 805 freed the Czechs and Slovaks from Avar rule. *LC.* The brothers Saint Cyril and Saint Methodius—renowned Byzantine missionaries who in the ninth century converted Moravia and Bohemia to Christianity. *NYPL*

and customs alive with encouragement from their only leaders—the local Catholic clergy.

With its empire destroyed by the Magyars, Moravia survived as a weak principality that fell more and more under Bohemian leadership and control. Meanwhile, Bohemia, never conquered by the Magyars, flourished under the rule of the Premyslide dynasty whose princes claimed to be descendants of the legendary Premysl. During the tenth century, when Bohemia was strong, the Premyslide princedom included Bohemia, Moravia, German Silesia, and even part of Hungary.

Best remembered of the early Premyslide rulers is Saint Wenceslaus, a Catholic murdered about 935 by his allegedly pagan brother Boleslav. In cold fact Boleslav was also probably a Christian whose motive for murder was desire for power rather than antireligious fervor. But regardless of historical accuracy, Wenceslaus became the patron saint of the Czechs and is still revered today.

During the eleventh century Bohemia grew weaker, and by mid-century the Premyslide princes began to pay tribute to Germany's Holy Roman Emperor. Thus, Bohemia and Moravia joined this

Duke Boleslav II, reigning 967–99, created a Bohemian empire including Moravia, Silesia, and part of Poland. Here his wife Emma kisses the feet of a statue of Saint Wenceslaus, whom her father-in-law murdered. *NYPL*

Bohemia's "Good King Wenceslaus," murdered around 935 by his brother, became Czechoslovakia's patron saint. *Sphinx Publishers*

Tomb and death statue of Bohemian King Ottokar II (1253–78), who created an empire extending south to the Adriatic Sea. *NYPL*

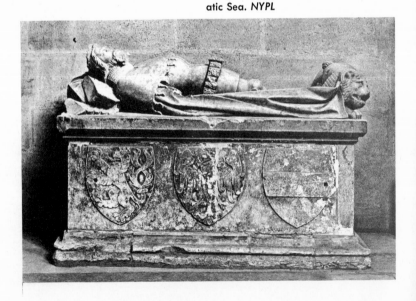

Bohemian King Vladislav. *NYPL*

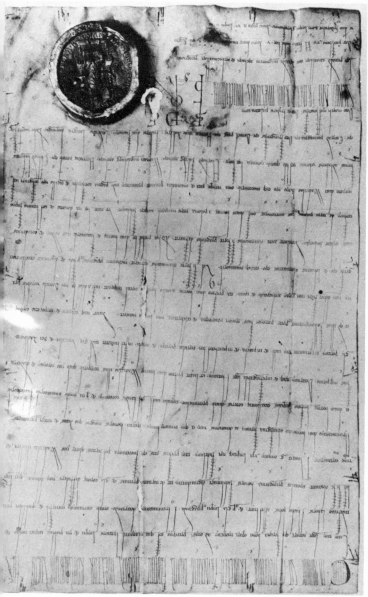

Oldest of all documents in the Bohemian state archives is this 1158 edict of Holy Roman Emperor Frederick Barbarossa granting the title of "king" to Prince Vladislav of Bohemia. *Eastfoto*

King Ottokar II kneeling in homage to Holy Roman Emperor Rodolf, who had just defeated him in the Bohemian war. *NYPL*

empire, which for a hundred years had protected them from the fierce Magyars. German nobles started infiltrating Bohemia, creating estates tilled by Czech tenant farmers. From this medieval period come the first Czech and Slovak written documents —in Latin but with distinctive Slavic accent markings. Czechoslovak scholars claim, with some justification, that Czech was therefore the first of all Slavic languages to appear in written form.

In the twelfth century, Moravia was elevated in rank to a margravate with its own courts and administration, but still under Bohemian control. The earliest-known Czech hymns and folk songs date from this era. An unusual feature of such music was the absence of harmony, all voices singing the melody in unison. Later, after mastering harmony, Czech choruses often still sang this unison to perpetuate national tradition.

Very important for Czech prestige was the coronation of Prince Ottokar I (1197–1230) as King of Bohemia—a title granted by the Holy Roman Emperor. At the time, the empire was a loose confederation of several hundred principalities, duchies, counties, and free cities, but with no kingdoms. Henceforth, the Bohemian king outranked every noble in Germany except the emperor himself.

During the reign of Ottokar II (1253–78), the Bohemian kingdom temporarily controlled much of present-day Austria and owned ports on the Adriatic Sea. From 1300 to 1306, the Bohemian monarchs were also kings of Poland.

The Ottokar era witnessed the rise of Bohemian cities: their growth was officially encouraged, partly to reduce the power of the landowning nobility, and also because townspeople were a new source of taxes. Many of the new townsmen were immigrants from Germany. These cities brought prosperity to Bohemia, which became one of the most urban of all medieval European nations.

King Wenceslaus III (1305–6) of Bohemia and Poland was murdered in Poland by unknown persons for unknown reasons. Thus ended the Premyslide dynasty, which at the time was probably the oldest royal family in Europe.

A period of confusion followed until 1310, when the Holy Roman Emperor persuaded the Bohemian nobles to elect as king his son, Count John of Luxembourg. John added German Silesia and Lusatia to the Bohemian realm, but spent little time in Prague, preferring to be a wandering ad-

The last three Bohemian kings of the Premyslide dynasty *(from left to right):* Ottokar II (1253–78), Wenceslaus II (1278–1305), and Wenceslaus III (1305/6). *NYPL*

venturer. He was killed in France in 1346 at the battle of Crécy, which he foolishly fought in when already blind.

John's son Charles IV (1346–78) was the greatest of all Bohemian kings, and also the first King of Bohemia to be simultaneously the Holy Roman Emperor. Charles made Prague his imperial headquarters and there constructed many fine new buildings. In 1348 he founded Prague (now Charles) University—the first university in the Holy Roman Empire.

Until this time the Holy Roman Emperor had been chosen by six electors: three top German nobles and three archbishops. To increase the power of his kingdom, Emperor Charles in 1356 issued a Golden Bull decreeing that the King of Bohemia also be an imperial elector. As an elector the king

could coin his own money, and there was no appeal from the decisions of his court.

Despite Charles's efforts to make Bohemia great, the kingdom declined after his death. Both the Czech nobility and church leaders attempted to weaken the power of the Bohemian crown. In this confused situation arose a religious reformer named Jan Hus (1369–1415), who was to exert longtime influence on Czech history.

Hus was a highly educated Catholic priest and professor who once served as rector (president) of Prague University. His book reforming the spelling of Bohemian written language founded the Czech literary style. But Hus began to question the wealth and aristocratic power of the Czech Catholic Church, which he believed to have abandoned the humility and poverty of early Christian priests. Re-

◄ Statue of John of Luxembourg, Bohemia's king from 1310 to 1346. A military adventurer, he was killed battling the British in France. *NYPL*

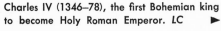

Charles IV (1346–78), the first Bohemian king to become Holy Roman Emperor. *LC* ►

The rector *(on the right)* and students of Prague University, which Emperor Charles IV founded in 1348. *NYPL*

Jan Hus—the great Czech priest, professor, and Protestant reformer—on trial for heresy before a council of Catholic bishops in the German city of Constance. *LC*

Near Prague, Charles IV built this stately castle, which today is a tourist attraction. *Eastfoto*

Jan Hus burning at the stake, after being condemned to death by the Council of Constance. *Eastfoto*

Giant statue of Jan Hus in modern Prague. *UPI*

Holy Roman Emperor Sigismund, whose Catholic crusades (Hussite Wars) of 1419–36 could not conquer Bohemia's Protestant Hussites. *LC*

garding church communion, he argued that the congregation should partake of both bread and wine like the priest, not just bread alone. By sharing the wine, the laity would be equal to the clergy. His emblem therefore became the chalice.

Preaching in Prague and to peasants in open fields, Hus began to attract a wide following. Alarmed by his success, the Catholic Church invited him to attend its Council of Constance with the Holy Roman Emperor's promise that he would not be harmed. But the Council immediately put Hus on trial, convicted him of heresy, and in 1415 burned him at the stake.

The martyrdom of Jan Hus only intensified the Hussite movement in Bohemia, with Prague University becoming known as the "university of heretics." Bohemian King Wenceslaus (1378–1419) tolerated the Hussites until just before his death, when he tried to wrest Prague churches from their control.

Wenceslaus's brother, the Holy Roman Emperor Sigismund, then demanded the Bohemian throne. The Hussites refused because the emperor had broken his promise to safeguard Jan Hus at the Council of Constance. With papal support, Sigismund launched a series of Catholic crusades against the Bohemian heretics. Thus in 1419 be-

gan the Hussite Wars that devastated Bohemia for seventeen years.

Most Czechs supported the Hussites, who established kingless Bohemian governments that repulsed Sigismund's crusades. Hussite leaders displayed great military genius by organizing peasant mobs into formidable armies whose armament included horse-drawn battlewagons—mobile forts put in position on hilltops to halt feudal enemy cavalry. After a while the Czech legions even invaded and harassed parts of Germany.

A weakness of the Hussites was their disunity. The moderate Utraquists desired reforms in the Catholic Church, while the radical Taborites wanted a Czech national church completely free from papal control. These groups fought civil wars among themselves only to reunite in common defense of Bohemia.

By 1436, Emperor Sigismund, weary of unsuccessful crusades, agreed at the Catholic Church Council of Basel that Czech laymen could receive wine in communion if they so desired. The Czech nobles, who meanwhile had suppressed the most radical Hussites, accepted this imperial promise and elected the emperor as King of Bohemia.

Statue of Jan Zizka, who led Czech Protestant peasants to victory in the Hussite Wars. Behind him are farm carts used by his troops as battlewagons. *Eastfoto*

Town hall of Tabor, a fortress city built by the Czech Protestants during the Hussite Wars. Underneath this square are vast catacombs where the Hussites hid from Catholic crusaders. *CTB*

Thereafter, for several decades, Utraquist and Catholic churches coexisted peaceably in Bohemia and Moravia.

Sigismund, the last of the Luxembourg dynasty, died in 1437 leaving no direct heir. After a period of confusion, a Czech nobleman named George of Podebrad became Bohemian regent (1452) and then king (1458–71). Bohemia's only Hussite king, George was an able ruler who revived his country's war-devastated economy. To papal displeasure he also protected the Hussites, the most radical of whom formed their own church —the Brethren. During his final years of power George had to repulse another papal crusade against Bohemia, this time originating from Hungary.

George was succeeded by Polish kings, of whom Louis II (1516–26) did Bohemia a great disfavor by tolerating peasant serfdom, which hitherto had been unknown. When Louis, who was also King of Hungary, died in battle against the Turks, he left no heir. Austrian Archduke Ferdinand was elected Bohemian king (1526–62), thus starting the Habsburg dynasty. Though exiling many radical Hussites, Ferdinand tolerated Hussite moderates as did his successor Maximilian II (1562–76). During the reign of King Rudolph II (1576–1611), the Hussite Church of the Brethren produced the first Bible written in Czech—the

beautifully worded Kralice volumes, which exerted much influence on Czech literary style. When Bohemia was threatened by another Catholic crusade from abroad, Rudolph in 1609 decreed freedom of religion for all Protestants, including members of the Lutheran Church, which had attracted a wide Czech following. By this time, two of every three Bohemians were either Hussite or Lutheran.

Rudolph was eventually forced to surrender the Bohemian throne to his brother Matthias, who ruled briefly (1611–17) and then died childless. Foolishly, the Czechs gave the kingship to Habsburg Archduke Ferdinand, despite his known record of violent anti-Protestantism. Once in power, Ferdinand immediately began to suppress Bohemia's Lutheran and Hussite churches. In anger, the Czech Estates (national assembly) during 1618 hurled three royal councilors out the windows of the Hradcany Castle in Prague. Luckily for the councilors, they landed on a pile of manure, dirty but unharmed.

In 1619 the Czechs dismissed Ferdinand as king, and invited Protestant count Frederick V of the Rhineland to be their ruler. Frederick accepted the Bohemian throne, Ferdinand invaded Bohemia, and so began the Thirty Years' War which was to devastate all central Europe.

At the Battle of the White Mountain near Prague in 1620, Ferdinand's Austrian troops

George of Podebrad (1458–71), the only Bohemian king belonging to the Hussite Church. *LC*

Martin Luther in 1517 introduced his Protestant reforms by nailing to a German church door his ninety-five theses criticizing the Catholic clergy. Soon countless Czechs became his followers. *NYPL*

A Hussite Bible, printed in 1500. *NYPL*

The "Defenestration" of 1618, when Czech Protestants threw King Ferdinand's Catholic viceroys out the windows of Hradcany Castle. *LC*

Execution in Prague (1621) of twenty-seven leaders of the unsuccessful Czech revolt against Habsburg King Ferdinand. *Orbis*

routed the Czech army. His punishment of the Czechs was horrible. The Bohemian kingdom was abolished, becoming for three hundred years a mere Austrian province. All nobles who had supported the Hussites lost their lands. Three-fourths of all Bohemian estates were handed over to alien nobles imported from abroad.

One-quarter of the old nobility and town burghers fled to other countries, usually never to return. Among them were some of the greatest Czech writers and intellectuals.

Protestantism was ruthlessly suppressed, and the Hussites who remained in Bohemia had to go underground. About 200,000 members of the Church of the Brethren were exiled to Poland and Germany, where their descendants founded the Moravian church that today has branches in both Europe and America.

Ferdinand also decreed that the Habsburgs would be hereditary monarchs of Bohemia, which henceforth must use German as the official language. Catholic priests burned tens of thousands of Hussite books, and for a hundred years Czech literature almost ceased to exist.

Meanwhile, the Thirty Years' War continued, but with little Czech participation and for other goals besides the Bohemian throne. Bohemia was a battleground for many of the outside armies, so war destruction added to other woes. When the war ended in 1648, half of Bohemia's population was missing.

Economic recovery was slow, and Bohemia became increasingly Germanized, even to the point that Prague seemed more German than Czech. The War of the Austrian Succession (1740–42) briefly aroused hope that Prussia might free Bohemia from Austrian rule. But Prussia merely annexed Silesia, leaving the Czechs under the firm control of Austrian Empress Maria Theresa (1740–80).

Maria's son, Emperor Joseph II (1780–90), aided the Czechs and Slovaks by several liberal reforms. At the start of his reign he decreed religious

Bishop Jan Amos Comenius (1592–1670), greatest of the Bohemian scholars fleeing to west Europe after the failure of the 1618–20 Czech rebellion. His *Testament* predicted that "the rule of thy country will again return unto thee, O Czech people." *Sphinx Publishers*

Austrian Empress Maria Theresa (1740–80), who converted Bohemia into a mere Austrian province. *LC*

Prussian King Frederick the Great, who defeated Austria in the War of the Austrian Succession (1740–42). Czechs hoped that he might free them from Austrian tyranny. *LC*

Prince Metternich (1773–1859), reactionary Viennese statesman, who opposed any attempts at Czech autonomy within the Austrian Empire. *LC*

Abbé Joseph Dobrovsky (1753–1829), the first Czech scholar to analyze the kinship of all Slavic languages. *Sphinx Publishers*

The writings of Frantisek Palacky (1798–1876) recalled the grandeur of Bohemian history and the eternal conflict between Czechs and Germans. *LC*

Ludevit Stur (1815–56), poet and politician, whose works romanticized the virtues of the Slovak people. *LC*

Among the wave of European revolutions during 1848, both Czechs and Slovaks rebelled against Austrian rule. Above are Czech civilians battling Austrian troops in a Prague square. *Orbis*

freedom for all Protestants, thus permitting the Lutheran and Hussite churches to revive. He liberated the serfs, who increased their incomes as free tenant farmers. Former serfs also helped Czech industrialization by migrating to the cities to man infant industries. In 1784 Joseph founded the Royal Bohemian Academy of Sciences, which did much to revive Czech culture.

Joseph was succeeded by several mild Hapsburg rulers, who continued the Austrian encouragement of Bohemian cultural life. A conservatory, an art academy, and a national museum arose in Prague. These institutions contributed to a Czech renaissance with noted scholars who included Abbé Josef Dobrovsky (1753–1829), the world's first analyst of the structure of all Slavic languages; Josef Jungmann (1773–1847), historian of Czech literature and compiler of a voluminous Czech-German dictionary; and Frantisek Palacky (1798–1876), popularizer of Czech history and founder of Pan-Slavism. The Czech renaissance aided the revival of Slovak culture, one of whose greatest spokesmen was poet and author Ludevit Stur (1815–56), who created the modern Slovak literary language.

Czech and Slovak cultural rebirth inspired mass nationalistic sentiments that erupted into mild rebellions during 1848—the year of revolutions throughout Europe. The Czechs led by Palacky demanded freedom of the press, political autonomy, and equality of the Czech and German languages. But Palacky still desired Bohemia to remain in the Austrian Empire, which he hoped to transform into a democratic federation of self-governing nationalities.

Meanwhile, the Slovaks were rebelling against the Hungarians who were rebelling against the Austrians. Slovakia, among whose leaders was Ludevit Stur, asked for political autonomy, official use of the Slovak language, creation of a Slovak-speaking school system from first grade to university, and Czecho-Slovak unity. But like the Czechs, the Slovaks envisioned their future as part of the Austrian Empire.

Both the Czech and Slovak revolts were easily suppressed. To weaken the Czechs, Moravia was detached from Bohemia and became a separate Austrian province.

The Slovaks fared much worse than the Czechs. As long as Hungary had been under direct Austrian control, Austria gave Slovakia some protection from excesses by the Magyar nobility. But in 1867, after defeat by Prussia in the Seven Weeks' War, enfeebled Austria had to elevate Hungary to equal partnership in the Austrian Empire. Thereafter, Hungary was in complete control of its

Austria's Emperor Franz Josef (1848–1916), who appointed Czechs to high posts in his Vienna government. *Photoworld*. Art flourished in nineteenth-century Bohemia. This charming portrait was painted by Josef Manes (1820–71). *Eastfoto*

Rebels barricading the gateway to a Prague bridge during the 1848 revolution. *UDS*

Bedrich Smetana (1824–84) *(below left)* founded Czechoslovak modern classical music. Most famous of his eight operas is *The Bartered Bride*. *NYPL*. Antonin Dvorak (1841–1904) composed many symphonies, one of which, *From the New World*, honors the United States, where he lived for several years. *NYPL*

A Czech Amazon of 1848 on the Prague barricades. *Sphinx Publishers*

internal affairs, including the fate of its Slavic minorities. The result was greater Magyarization of Slovakia than ever before. In 1874 Hungary even closed all Slovak high schools and colleges because they were teaching Pan-Slavism.

Fortunately for the Czechs, Bohemia and Moravia were under Austrian rather than Hungarian rule. By the late nineteenth century, the Austrian Emperor Franz Josef (1848–1914) granted important concessions to his Czech domains. Prague University, where the language of instruction had been German, was divided into Czech and

Some Czechoslovak opera stars were famous in the United States as well as Europe. *(Left)* Emmy Destinn (1878–1930), Bohemian soprano, sang leading roles at the Metropolitan Opera House in New York for almost a decade. *NYPL. (Center)* Maria Jeritza, born in 1887 in the Moravian city of Brno, joined the Metropolitan Opera Company in 1921. After a glorious career, she retired in 1935 to live quietly in California. *NYPL. (Right)* Thomas Masaryk (1850–1937)—professor, philosopher, and politician—was a realist who considered past leaders of Czechoslovak nationalism to have been impractical idealists. *UPI*

During World War I, Masaryk was in the West, where he became president of the Czechoslovak National Council agitating for his country's independence. Here he sits *(center)* before the Liberty Bell in Philadelphia, at a meeting of East European exile leaders. *UPI*

German faculties of equal size and importance. Czech became the official language of Bohemian law courts along with German. Since many Czechs spoke German but few Germans mastered the Czech language, these bilingual courts helped create an efficient Czech civil service. Czechs also held high posts in the Austrian imperial government, some even serving as cabinet ministers.

All these concessions did not satisfy the Czech politicians, who demanded that Bohemia become an equal partner of Austria and Hungary in the empire. Though the emperor seriously considered this request, he vetoed it to please the Austrians, Bohemian Germans, and Hungarians—all of whom feared Czech nationalism.

Czech politicians expressed their frustration by boycotting or disrupting meetings of the Bohemian and Austrian imperial parliaments. At the crucial moment when World War I began, neither parliament was functioning because of disorders by Czech deputies.

Meanwhile, a new Czech leader had arisen: Prague university professor Thomas Masaryk (1850–1937). Born in Moravia of humble Czech and Slovak parents, Masaryk worked his way through college to become a great philosopher. He authored several books, one of which was a brilliant criticism of Marxism. Western in outlook, he married an American whose last name (Garrigue) he gallantly adopted as his own middle name.

Eduard Benes (1884–1948) during World War I at his desk in Paris, where he was secretary of the Czechoslovak National Council. *UPI*

The brilliant Slovak astronomer Milan Stefanik, while serving in the French air force during World War I. He induced important French statesmen to champion Czechoslovak independence. *LC*

The Czechoslovak National Council organized exiled Czechs and Slovaks into troop units to help the Allies win World War I. Above are Czechoslovak soldiers on the French front. *UPI*

Thomas Garrigue Masaryk called himself a realist, believing past Czech politicians to have been overly romantic and idealistic. By writing and

lecturing at home and abroad, he achieved great fame both in the West and among all Slavs of the Austro-Hungarian Empire. Even before World War I began, he was the main leader of the Czech national movement.

At the start of the World War in 1914, Masaryk was in the West, where he stayed to agitate for Czechoslovak postwar independence. In this noble endeavor he was ably assisted by a younger Prague University professor, Eduard Benes (1884–1948), and by the brilliant Slovak astronomer Milan Stefanik. This triumvirate formed a Czechoslovak National Council in Paris, and visited other Entente capitals (and Washington as well) to gain international support. During 1918 before World War I ended in German and Austrian defeat, all major Entente Powers recognized Marsaryk's council as the government in exile of a future free Czechoslovakia.

In Russia of World War I were other Czechoslovak exile troops— the Czech Legion, shown here at ceremonies in a Ural city. *LC*

When Russia went Communist, concluding peace with Germany and Austria-Hungary, the Czech Legion fought its way across Siberia to embark on Allied ships at Pacific ports. Here are Czech soldiers wearing Siberian coats to stay alive at 40° below zero. *LC*

Czech troops beside the boxcars that carried them from European Russia to the Pacific coast. *LC*

Meanwhile the government in exile had formed an army in exile. Czechs and Slovaks living abroad organized small troop units aiding the French and Italian forces. More important was the Russian front, where 45,000 Czech and Slovak deserters from the Austro-Hungarian army formed a "Czech Legion" eager to fight their former masters. Tsarist Russia made little use of these troops, but the succeeding Provisional Government sent them into battle against Austria in 1917. This Provisional Government was soon overthrown by the Bolsheviks, who concluded peace with Germany and Austria-Hungary, leaving the Czech Legion stranded in western Russia. The Bolsheviks agreed that the Legion could cross Siberia for embarkation at Pacific ports on Entente ships heading for West Europe.

The Legion began battling the Bolsheviks before it even reached Siberia, with both sides claiming the other had broken the peace. Then the

Czech Legionnaires arriving at the Pacific coast port of Vladivostok to sail for France on Allied ships. By the time they reached Europe, World War I was over. *UPI*

Just before the 1918 surrender of Austria-Hungary to the Allies, a general strike in Czechoslovak cities undermined local Viennese viceroys. These are strikers in the Moravian city of Ostrava. *UDS*

The Czechoslovak National Council in 1918, when the Allies recognized it as a government-in-exile. *UPI*

Czechs seized control of the Trans-Siberian Railroad and aided anti-Bolshevik forces in the Russian Civil War. Finally reaching the Pacific coast, the Legion sailed halfway around the world to Europe and home.

The Czechoslovak homeland was a free nation before the Legion arrived, having declared independence in 1918 when the Austro-Hungarian Empire collapsed in defeat. The Paris Peace Conference drew boundaries giving Czechoslovakia the historic provinces of Bohemia, Moravia, and Slovakia, plus underdeveloped mountainous Ruthenia—a Ukrainian region east of Slovakia. Ruthenia had been annexed by the Austrian Empire during the eighteenth-century partitions of Poland. Since Ruthenia was separated from Russia by Polish and Romanian territory, Czechoslovakia inherited this isolated Ukrainian area.

The new independent Czechoslovakia was prosperous. Possession of most of the industry of the former Austrian Empire gave the Czechs economic superiority over other East European countries, which were mainly agricultural. New industries were developed with government support in overly rural Slovakia. A modernization program was started in impoverished Ruthenia.

Czechoslovak agriculture was aided by a land reform that divided the great estates (owned mostly by Germans and Hungarians) into peasant private farms. The peasants responded by working harder

on land now their own, sharing the general prosperity.

Some of the Czechoslovak economic success between World Wars I and II also resulted from the stability of the government. Masaryk was president of Czechoslovakia from 1918 till his retirement in 1935. Benes was Masaryk's foreign minister and succeeded him as president. Of all East European countries, only Czechoslovakia remained a democracy throughout the entire interwar period.

Nevertheless there were grave internal problems concerning national minorities. Czechoslovakia had been given natural boundaries: mountains on the north, east and west, and the Danube River on the south. These frontiers were not racial, so the total population of 13,600,000

Returning from the West in 1918, Foreign Minister Benes announces in Prague that Czechoslovakia is a free, democratic republic. *UPI*

With little fanfare, in 1920 left-wing Social-Democrats organized the Czechoslovak Communist Party which three decades later would convert their country into a Soviet satellite. This is the first issue of the Czechoslovak Communist newspaper *Rude Pravo* (Red Rights). UDS

Mass gymnastics are the most popular Czechoslovak sport. Here Prague stadium is host for no less than 25,000 girl athletes. *UPI*

Listening to a Hitler speech demanding German control over the Czech Sudetenland are Sudeten Nazi leader Konrad Henlein *(wearing glasses)*, his cruel assistant Karl Frank *(third from left)*, and former German foreign minister Von Neurath *(right)*. *UPI*

Henlein inspecting his illegal private army of Nazi Sudeten Germans, who in 1938 were ready to rebel against the Czechoslovak government. *UPI*

Nazi threats did not scare Czechoslovakia, which in 1938 prepared its million-man army to fight. Below are Czechoslovak cavalry reservists mobilized for action. *UPI*

included 3,100,000 Germans (mostly in the Sudetenland), 700,000 Hungarians (mainly in Slovakia), 600,000 Ruthenians, and about 100,000 Poles. Though all minorities used their own languages and had their own schools, they were restless and began looking for outside support from neighboring kindred nations.

Even the Slovaks, outnumbered by the Czechs three to one, considered themselves a mistreated minority. They accused Masaryk of betraying a 1918 promise, made in Pittsburgh, that Slovakia would have political autonomy within the Czechoslovak state. Some leaders of the Slovak national movement proved to be agents of Hungary.

Beset by these internal troubles, Czechoslovakia pursued a cautious foreign policy. In the early 1920s the Little Entente alliance was concluded with Romania and Yugoslavia to prevent Hungary from regaining territory lost to all three nations. High hopes were placed in the League of

Czechoslovak artillery taking up positions near the German frontier. *UPI*

President Benes at field maneuvers training the Czechoslovak army to fight Hitler's Wehrmacht. *UPI*

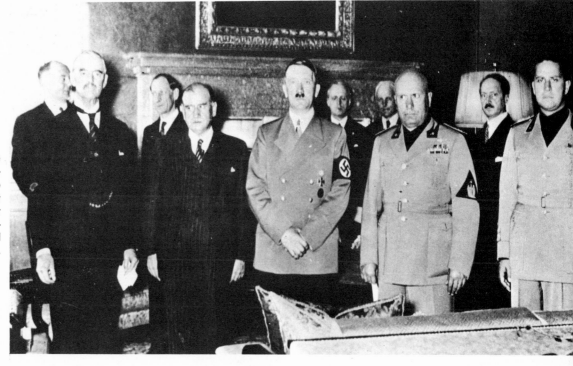

The Munich Conference in the fall of 1938, ordering Czechoslovakia to cede the Sudetenland to Nazi Germany. In front from left to right are British Prime Minister Chamberlain, French Premier Daladier, Hitler, Mussolini, and Italian Foreign Minister Ciano. *UPI*

Nations, and close Czech relations were maintained with France.

Hitler's rise to power in Germany frightened Czechoslovakia, which sought protection in 1935 by concluding a French-Czech-Soviet military alliance. To please the new Russian ally, Czech police in 1937 even warned Stalin about an alleged Red Army plot against him.

This alliance was of little use to Czechoslovakia in 1938, when Hitler demanded the Sudetenland, whose Germans were conducting pro-Nazi riots. Russia suggested referring the crisis to the impotent League of Nations. France refused to come to Czechoslovakia's defense. Both France and Britain warned Czechoslovakia not to fight alone, since such action would probably start another World War. Even if France and England got involved in this war and won, they would not recreate an independent Czechoslovakia.

Betrayed by its allies, Czechoslovakia decided

not to go to war. This was a fatal error, since at the time the Czech army was larger than the Nazi Wehrmacht.

In September 1938, without Czech participation, British, French, German, and Italian leaders met at Munich to settle Czechoslovakia's fate. The Sudetenland was given to Nazi Germany. Czechoslovakia also lost the Teschen industrial district to Poland, and Hungary obtained south Slovakia and southern Ruthenia. Hitler promised to respect the integrity of the remaining Czechoslovak territory.

This promise was broken in March 1939 when German troops occupied all Czechoslovakia, which again did not resist. Bohemia and Moravia became German protectorates (actually Nazi colonies). Slovakia declared itself an independent Fascist state, and Hungary annexed all Ruthenia. Thus Czechoslovakia disappeared from the map, not to be re-created until six years later.

Benes had resigned his presidency and fled abroad in 1938. After World War II began in 1939, he started forming a Czechoslovak government in exile, which gained Allied recognition in 1940. Headquartered in London, the exile government in 1943 concluded a Czech-Soviet military alliance that exists to the present day.

Meanwhile the German occupation of Bohemia and Moravia proved harsh, because Hitler needed the huge quantities of armament produced by Czech industry. Czech colleges, universities, and many schools were closed, and the Gestapo ruthlessly exterminated thousands of Czech intellectuals. The Czech people responded mainly by economic sabotage.

When Hitler invaded Russia in 1941, Slovakia dutifully declared war on the USSR. But as the war continued, most Slovaks learned to hate their oppressive Fascist regime. In 1944 a large-scale Slovak rebellion erupted against the German-dominated Slovak government. The rebels hoped for assistance from Soviet troops, who unfortunately were too far away to help. The revolt failed.

In 1945 Soviet armies arrived in force, American tank troops reached Pilsen, and President Benes returned to Czechoslovakia via Moscow. Bohemia, Moravia, and Slovakia were reunited, but at Stalin's request Ruthenia was ceded to Russia. The loss of backward Ruthenia was almost a blessing. Czechoslovak war losses were totaled and found to be gruesome: 38,000 dead, 2,000,000 people missing, and costly damage to railway rolling stock.

Once Benes was in power, Soviet and American troops withdrew from the country, and Czechoslovakia appeared to have an independent future. In agreement with the Allies, most Sudeten Germans were expelled into Germany and the Sudetenland was repopulated with Czechs and Slovaks. Many Hungarians were also exiled into Hungary. Loss of the Germans, Hungarians, and Ruthenians gave Czechoslovakia a much more homogeneous

Returning to England from the Munich Conference, Prime Minister Chamberlain proudly displays the Munich agreement, which he said would bring "peace in our time." (World War II started a year later.) *UPI*

After surrendering the Sudetenland to Hitler, Benes resigned his presidency and went abroad, leaving Czechoslovakia under a caretaker government headed by *(left to right)*: Premier Josef Tiso, Army Commander in Chief Jan Syrovy, and Foreign Minister Frantisek Chvalkovsky. *UPI*

Rather than live under Hitler, many Czechs fled in 1938 from the Sudetenland. These refugees have just arrived in Prague railway station. *NYPL*

When Hitler occupied all of Czechoslovakia during March 1939, General Syrovy was forced to watch the Nazi victory parade in Prague. On the reviewing stand he sadly shakes hands with a German general. *UPI*

Hitler's first viceroy in German-occupied Bohemia was Baron Von Neurath *(front left)*, here leaving his headquarters in Hradcany Castle on a sight-seeing stroll through Prague. *UPI*

Triumphant Hitler in Prague, greeting local Germans. The smiling officer with spectacles is Heinrich Himmler, head of the dread Gestapo. On the far left is sadist Reinhard Heydrich, who later replaced Von Neurath as German boss of Bohemia. *UPI*

Hitler converted Slovakia into a puppet state. Here the Slovak ambassador and Nazi Foreign Minister Von Ribbentrop sign the 1939 German-Slovak treaty of alliance. *UPI*

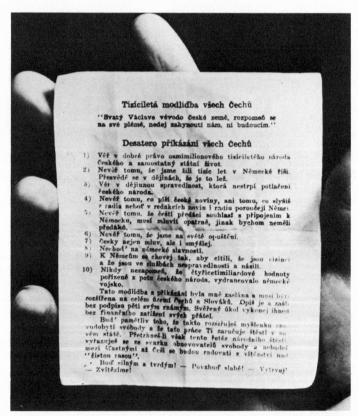

Tiny anti-Nazi leaflet, easy to conceal, issued by the Czechoslovak wartime underground which constantly sabotaged the German occupation. *NYPL*

Rubble of Lidice, a Czechoslovak village destroyed by the Nazis in revenge for Czech assassination of gauleiter Heydrich. *UPI*

Benes and his wife in England, where he spent World War II organizing an exile Czechoslovak government and army. *UPI*

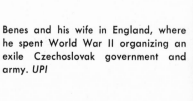

Polish General Sikorski and Czechoslovak president-in-exile Benes review Czech and Slovak troops in wartime England. *UPI*

Cheerful Czechoslovak fighter pilots serving with the Royal Air Force in the Battle of Britain. *UPI*

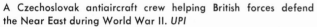

A Czechoslovak antiaircraft crew helping British forces defend the Near East during World War II. *UPI*

The Czechoslovak Brigade attached to Russia's Red Army fighting in the 1943 Battle of Kiev. *UDS*

U.S. General George Patton in 1945 receiving a Czech ornamental vase and a grateful Czech kiss after his army liberated Susice. Russia asked his troops not to advance to Prague. *UPI*

population. Czechs and Slovaks now comprised 92 percent of all inhabitants compared to 66 percent before the war.

In true democratic fashion Benes held parliamentary elections during 1946. The Communists received 38 percent of the total vote—more than any other party. The Czech Communist Party had been organized as early as 1920, was never banned in prewar Czechoslovakia, and had a sizable following among Czech workers.

Benes appointed Klement Gottwald as premier, with orders to form a coalition cabinet. Gottwald was one of the founders of the Czech Communist Party, and since 1927 had been its secretary-general. Deceiving Benes, he used the premiership to pack the police, army, and communications network with trusted Communists and fellow travelers. Meanwhile, in 1947, when Czechoslovakia wanted to receive U.S. economic aid from the Marshall Plan, Stalin commanded Gottwald to refuse.

In 1948 new parliamentary elections were to be held, and the Communist Party was losing support among the Czech workers. To retain power, Gottwald had to act fast. When non-Communist members of his cabinet complained about Communist infiltration of the police, he delivered an ultimatum to President Benes: Let Communists take control of the entire government, or face civil war! Knowing that Stalin supported Gottwald and

that Soviet troops were on the alert around the Czech frontiers, Benes submitted. Thus, in a bloodless one-day coup, Communists seized control of all Czechoslovakia. Benes soon retired; he died heartbroken in a country home outside Prague. Foreign Minister Jan Masaryk, the son of Thomas Masaryk, plunged or was pushed to his death from a ministry window.

Then for twenty years Czechoslovakia was a faithful Soviet satellite. All industry was nationalized, agriculture was collectivized, the press was heavily censored, and concentration camps filled to bursting with political prisoners. The USSR share of Czech foreign trade rose to 60 percent, compared to 1 percent before the war.

Purging of dissidents was almost continual. The first victims were the bourgeoisie and intellectuals. In 1949, 100,000 Czech Communist Party members were purged for allegedly sympathizing with heretical Communist Yugoslavia. In 1950 the purge struck the army and high Communist officials. Rudolf Slansky, Communist Party secretary-general, was one of the worst purge executioners until 1952, when he himself was executed. By that time there was almost no one left to purge.

Meanwhile Czech foreign policy slavishly copied the Soviet by fighting the Cold War against the West and Yugoslavia. Also imported from the USSR was Stalin worship, which Czech Communists developed into a fine art. A Prague newspaper

After driving out the Germans, Russian tanks are cheered by Prague crowds. *UDS*

The postwar Czechoslovak government, again headed by President Benes, punished war criminals quickly and severely. Here is Karl Frank, the "Butcher of Lidice," after execution by hanging. *UPI*

Josef Tiso *(left)*, wartime fascist premier of puppet Slovakia, on trial in 1946 for mass murder of Slovaks and Jews. *UPI*

Early in 1948, a bloodless Communist coup ended Czechoslovak democracy. Here a Prague crowd listens to Communist demands against President Benes. *UPI*

Social-Democratic leader Zdenek Fierlinger, who betrayed his own party to help the Czechoslovak Communists seize power. *UPI*

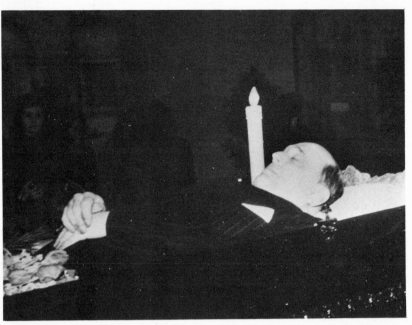

Jan Masaryk, Czechoslovak Foreign Minister and son of Thomas Masaryk, died soon after the Communist coup by falling to the street from a high window. Still uncertain is whether his death was an accident, a suicide, or "defenestration" murder. *UPI*

So popular was anti-Communist Jan Masaryk, even in death, that Communist Premier Klement Gottwald (*at mike*) had to read the funeral oration. *UPI*

The Czechoslovak high command, soon after the Communist takeover. *From left to right:* Defense Minister Ludvik Svoboda, Premier Gottwald, Communist party Secretary-General Rudolf Slansky, and the premier's military aide—General Bulander. *UPI*

mentioned Stalin's name six hundred times in a single issue. The highest peak in the Tatra Mountains was renamed Mount Stalin.

Stalin's death in 1953 brought little change in Czechoslovakia, even though Gottwald died from a cold caught at the Moscow funeral. Gottwald's successor, Zapotocky, held the Czechs under iron control during the 1956 Polish and Hungarian revolutions. When he died in 1957, strongman Antonin Novotny continued the same tough policy.

Czechoslovakia fell increasingly under Russian control. The country was a founding member

Communist dictator Gottwald gaily warning a Prague crowd of 120,000 that he would soon purge all Czechoslovak "reactionaries." *UPI*

Communist purge victims: a group of democratic Czechoslovaks hearing a judge sentence them to prison for alleged treason. *UPI*

Even prominent Communists were caught by the purge. *(Left)* Foreign Minister Vladimir Clementis, a longtime Marxist, was executed in 1952 as an alleged foreign spy. *UPI (Right*, Rudolf Slansky *(second from left)* was one of the chief purge executioners, until he himself was executed in 1952. *UPI*

of the Warsaw Pact military alliance in 1955. During 1963 all large Czech electric power stations were attached to a grid connecting with the Soviet Ukraine. By 1964 most petroleum was imported from the Volga valley via a thousand-mile "Friendship Pipeline." After 1966 the huge Kosice steel plant in Slovakia received most of its iron ore on direct trains from Russia. Politically, militarily, and economically, Czechoslovakia was a mere protectorate of the USSR.

Then in 1968 came a short-lived burst of Czechoslovak independence. Novotny was removed

as Czech president and party first secretary for mismanaging the economy. The presidency was assumed by Ludvik Svoboda, an old general, and the secretaryship fell to a kindly Slovak named Alexander Dubcek. Both men were moderate Communists who instituted economic reforms, ended police terror, and abolished censorship of the press.

Russian officials began visiting Czechoslovakia to warn against excessive liberalization, which might endanger Communist control. Some Soviet troops conducted Warsaw Pact maneuvers on Czech territory, then delayed departing. Huge So-

Under Communism, the already large industry grew much larger. Above is a daring rigger, stringing cables for a new hydroelectric power dam. *Stebou, Zemé*

During the Soviet dictator's lifetime, Czechoslovak officialdom worshiped Stalin like a god. Here fireworks illuminate his statue *(fifth from left)* in Prague. *Eastfoto*

Czechoslovak Communist "art" was forced to glorify industrial might, as in this 1952 painting of turbine installation. *Eastfoto*

Left: Antonin Zapotocky, Czechoslovakia's cruel Communist chief after Gottwald died in 1953 from a cold caught at Stalin's funeral. *UPI. Right:* Stalinist Antonin Novotny, who ruled Czechoslovakia from 1957 until early 1968, when he was ousted by Communist liberals. *UPI*

Liberal Ludvik Svoboda *(right)*, after replacing Novotny as Czechoslovak president, immediately helped introduce democratic reforms. Here he addresses an admiring crowd of Skoda workers. *UPI*

Worried by Czechoslovakia's new democracy, top Soviet statesmen came in the summer of 1968 to the Slovak town of Cierna to argue with Prague liberal leaders. Facing the camera are Czechoslovak President Svoboda *(fourth from right)* and Communist party chief Alexander Dubcek *(third from right)*, both refusing to repeal their reforms. *UPI*

Smiling in Bratislava after a Warsaw Pact Conference (which followed the Cierna meeting) are Dubcek and treacherous Soviet leader Brezhnev, who promised to respect Czechoslovak freedom. *UPI*

viet armies encircled the Czechoslovak frontiers. But Dubcek and Svoboda still continued liberalization.

At the Slovak city of Bratislava, leaders of the USSR, East Germany, Hungary, Poland, Bulgaria, and Czechoslovakia met in a conference that seemed to settle the crisis. But on the night of August 20, 1968, Czechoslovakia was invaded by 200,000 Soviet troops plus small detachments from East Germany, Hungary, Poland, and Bulgaria. Soviet soldiers occupied historic Prague, kidnapped Dubcek, and spirited him into captivity in the USSR.

The Czech government ordered the population not to resist. A joint treaty of Czechoslovakia, East Germany, Hungary, Bulgaria, Poland, and the USSR then provided that most occupation troops would leave the country. But some Soviet forces would remain indefinitely until the Czechoslovak situation "normalized." Dubcek returned from Moscow, and sadly commenced deliberalization. Within a year he and most other Czechoslovak moderates were dismissed from governmental and Communist Party leadership. A new party chief, Gustav Husak, even praised the Soviet occupation. Slowly but surely, all Czechoslovak liberty was liquidated by neo-Stalinist dictatorship.

But the Czechs and Slovaks have not lost hope for future freedom. They survived Habsburg and Hitlerite tyranny and will survive again.

Double-crossing Dubcek, Brezhnev in August 1968 ordered Soviet troops to invade Czechoslovakia, which saved lives by not going to war. Above is a Russian tank policing Prague. *UPI*

A Czech girl cursing the Russian invaders. *UPI*

A Russian tank set on fire by Czech civilians. The flag is stained with the blood of Prague youths slain by Soviet gunfire. *UPI*

Prague students storming the gates of Hradcany Castle in protest against Soviet occupation. *UPI*

What Russia fears is a future Czechoslovak uprising, like this anti-Soviet outburst in Bratislava. *UPI*

BALTIC SEA

•Rostock

MECKLENBURG

⊚Berlin

Potsdam•

BRANDENBURG

Oder River

Elbe River

•Leipzig

Dresden•

SAX

THURINGIA

EAST GERMANY

————— Present Boundary

0   50   100

East Germany

WHEN LIGHTS are low and Communist police are far away, East Germans whisper:

"Dictator Walter Ulbricht finally died and went to the hell he long deserved. Next morning the devil knocks at the pearly gates. A surprised Saint Peter asks what is wrong. The Devil complains:

" 'Ulbricht has arrived in hell, and I am his first refugee.' "

This joke contains much bitter truth. During the first fifteen years (1946–61) of Ulbricht's unkind regime, one of every five East Germans fled to freedom in West Germany. Most of the 4,000,000 escapees were not aged or unskilled but were serious students or youthful workers, farmers, teachers, lawyers, dentists, and doctors. Loss of their skills threw East German life into daily confusion. Without warning, local bus service would stop, stores close, factories stall, or a hospital shut down because key personnel had suddenly skipped the country. West Germany welcomed these capable refugees, whose skills aided rapid recovery from war devastation.

The early exodus from East Germany was easy. Though the East German territories were conquered by Russia's Red Army in mid-1945, no real Iron Curtain was erected until 1952. At first many runaways simply walked abroad through frontier forests. Then Ulbricht's "People's Police" sealed the border with minefields, barbed wire, and a horde of watchmen and vicious watchdogs. Yet the city of Berlin remained a huge escape hatch because it was under both Soviet and Western Allied control. A mere ride by subway, elevated railway, or bus would bring a refugee from Communist East Berlin into the British, French, or American sector, where he could catch a plane to fly 100 miles to the German West. Emigration actually increased after the Iron Curtain was constructed: during 1950 about 198,000 East Germans went westward, and the 1956 total rose to 396,000.

Finally the unpopular Ulbricht regime became so desperate that in 1961 the People's Police built a twenty-eight-mile barricade completely around West Berlin. This so-called Berlin Wall in park forests or fields is a high, double-barbed-wire fence, backed by mined earth. Where there are many buildings, one sees a real stone wall eight to ten feet high with a low barbed-wire fence on top slanting toward the East German side. Broken glass is often glued to the top of the wall. Windows and doors of buildings along the wall are bricked up, sometimes leaving little loopholes from which the People's Police can observe and fire. If a building has a flat roof, a sort of barbed-wire fence is attached along the gutters. Behind the stone wall are one or more high barbed-wire fences and many small cement blockhouses where the People's Police sit with machine guns. There are only eight

Forests and fields in the Ore Mountains of the "Saxon Switzerland" in southern East Germany. Most of the silver, tin, and uranium ores must now be exported to Russia. *EPA*

Some of the four million refugees who fled to West Germany from East Germany to escape Ulbricht's unkind regime. This forlorn group is resting in a West German village, just after sneaking across the border. *Photoworld*

Cruel Walter Ulbricht, East Germany's Communist dictator since 1946. *UPI*

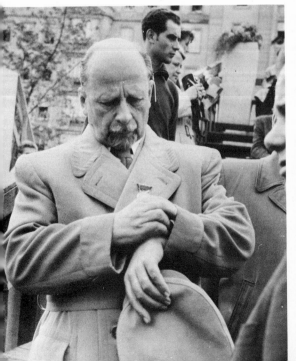

Infant Iron Curtain in 1952 Berlin—a trench easy to jump but hard to cross with bikes. *UPI*

At first after World War II there was no impassible Iron Curtain between the Soviet and Western zones of Allied-occupied Berlin. But this cautious West German stays safely behind the border to photograph Communist Berlin with his telescopic camera. *UPI*

Finally in 1961 comes a real Iron Curtain—the Berlin wall. First, East German troops build a border fence of barbed wire. *Photoworld*

Behind the barbed wire, East Berlin workmen build a concrete border wall. *Wide World Photos*

cross-points, each honeycombed with huge, iron, antitank barriers to stop autos and trucks from crashing through. Crossing a cross-point requires special East German permission, which is difficult to obtain.

Once the wall was completed, the huge refugee flood shrank to a mere trickle of about 1,000 runaways per year. With its footloose population forced to stay home, East Germany finally had a stable labor force, which soon converted economic depression into partial prosperity. Today East German industry is the second largest in the Soviet bloc (after Russia's), sixth in Europe, and eighth in the world. Though still one-third below the West German level, East Germany's standard of living is the highest of any Communist country. Almost all East German families possess home radios, and 60 percent own television sets. No other European nation, east or west, has such a large proportion (one-sixth) of its college-age youth actually en-

The completed Berlin Wall, shown here blocking off the historic Brandenburg Gate. *EPA*

One of the few crossing points along the twenty-eight-mile Berlin Wall. No less than three walls guard this entrance into Communist territory. *EPA*

Shopping for a new TV. Three of every five East German homes have television sets. *Eastfoto*

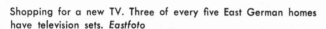

The largest teachers college in East Germany, which leads all Europe in percentage of college-age young people taking higher education. *Eastfoto*

THE EAST GERMAN NATION

	Pre- World War II	Post- World War II	Present
Area (square miles)	—	41,800	41,800
Population	15,100,000	19,000,000	17,000,000
In percent of total population			
Rate of literacy	100%	100%	100%
Urban populace	50%	40%	73%
Major Nationalities			
Germans	97%	99.8%	99.8%
Jews	2%	.02%	.01%
Main Religions			
Protestant	81%	81%	80%
Catholic	12%	12%	9%

THE EAST GERMAN ECONOMY

	Unit of Measurement	Pre- World War II	Post- World War II	Present
Industrial Production				
Electricity	(kilowatt-hours)	26,000,000,000	19,500,000,000	63,200,000,000
Black coal	(metric tons)	3,500,000	2,500,000	1,800,000
Brown coal	" "	118,000,000	109,000,000	242,000,000
Steel	" "	1,700,000	200,000	4,600,000
Agricultural Production				
Wheat	" "	1,500,000	480,000	2,000,000
Rye	" "	2,100,000	1,400,000	2,000,000
Potatoes	" "	13,600,000	8,100,000	14,100,000
Sugar beets	" "	5,500,000	3,100,000	6,900,000
Number of Livestock				
Cattle		3,600,000	2,800,000	5,000,000
Swine		5,700,000	2,000,000	9,200,000
Communications				
Length of railways	(miles)	8,900	7,000	9,200

rolled in higher education. Some East German magazines are banned in Russia because they portray comforts of life still unknown in the less-developed USSR.

Such Teutonic successes have been achieved by a small country with a small population. Surrounded by the Baltic Sea on the north, Poland to the east, Czechoslovakia at the southeast, and West Germany on the west and southwest, East Germany has an area of 41,800 square miles—about the same as that of Tennessee. The population was 19,000,000 in 1946, but is now only 17,000,000

Though this agricultural exhibit displays fine crops, East Germany cannot feed itself and must import some food to survive. *Eastfoto*

Smelting steel at East Germany's largest metallurgical mill. Most of the iron ore for steelmaking is imported from Russia. *Photoworld*

Polish turkeys and geese arriving for an East German holiday. Most imported food comes from other Communist countries. *Eastfoto*

Below, left: Smooth sheet steel from an East German factory. Under Communism the national steel production has almost tripled. *Eastfoto.* Right: A skilled craftsman completing a diesel engine. Machinery manufacture is East Germany's biggest industry. *Eastfoto*

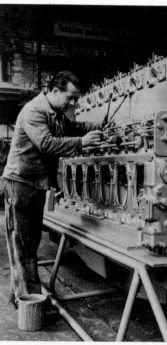

Giant chemical plant constructed by the Communist regime. East Germany ranks second in the world (after the United States) in per capita output of chemicals. *Eastfoto*

A new chemical factory providing fertilizer for farm fields in the Baltic coastal plain. *Eastfoto*

Mass production of lace by machine in Europe's largest lace factory, located in East Germany's southern mountains. *Eastfoto*

because the birthrate has not yet overcome past loss of refugees. Even this smaller populace cannot be completely fed from East German farms, so grain, meat, and butter are imported from both East Europe and the USSR.

Sandy soil is East Germany's perpetual agrarian problem, both in the northern coastal lowland (Mecklenburg) and around Berlin on the central plain (Brandenburg). Many ponds and lakes interrupt farm fields in moist Mecklenburg, whereas most of Brandenburg is too dry for good crops. The most fertile soil lies at the south of the central plain, just before the rise of the southern mountains (Saxony and Thuringia), where large-scale agriculture is impossible. Potatoes, grain, and sugar beets are the chief East German crops, providing a very sweet and starchy diet.

Because farming is so difficult, less than one-third of the East Germans live in rural villages. Most people live and work in industrial cities, which cover almost one-tenth of the country's entire territory.

Yet mineral resources are inadequate for a huge heavy industry. East German earth contains a little iron, a little black coal, no oil, some salt and potash (a fertilizer). Sizable uranium deposits have been almost exhausted by greedy Soviet mining. The only great mineral wealth is brown coal, which East Germany leads the world in mining. This low-grade fossil is burned for fuel, converted into gas for cooking, and even distilled into gasoline for automobiles. Without brown coal, the entire East German economy would grind to a halt.

Poverty in minerals has forced manufacturing to specialize in products demanding immense skill. Largest of all industries is metalworking, which mass-produces trucks, railway cars, ships, machines, munitions, and every type of electrical equipment. Second in size is a chemical industry famous for artificial rubber, synthetic gasoline, farm fertilizer, and military explosives. Per capita output of chemicals is second in the world (following the United States). Also, there are many factories creating consumer goods like clothing, cameras, clocks, china, and Christmas toys. Much industry is located in the southern mountain region (the Saxon Switzerland), one of Europe's most heavily populated areas.

East Germany's foreign trade mirrors its manufactures. Almost half the trade is with the USSR, which supplies oil, coal, metals, and ores. In return, Russia receives East German ships, railway cars, machinery, chemicals, and consumer goods.

Of the many East German cities the largest is Berlin, whose Soviet sector alone houses more than 1,000,000 people. Another 2,000,000 live in the Western sector, which still remains under Anglo-French-American control. Both sectors are great cultural centers, with many colleges, research institutes, theatres, museums, and old historic palaces. No less than twelve railway lines radiate from the

New box buildings on East Berlin's main avenue, the Karl-Marx-Allee, which before de-Stalinization was called "Stalinallee." *EPA*

Stately grandeur of an old East Berlin building—the city hall completed in 1869. *EPA*

East Berlin's Humboldt University, named after the Prussian Minister of Education who founded this cultural center in 1810. Among its former professors were the great philosopher Hegel and the great physicist Albert Einstein. *EPA*

In contrast to West Berlin, battle and bomb damage in East Berlin was repaired very slowly after World War II. As late as 1961, the sixteenth postwar year, the Brandenburg Gate still stood unrepaired while the Communist regime built the Berlin Wall. *UPI*

Model of East German radar tower on display at the Leipzig trade fair, which is held twice every year. *Photoworld*

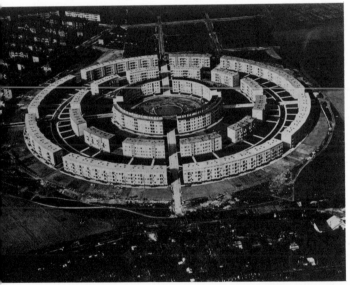

The "Round" housing complex in Leipzig, East Germany's second largest city. *Photoworld*

Many Western firms advertise their wares at the Leipzig fairs, like this exhibit featuring American and British books. *Eastfoto*

city, whose huge industries specialize in textiles, precision machinery, tough steel, and tasty beer.

No other city in the world has the excitement of divided Berlin, where communism and capitalism coexist only a wall apart. West Berlin is gay, bright, and cheerful, with bustling traffic and stores bursting with reasonably priced goods. Across the wall are dirty decaying buildings, empty streets, and stores with barren shelves. Dreary East Berlin is the capital of East Germany, whose Communist regime is constantly embarrassed by West Berlin's beauty and glamour.

In the Saxon Switzerland is Leipzig—East Germany's second largest city, main book publisher, and site of biannual trade fairs where Western businessmen confer with Communist bureaucrats.

The huge "market square" in Dresden—third largest of the many East German cities. *EPA*

The world-famous Zwinger art gallery in Dresden was first intended to be the entrance to a palace never completed. *EPA*

Among the many beautiful buildings in Dresden is this "court church" constructed 200 years ago for Saxon kings. *EPA*

Busy docks at the boom town of Rostock—East Germany's biggest Baltic port. *Eastfoto*

Badly damaged by wartime bombing, Leipzig's present population of 596,000 is still below the prewar 700,000.

Next in size is nearby Dresden, called the "Florence of the Elbe River" because of its many museums, art galleries, and old monumental buildings. Half-destroyed during World War II, the city has been rebuilt and its population of 500,000 is larger than its prewar size.

Biggest of East Germany's Baltic ports is the boom town of Rostok, whose 200,000 inhabitants are almost double the prewar total. Once a sleepy provincial harbor, Rostok now operates a communist-constructed shipbuilding yard—one of the ten largest in the world. There is also a yacht basin sheltering the pleasure boats of high Communist officials.

Thanks to Rostok, the East German merchant marine has mushroomed from one ship in 1952 to more than three hundred today. In contrast to this great gain in ocean shipping, inland waterway traffic has declined. The Elbe River along the western

Streamlined cargo ship built by Rostosk's new giant shipyard. *Eastfoto*

Besides big ships, East Germany builds small pleasure boats, many of which are sold abroad. *Eastfoto*

A medieval tower overlooking one of East Germany's lengthy canals. *Photoworld*

Transferring a ten-ton cargo container from truck to train. These modern containers speed the handling of fast freight. *Eastfoto*

East German terminus of the "Friendship Pipeline" that supplies Soviet oil to East German industry. The petroleum in these tanks has been piped from the Volga Valley more than 1,000 miles away. *Eastfoto*

A reminder of medieval grandeur: Brandenburg's 600-year-old city hall. *Photoworld*

frontier and the Oder along the eastern are both navigable, but both reach the Baltic Sea through foreign territory (West Germany and Poland respectively). Such streams are less useful than they were in the prewar period, when their estuaries lay within a united Germany. Linking the Elbe and Oder are old Brandenburg canals, whose barges still carry slow bulk freight. But fast freight hurries along the good railways and roads inherited from Hitler.

Russia uses communications as a club to control Red German industry. East Germany depends on Soviet oil via pipeline from the Volga, and it has been forced to merge its power stations into the European USSR electrical grid. By just closing a pipeline valve or flicking a power switch, Russia can stifle the East German economy.

Before and during World War II, there was no country of East Germany. Mecklenburg, Brandenburg, Saxony, and Thuringia were merely provinces of the German Reich. Their territories were considered "central" rather than eastern, since German Silesia, Pomerania, and East Prussia lay still farther east. Brandenburg was the former Kingdom of Prussia, whose military autocracy in the nineteenth century united all Teutonic territories into a German Empire. Saxony was the homeland and stronghold of German socialism. Mass executions of German Jewry by the Nazis left central Germany

Tanks, horsecarts, and foot soldiers: the Russian army invading East Germany in 1945. Despite their sloppy appearance, these troops were fierce fighters. *UPI*

Majestic appearance of East Berlin, just before being captured by Russia's Red Army. *UPI*

Ruins of Berlin after the Russians stormed the city. The marching men are captured Nazi soldiers. *UPI*

During the Battle of Berlin Hitler committed suicide in his fortress-like chancellory. These Soviet soldiers examine the shallow grave in the chancellory yard where his corpse was found after Berlin surrendered. *UPI*

with an incredibly homogeneous population—99.8 percent German.

Present-day East Germany was first mapped out by the Yalta Conference of U.S. President Roosevelt, British Prime Minister Churchill, and Soviet Premier Stalin. At the time (February 1945), the Allied armies were poised to invade Germany and had to be assigned separate battle spheres which, after Germany's surrender, would become separate zones of military occupation. Russia's zone was all Teutonic territories east of the Elbe River.

Germany ceased fighting in May 1945, so U.S. President Truman, British Prime Minister Attlee, and Stalin met during July in the Berlin suburb of Potsdam to confirm the Yalta decisions. Meanwhile the USSR had annexed the eastern section of East Prussia, and had given Silesia, eastern Pomerania, and the rest of East Prussia to Poland. So the Reich's real eastern regions were already gone, and central Germany had become "East Germany." The Potsdam Conference condoned the Russian and Polish land grabs as supposedly temporary, and divided

The Potsdam Conference of July 1945 divided both Germany and Berlin into American, British, French, and Soviet zones of occupation. At the conference table, surrounded by their aides, are U.S. President Truman (*left*), British Prime Minister Churchill (*center*) and Soviet Premier Stalin (*right*). *UPI*

The Oder River, which the Potsdam Conference accepted as the new eastern frontier of East Germany. On the opposite shore are longtime German lands now given to Poland. *Eastfoto*

Postwar divided Berlin: Both the bridge lettering and road sign warn motorists that the American zone ends here. The Soviet sector lies straight ahead. *UPI*

114

Soviet officer (*left*) watching workmen dismantling German factory machinery going to Russia as war reparations. *Photoworld*

Repairing what was left of East German railways, after all second tracks had been removed by the Red Army and sent into Russia. *Photoworld*

East German dictator Ulbricht, and the wife he met and married in Moscow. *Photoworld*

Few German Communists survived the Hitler regime, which destroyed the entire Communist party. Here Nazi police are arresting German Reds before World War II. *UPI*

the rest of Germany into American, British, French, and Soviet zones of occupation. Germany's capital city of Berlin was similarly split into four sectors. Britain, France, and the United States took zones west of the Elbe, plus West Berlin. The Soviet zone included East Berlin and the entire area between the Elbe and Oder rivers. But Germany was supposed to remain united, with all four zones coordinating their occupation policies.

From the very start this coordination was sabotaged by the Soviets. Because the Western Al-

lies allowed Russia's Red Army to capture Berlin in May 1945, American, British, and French troops were not stationed in West Berlin until July. Before they arrived, the Red Army stole West Berlin's movable property such as bank cash, stocks, bonds, bicycles, autos, trucks, factory machines, trolleys, trolley tracks, sewer pipes, and even toilet seats. Western troops inherited an urban wasteland which they had to revive and rebuild.

Similar Soviet looting was inflicted upon all East Germany. More than sixteen hundred factories

(40 percent of East German industry) were dismantled and carted into the USSR. Also taken were technical libraries, scientific laboratories, half of East German printing presses, all second tracks of railways, and tens of thousands of farm horses, cows, tractors, and plows. Hitler's many noise machines for jamming foreign radio broadcasts migrated to Moscow to augment Russia's noise network. Saxon uranium mines were simply seized by Soviet troops, who forwarded all explosive ore to USSR plants producing nuclear bombs.

Outright Russian looting ended around 1948, but the East German industry still intact was forced to give part of its production free to the USSR. Both the loot and gift products were Russia's war reparations, which the Potsdam Conference limited to equipment and goods worth $10 billion. When these Russian reparations were finally finished in 1953, East Germany's Ulbricht confessed that they had totaled $22.5 billion—more than twice the legal limit. Despite this enormous drain of exports, hardworking East Germany managed to regain its pre-World War II level of industrial output just as

reparations ended. Freed from reparations, industry then grew like lightning and is now four times larger than it was before the war.

Meanwhile East Germany was Communized, slowly but surely. Spearheading this socialization was Walter Ulbricht (1893–)—bald, dull, shrill voiced, and with a beard aping Lenin's goatee. Son of a poor Saxon tailor, Ulbricht in 1919 was one of the founding fathers of the German Communist Party. During the 1920s and 1930s, he was busy sometimes as a German Communist leader, then as a Soviet agent in Europe, and finally in the early 1940s as a student in a secret Moscow school training foreign Communists for future satellite leadership.

Ulbricht and his closest companions were flown from Moscow to Berlin in 1945 just after Nazi surrender. A faithful Soviet servant, he was smooth and skillful in setting up a Communist state. One problem was that in the East Germany of 1945 Communists were few and far between. The problem was solved a year later by merging the large Social Democratic and small Communist po-

After World War II the tables are turned: A Communist court sentences a Nazi warden (left) to death for murdering 500 prisoners. *Eastfoto*

Every trick was used by Communist East Germany to rearm quickly. These youngsters in uniform are joining the "People's Police," a fighting force organized as early as 1948. *Photoworld*

Supporting the People's Police is the "Workers' Militia" numbering a quarter of a million men. *UPI*

Even girls learn to shoot guns in heavily armed East Germany. *UPI*

Cheerless East Berlin celebration in 1949, when the Russian occupation zone of Germany was renamed the German Democratic Republic. The huge portraits show East German President Pieck (*left*) and Soviet dictator Stalin. *UPI*

Watching an East Berlin parade are two Communist chiefs: Soviet Marshal Chuikov (*in white uniform*), commander of Russian armies in East Germany, and (*next to Chuikov*) Otto Grotewohl, first premier of the German Democratic Republic. *Photoworld*

117

litical organizations into a new "Socialist Unity Party" that was forced to accept Ulbricht as its leader and first secretary.

Since the Socialist Unity Party consisted largely of workers, the middle class was given a political home by continuing two small prewar parties: the Liberal Democratic Party and the Christian Democratic Union. Both these bourgeois groups participated in elections, pretended to be free, but were actually controlled by Communist agents.

Another problem was the hundreds of thousands of former Fascists. A few Nazi leaders were quickly caught, tried as war criminals, and put to death. Denazification was then considered com-

plete, and all low-level Nazis were granted mass pardon. By 1948 a "National Democratic Party" was formed to give former Fascists their own political organization (under careful Communist control). In the same year began the People's Police, which eagerly enlisted former members of Hitler's Gestapo. A "Democratic Peasants' Party" was also created to placate private farmers. Thus labor, peasants, bourgeoisie, Nazis, and Nazi police were all taken over by Ulbricht and used to strengthen his Red regime.

When the Western Allies granted independence to West Germany in 1949, Russia converted its occupation zone into an allegedly free "German Democratic Republic" with the aged Communist

Addressing the East German parliament is Willi Stoph, who became the new premier in 1964 after Grotewohl's death. *Eastfoto*

At first the Communist regime did not collectivize agriculture, but divided large estates into small peasant farms. Here a new petty landowner drives his oxen past the manor house of his former landlord. *Photoworld*

Later came slow collectivization. This Russian-made machine harvests potatoes on an East German collective farm. *Eastfoto*

Trying with little success to sell Communist newspapers in anti-Communist West Berlin. *Sovfoto*

Dominating the skyline is this new television-transmission tower in East Berlin. But most East Germans prefer to watch West German telecasts, which are more entertaining. *Eastfoto*

Soviet military instructors at a college training officers for the East German police. *UPI*

Wilhelm Pieck (1876–1960) as president and the former Social Democrat Otto Grotewohl as premier. Both men were mere puppets of Ulbricht, who remained head of the dominant Socialist Unity Party. When Pieck died in 1960, Ulbricht promoted himself to president. Grotewohl died in 1964, leaving his premiership to a popular Communist—handsome Willi Stoph, whose cabinet has included as many as five former Fascists. President Ulbricht can hardly complain because his own bodyguard is under the command of an ex-Nazi.

All Communist countries try to nationalize industry and collectivize agriculture, but East Germany proceeded very cautiously. The great estates,

East Berlin rioters in 1953 burning Communist posters and news-stands. They also wrecked government buildings and tore down Communist flags. *Photoworld*

Production rally pressuring East German workers to speed up industrial output. Crude campaigns like this helped cause the 1953 worker riots. *UPI*

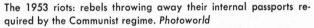

The 1953 riots: rebels throwing away their internal passports required by the Communist regime. *Photoworld*

The East German army, which could not or would not suppress the 1953 riots. *UPI*

The East German riots were finally crushed by Russian troops like these, who came from rural camps to subdue the rebellious cities. *UPI*

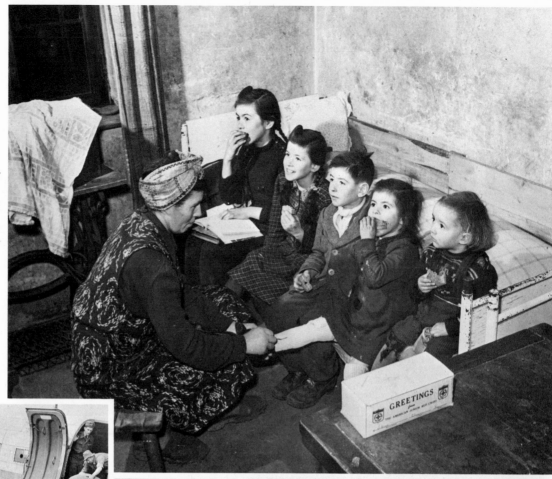

West Berliners will never forget the blockade of 1948/49, when Soviet troops stopped all rail, road, and canal shipments of food into Western sectors of the city. Large families like this became very hungry. *Photoworld*

Loading a plane in the great Anglo-American airlift, which broke the blockade by flying food and fuel from West Germany into West Berlin. *Photoworld*

Raising vegetables in West Berlin flower gardens during the 1948/49 blockade. *Photoworld*

Hapless victim of the Berlin Blockade was this Berlin suburb, first under French control, then seized by Soviet troops. *Photoworld*

East German leaders Ulbricht (*hat in hand*) and Stoph (*holding gloves*) attending one of the first meetings of the Warsaw Pact military alliance. *Photoworld*

Puppet leader and puppeteer: East Germany's Ulbricht (*left*) and Soviet Premier Khrushchev. *Photoworld*

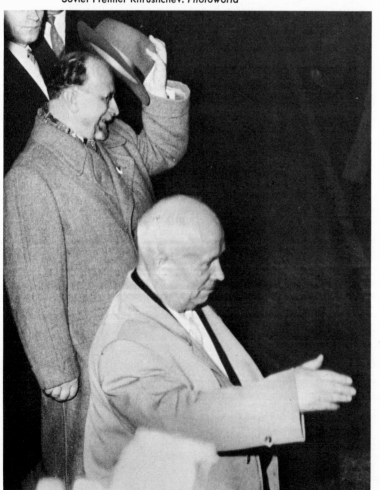

which had tilled 40 per cent of all farmland, were divided into half a million small farms for previously landless peasant families. Collectivization did not even start until 1952 and took eight years to complete. There are three types of collective farms —one like a Soviet total collective, the others merely mild partial cooperatives. Thus peasants were eased into collectivization by first being induced to join the milder types.

Industry has never been fully nationalized, though the private portion has shrunk from 25 percent in 1948 to about 10 percent today. There are two forms of private manufacturing: purely private plants, and enterprises where the entrepreneur and government are partners. Many stores and restaurants are also under private management. Motivated by personal profit, these Communist capitalists are often more efficient than the bureaucratic bosses of state-owned businesses.

At first much of nationalized industry operated at a loss, and had to be subsidized by the state treasury. Then in 1963 the government ordered its factories, mills, and mines to make a profit or cease operation. The result was great industrial improvement. East Germany is very proud of this 1963 "economic reform," which was copied by Russia three years later.

A Communist youth festival in East Berlin. Though forced to attend such spectacles, many East German youths are anticommunist and anti-Russian. *UPI*

Though progressive in industry, the East German regime is ruthless and reactionary in preserving its political power. No other Communist country is so heavily guarded as the German Democratic Republic, where police security troops outnumber the regular army three to one. At frontier railway checkpoints each train is stopped and immediately surrounded by border police armed with rifles and submachine guns. Some policemen search the railway car undercarriages, while others lock all passenger car doors. Then officers take an hour to inspect the passports, tickets, and visas of every passenger. One can hear the screams of stowaways as they are seized and hauled off the train.

These brutal border checks are conducted at every frontier, even those facing friendly Communist countries. No wonder many East German youths complain: "Our country is a prison!"

Crude government censorship of art, music, literature, and theatres has converted the German Democratic Republic into a cultural desert. In some years Western jazz has been forbidden to be played for dancing. Certain Soviet movies are banned, because they reveal flaws in the communist way of life. But no censorship can stop East Germans from quietly tuning their radio or television sets to West German broadcasts, which are so lively compared to the dull domestic programs. Wavelengths are a window to the West, keeping East Germans in touch with the news, views, and entertainment of the free world.

Russia does not trust the East German population, so 183,000 Soviet troops are stationed in the German Democratic Republic to keep order. These Soviet soldiers outnumber the East German armed forces almost 50 percent and are forbidden to fraternize with Teutonic civilians. Need for Russian military might was proved in 1953, when workers in most East German cities rioted against a cut in wages. Ulbricht's puppet army was either unable or unwilling to subdue the rioters, who burned government buildings and tore down communist flags. So Russian troops rushed to Ulbricht's rescue, crushing the rebels in just two days.

Dominated by Soviet military occupation, the Red German regime slavishly pursues a foreign policy made in Moscow. When Russian troops blockaded West Berlin during 1948/49, Ulbricht applauded this cruel USSR attempt to control the city by starvation. Later he lauded Stalin's kindness in ending the blockade, which failed because West Berlin was fed with food flown in by a giant Anglo-American airlift. The German Democratic Republic in 1948 condemned Yugoslav leader Tito for

East Germany longs to be free, and again practice democracy in this great House of Parliament. *EPA*

splitting with Stalin, in 1956 praised Tito for be-friending Khrushchev, then two years later cursed Tito for his new quarrel with the Kremlin.

East Germany was a founding member of the 1955 Warsaw Pact that subordinated the armies of East Europe's Soviet satellites to overall Russian command. A separate Soviet-East German alliance of 1964 made military cooperation even closer. When the USSR invaded Czechoslovakia in 1968, faithful Ulbricht sent some Teutonic troops into Czech territory to aid the Russians. But at home many East German youths held illegal meetings sympathizing with the conquered Czechs.

The German Democratic Republic faces an uncertain future. Most of its citizens resent Communism, hate Russia, and long to unite with West Germany in a free Teutonic nation. Shrewd, pro-Soviet President Ulbricht is very old and must soon die. His successors may be less capable in controlling their restive people. Just in case, the Russian army has war plans ready for fighting future East German rebellion.

Hungary

"There is no life outside of Hungary."
"I believe in one God. I believe in one country. I believe in one eternal Divine Justice. I believe in the resurrection of Hungary. Amen."

THESE HUNGARIAN sayings are typical, portraying the pride, patriotism, and profound religious faith of Hungary's romantic people. Despite the heavy hand of communism, gypsy violins still play softly in Hungarian cafes, where pleasant hours can be spent sipping Tokay—"king of wines, and wine of kings." The music starts with sadness, bursts into gladness, then madness, and subsides again into moody sadness. This is a land of dreams, which often erupt into revolution. No other East European country has so many statues of revolutionary heroes who, regardless of failure or success, are still revered. Hungary's 1956 anticommunist revolt, which stunned the world, proved that Hungarians have not forsaken their long revolutionary tradition. Like all past oppressors of Hungary, Russia is ever fearful that revolt may arise again.

Who are these fiery Hungarians? In ancient times they were Finno-Ugric nomads roaming the steppes of Siberia east of the Ural Mountains. They absorbed neighboring Turkic tribes, thus creating the Hungarian or Magyar nationality. This mix survives today in the Hungarian language, which is not Indo-European but Ural-Altaic.

Little now remains of the ancient Magyars except their language. Intermarrying with the many European peoples they conquered, the Hungarians absorbed many racial strains. But they are still proud that their ancient ancestors were fierce horsemen of the steppes.

Present-day Hungary is a small part of the large empire that Hungarians proudly ruled in the past. After Hungary lost World War I, most imperial domains had to be surrendered to Czechoslovakia, Romania, and Yugoslavia. Still, Hungary longed for its lost territories. Between World Wars I and II, Hungarian schoolchildren were taught to hate shrunken national boundaries by chanting: "No, no, never!" But defeat in the Second World War kept the boundaries as shrunken as before.

So Hungary today has a modest area of 35,-900 square miles—about the same as the state of Indiana. The population is also small—10,300,000 —and under Communist control the birthrate has declined. Many Hungarian couples prefer to have few or no children because living conditions are so poor.

Despite intensive industrialization before and during the Communist regime, Hungary still remains a predominantly agricultural country. Over half of the population lives in rural villages, mostly raising corn, wheat, potatoes, sugar beets, and, of course, grapes for the renowned Tokay wine. Hungary consists almost entirely of a fertile Danubian plain with few mountains and few minerals. The only real mountains are the Austrian Alps on the western frontier. Minerals are found mostly in west Hungary: some coal (usually low grade), some

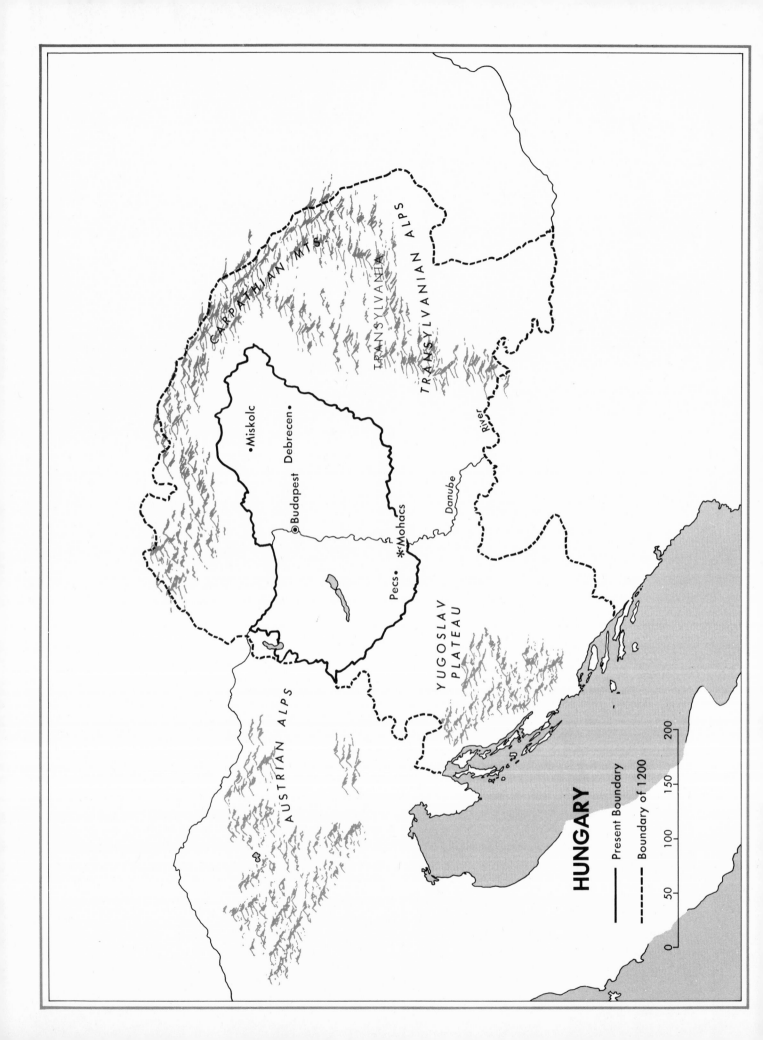

HUNGARY

——— Present Boundary
– – – Boundary of 1200

CARPATHIAN MTS.

TRANSYLVANIA

TRANSYLVANIAN ALPS

•Miskolc

Debrecen•

⊙Budapest

*Mohács

Pecs•

Danube River

YUGOSLAV PLATEAU

AUSTRIAN ALPS

0   50   100   150   200

Hungary has been the battleground for many revolutions, so there are countless statues of revolutionary heroes. This monument in Budapest honors Lajos Kossuth (1802–94) who led the anti-Austrian revolt of 1849. *EPA*

A country cafe with two shepherds and a gendarme sipping tasty Hungarian wine. *Photoworld*

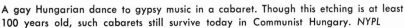

A gay Hungarian dance to gypsy music in a cabaret. Though this etching is at least 100 years old, such cabarets still survive today in Communist Hungary. *NYPL*

iron, a little oil and manganese. Uranium is mined in great secrecy and immediately shipped under guard into the USSR. The only great mineral resource is bauxite, the raw material for aluminum, with Hungary containing one-tenth of known world deposits. Like the uranium, most bauxite is exported to Russia for processing.

But Hungary's main wealth is its fertile soil, much of which is lush black earth. Like a valley of grain, Hungary lies surrounded by mountainous neighbors: Austria on the west, Czechoslovakia on the north, Romania to the east, and Yugoslavia to the south. A short mountain frontier on the northeast links Hungary with the USSR. Besides field crops the valley breeds large numbers of cattle, sheep, and hogs, and meats like ham are still major Hungarian exports. Though the Hungarian pedigree horse herds are decreasing, they still exist, guarded by cowboys wearing the traditional cloak and upturned round hat. Some horses are trained for international shows.

Hungary has few cities, and most of them are small. Miskolc, second largest city and a big armament center, has a population of 181,000. The

THE HUNGARIAN NATION

	Pre- World War II	Post- World War II	Present
Area			
(square miles)	36,000	35,900	35,900
Population	9,300,000	9,200,000	10,300,000

In percent of total population

Rate of Literacy	95%	95%	97%
Urban Populace	32%	33%	45%
Major Nationalities			
Magyars	93%	97%	97%
Germans	5%	2%	2%
Main Religions			
Catholic	66%	68%	67%
Protestant	27%	26%	27%
Jewish	4%	1%	1%
Orthodox	3%	2%	2%

THE HUNGARIAN ECONOMY

	Unit of Measurement	Pre- World War II	Post- World War II	Present
Industrial Production				
Steel	(metric tons)	650,000	890,000	2,700,000
Iron ore	" "	300,000	200,000	700,000
Coal	" "	1,042,000	711,000	4,300,000
Brown coal	" "	8,300,000	3,600,000	26,000,000
Oil	" "	42,000	500,000	1,800,000
Bauxite	" "	540,000	300,000	1,600,000
Agricultural Production				
Wheat	" "	2,300,000	1,600,000	2,200,000
Corn	" "	2,500,000	1,680,000	3,900,000
Potatoes	" "	2,300,000	1,880,000	2,400,000
Sugar beets	" "	1,000,000	1,230,000	3,600,000
Number of Livestock				
Cattle		2,400,000	2,000,000	2,200,000
Sheep		1,800,000	600,000	2,300,000
Swine		4,700,000	2,000,000	5,500,000
Communications				
Length of railways	(miles)	5,400	4,800	5,000
Length of highways	"	18,900	12,800	18,200
Number of telephones		150,000	12,000	634,000

Threshing grain on the Hungarian plain. Hungary is one of the greatest granaries in Eastern Europe. *EPA*

Picking peppers on a large mechanized collective farm. *EPA*

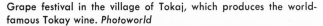

Grape festival in the village of Tokaj, which produces the world-famous Tokay wine. *Photoworld*

A giant bauxite refinery being built in northern Hungary near the Czechoslovak frontier. Hungary contains one-tenth of all world reserves of bauxite—the raw material for aluminum. *Photoworld*

third largest town, historic Debrecen, contains only 154,000 people.

Budapest, "queen of the Danube," is Hungary's capital and sole large city. With 2,000,000 inhabitants, Budapest houses almost one-fifth of Hungary's entire population. There are two main sections: Buda and Pest, divided by the Danube River. On the west bank, Buda rises on terraced hills, overlooking low-lying Pest on the other side of the river. Buda, now mostly residential, was founded in ancient times by the Romans. Pest, the more modern business district, is a tangle of broad boulevards and narrow winding streets. Over half of Hungarian industry operates in Budapest, producing such diverse manufactures as locomotives, farm machinery, textiles, tanks, and riverboats. The city also is Hungary's main railway center, with rail lines radiating outward like spokes from a wheel hub.

Now sadly lacking repairs and modern equip-

Factory apartments at a new steel mill on the Danube. When first built, this settlement was called "Stalin town." *Photoworld*

A Hungarian cowboy in national costume guards his herd of fine pedigree horses. *EPA*

Hungarian cowboys cooking on the field. Their long-horned cattle are a breed raised by the Magyars for a thousand years. *Photoworld*

Sheep raising is a major Magyar occupation. *EPA*

The heavy-industry college at Miskolc, Hungary's second largest city. Under Communist rule, heavy war-potential industry has greatly expanded. *EPA*

The fine university at Debrecen, the third largest Hungarian city and center of the 1849 rebellion against Austrian misrule. *EPA*

The Debrecen museum, containing many valuable revolutionary relics. *EPA*

Beautiful Budapest, Hungary's capital and only large city. Originally it was two cities divided by the Danube: ancient Buda (*on the left*) and the more modern Pest (*on the right*). *EPA*

Old highly decorated houses in Buda. *Photoworld*

The new Budapest Hotel, built by the Communist regime to attract foreign tourists. *Eastfoto*

Budapest is one of the largest industrial centers of Eastern Europe. This huge new plant rises in the city outskirts. *EPA*

Busy river docks at Budapest, which is Hungary's greatest Danubian port. *EPA*

ment, Hungary's rail network is among the most strategic in Europe. No other country has the roads of iron linking Central Europe, northern East Europe, Russia, Romania, and the Balkans. During World War II, Hitler was desperate to control Hungary, not because of its people or economy but for the sake of its vital railways.

Not blue as described in the famous Viennese waltz, but a muddy brown, the Danube River flows through Hungary as a major artery of water transport. Entering Hungary from Austria, the river at first forms the northwest frontier dividing the Hungarian realm from Czechoslovakia. Then the Danube abruptly turns south, literally cutting Hungary into almost equal halves. At Hungary's southern frontier the river exits into neighboring Yugoslavia.

Rarely within Hungary can the Danube be seen empty. Barges hauled by tugs, river steamers and small pleasure craft are almost always present. Located on the Danube shortly after it bends south, Budapest is Hungary's main river port.

The origin of the Hungarians is lost in obscurity. At the dawn of the Christian era, they were pagan tribes living in west Siberia east of the Ural

Mountains. About the fifth century A.D., they moved westward into the north Caucasian plain and settled along the lower reaches of the Don River. In the seventh and eighth centuries they became allies and vassals of the Khazars—a Turkic people who adopted the Jewish faith. When the Khazar Empire disintegrated during the ninth century, the Magyars migrated westward all across the Ukrainian steppes into the fertile region now called Bessarabia.

Behind them, also surging west, were a more fierce Asian horde—the Pechenegs whose bravery and cruelty were unlimited. Hard pressed by the Pechenegs, the Magyars made a fateful decision to cross the East Carpathian Mountains and enter the Danubian basin. Seven chieftains of the seven Hungarian tribes slit their veins and mixed their blood,

solemnly swearing to unite under the leadership of the mighty Arpad (?–907), who then led his people through the difficult Carpathian passes down into the present Hungarian plain. Easily, the tough Hungarians overwhelmed the Great Moravian Empire of the Czechs and annexed Slovakia, which remained under Hungarian rule for almost a thousand years.

At first the Magyars continued as adventurist nomads, using the Danubian basin as a military base for raids into the Balkans, Italy, Germany, and even distant France. "From the Magyars' wrath, deliver us, O God!" was intoned by West European priests during the first half of the tenth century. But in 955, at a battle near Bavaria's Augsburg, the combined Italo-German forces of the Holy Roman Empire crushed the Hungarian horsemen. So-

In ancient times part of the Hungarian plain was ruled by the Romans. These ruins were once a Roman town in western Hungary. **EPA**

The Magyars invading the Hungarian plain at the end of the ninth century A.D. For several centuries they had been slowly migrating westward from their original homeland east of the Ural Mountains. *LC*

The mighty Arpad *(right on white horse)* who led the Magyar invasion into the Hungarian plain. Here he receives tribute from Slavs whom he found and conquered in the Danubian basin. *NYPL*

Early Magyar soldiers with their maces and tall shields. *NYPL*

Giant statues of Arpad and his warriors dominate this meeting of the 1930s honoring the first Hungarian aviators to fly across the Atlantic Ocean. This multiple monument is in Budapest. *Photoworld*

bered by defeat, the Magyars withdrew into their Danubian plain, ceased raiding, forsook nomadic life, and settled down as an agricultural nation.

With Slavs to the north and south, plus Germans on the west, the pagan Hungarians felt insecure. By adopting Christianity they might avoid crusades from their already Christianized neighbors. At the time there was a choice of two types of Christianity: the Orthodoxy of Byzantine Constanti-

nople or the Catholicism of Rome. Hungary chose distant Rome, which could exert only weak political authority, rather than the Orthodox Church of the nearby Byzantine Empire which controlled most of the Balkans. Arpad's great-grandson Geza (972–97) became a Catholic in 973.

Geza's son, Saint Stephen (997–1038), is among Hungary's most revered rulers. In the year 1000 he asked the Pope to be crowned an "Ap-

At first the Magyars used the Hungarian plain as a base for raids against Germany, Italy, the Balkans, and even far-off France. Then in the year 933, King Henry of Saxony refused to pay tribute to the Magyars, giving them only a sickly dog. *NYPL*

In 955 at the battle of Lechfeld, King Otto I of Saxony defeated the Magyars, who thereafter ended their raids against western Europe. *NYPL*

The ornate crown of Saint Stephen, bestowed to the Hungarian kingdom in the year 1000 by the Pope of Rome. Proudly all Hungarian kings wore this crown, until there were no more kings.

Saint Stephen (997–1038), Hungary's first king, while still a prince is baptized into the Christian religion.

Monument to Saint Stephen in Budapest, in front of the Fisher Bastion which was part of a medieval city wall. *EPA*

Learned King Kalman (1095–1116) expanded the Hungarian domains into the lush Dalmatian coast of the Adriatic Sea. *NYPL*

◄ High on a Buda hill rises this imposing statue of Saint Gellert, a Catholic bishop sent into Hungary in 1015 to help convert the country to Christianity. *Eastfoto*

Heavy Hungarian silver coins of the thirteenth century. At the time of their minting they were worth two suits of armor. *East-foto*

The heathen Mongols conquer Christian Hungary, 1241–42. These barbarians soon withdrew, cruelly slaughtering tens of thousands of Hungarian prisoners who became a burden as the Mongols went back east. *NYPL*

Ingreſſus tartaroz in hungariã temporibus regis Bele quarti

First built before the Mongol invasion, this stately church reveals the artistry of early Hungarian architecture. *NYPL*

ostolic King." The Pope gladly agreed, sending a gold crown that became one of Hungary's most precious treasures. In times of invasion from abroad, the crown was carefully hidden. All Hungarian kings wore it until World War I, after which there were no more kings. Today the crown is in American hands, having been spirited out of Hungary at the end of World War II so that the sacred relic would not fall under atheist communist control.

Besides completely Christianizing Hungary, Saint Stephen also adopted the German "county" system of local government, which with some modi-

fications lasted until World War II. Medieval Hungary was divided into counties, each headed by a count who collected taxes, mobilized soldiers, and served as highest regional judge.

Soon after Saint Stephen, Hungary started on a longtime expansion. During the reign of Saint Ladislas (1077–95), a royal marriage brought Yugoslavian Croatia under Magyar rule. This was only the beginning of the Hungarian Empire, which was to grow into one of the vastest imperial domains of medieval Europe.

Foreign conquests became a parade. Dalmatia, the scenic north Yugoslav coast of the Adriatic Sea, was taken during the reign of Hungary's "bookish" King Kalman (1095–1119). Romania's Wallachia fell under Hungarian control in 1128, Yugoslavian Bosnia in 1137, Polish-Ukrainian Galicia during 1187, and northern Serbia in 1201.

By the thirteenth century, Hungary was one of the world's largest Christian kingdoms. But a weak king, Endre II (1205–35), had to yield important royal rights to the "little kings"—the powerful nobility. He was forced to issue a Golden Bull (1222) that freed the nobles from taxes, made the king pay all costs of wars outside the frontiers, and even permitted the nobility to overthrow a royal tyrant. Thus real political power fell into the hands of the "magnates"—the great nobles owning vast estates who "on constitutional grounds" refused to pay taxes until the mid-nineteenth century.

Endre was succeeded by Bela IV the Rebuilder (1235–70), a kindly king who was almost overthrown by the Mongol invasion of 1241–42. Even the tough Hungarians could not stop the Mongol Horde, which devastated the entire country. King Bela had to flee for his life, finally finding safety on an island in the Adriatic Sea. But the Mongol emperor, or so-called khan, died in Mongolia. His generals had to return home to elect a successor. So the Horde withdrew from Hungary, and King Bela returned to rebuild an almost lifeless nation. As a safeguard against future invasions, Bela fortified Hungary's frontier towns and invited German immigrants to become the townsmen. He also permitted the nobles to convert their mansions into strong castles behind whose walls the magnates became even more independent of the king.

The Arpad dynasty died out with King Endre III (1290–1301), after which the magnates decided to make the monarchy elective. They became the electors, usually choosing foreigners to be the Hungarian kings.

First elective king was the French noble Charles Robert I (1307–42), who founded the Anjou dynasty. His son Louis I the Great (1342–82) occupied the thrones of both Hungary and Poland. Louis fostered art, created Hungary's first university at the city of Pecs (1367), and annexed Romanian Moldavia. Unwisely he strengthened the magnates by introducing "entail," which required estates to be inherited intact, rather than being divided among heirs after a landlord's death. Louis left no sons, so his funeral ended the Anjou dynasty.

The Fisher Bastion—a surviving rampart of Budapest's medieval fortifications. *EPA*

City square of Pecs, where King Louis the Great founded Hungary's first university in 1367. *EPA*

As befitting royalty, the drinking cup of King Sigismund (1387–1437) was of giant size.

Far from Budapest, King Ladislas of both Hungary and Poland died in battle in 1444 fighting the Turks at the Bulgarian seaport of Varna. *NYPL*

After the Anjous, the Hungarian empire began to decline. Again Hungary was threatened by fierce Asians—this time the Turks, who surged into the Balkans from Asia Minor. Though Hungary's king Sigismund of Luxembourg (1387–1437) was also Holy Roman Emperor and King of Bohemia, he was not strong enough to stop the Turks from seizing Serbia. Meanwhile, Venice conquered Dalmatia, and the Romanian provinces of Wallachia and Moldavia freed themselves from Hungarian rule.

Trying to stop the Turks, Hungarian and Polish King Ladislas (1440–44) of the Polish Jagiellon dynasty led a crusade into Bulgaria, where he was defeated and killed by Turkish troops near the city of Varna.

Temporarily, Hungary was saved by a royal Hungarian, Regent Janos Hunyadi (1446–56), who defeated the Turks at Belgrade, then died of disease on the Belgrade battlefield. Europe was so impressed by the victory over the Turkish Moslems that the Hungarians were hailed as "shields of Christianity."

Janos was succeeded by his son Matthias I Corvinus the Just (1458–90), who loved to don simple clothes and mingle incognito with his people. After befriending a commoner, Matthias would sometimes invite him to visit him in Budapest.

Far Left: Janos Hunyadi, a Hungarian royal regent, halted the Turkish invasion of Europe in 1456 at the Serbian city of Belgrade. *NYPL.*

Left: Hunyadi defeating the Turks at Belgrade. Soon after the battle he died from disease. *NYPL*

After Hunyadi died in victory, his eldest son was beheaded in Budapest because of palace intrigues. *NYPL*

Matthias I Corvinus the Just, another of Hunyadi's sons, became one of Hungary's greatest and most beloved kings (1458–90). He added Austria and Bohemia to the Hungarian realm. Here he is shown with his Italian wife, the Princess Beatrix.

Royal wedding of Matthias and Beatrix in 1476, showing the walled city of Budapest before it was destroyed by the Turks.

In the background is a sturdy Budapest castle built by Janos Hunyadi in 1446. *Photoworld*

King Matthias allegedly planted this giant tree in 1480 in a wood near Budapest where he loved to hunt. *Eastfoto*

King Louis II (1516–26) died at the Battle of Mohacs, trying in vain to stop the Turkish advance into Hungary. *NYPL*

Sad discovery of the corpse of King Louis II on the battlefield at Mohacs. After his forces were defeated, he drowned while fording a stream in an attempt to escape.

As the Turkish tide engulfed Hungary, Countess Zrinyi blew up ▶ her castle (1566) rather than surrender it to the Turks. *NYPL*

142

When he arrived at the Budapest address, it was the royal palace.

Holding the Turks at bay, Matthias turned westward, conquering Austria and Bohemia. Such conquests were futile, since both countries seceded after his death.

Matthias died childless, so the Jagiellons returned to the Hungarian throne. Jagiellon King Louis II (1516–26) tried and failed to halt the Turkish northward advance. After losing Belgrade, he led his Hungarian forces into battle against the Turks at Mohacs in south-central Hungary. Expected Hungarian reinforcements never arrived, and Louis's entire army perished (1526). So did he, drowning while fording a stream in an attempt to escape. All central Hungary fell under Turkish rule, which lasted more than 150 brutal years.

West Hungary was saved by Austria, whose Habsburg archduke was elected Hungarian king. Thus began Habsburg Hungarian rule, which continued until World War I.

Hungarian Transylvania stayed free from both Austrian and Turkish control. This mountainous plateau northeast of the Hungarian plain was too difficult for the Turks to conquer and too remote for Austria to annex. So Transylvania was ruled by its own Hungarian princes, among them Stephen Bathory (1571–86), who was also an able king of Poland. At times Transylvania had to pay tribute to the Turks, but always repulsed Moslem military conquest.

To most Americans, Transylvania is a never-

Though most of Hungary fell to the Turks, they could never conquer Transylvania which remained free under Hungarian princes. One of the greatest (left) was Prince Stephen Bathory (1571–86), who also became King of Poland. (Center) Gabriel Bethlen, another great Transylvania prince (1613–29), whose court was a renowned center of science and art. (Right) During the Reformation, many Hungarians in Transylvania became Protestants. This painting shows a Lutheran sermon when Protestantism was just starting. NYPL

never land—mystic home of the vampire legends of Dracula. Though the legends exist, Transylvania is very real and is rich in many minerals. Europe's largest gold deposits are mined on this plateau, which also abounds in large timberlands and much fertile soil. As early as 1003, the Hungarian king, Saint Stephen, laid claim to the area, which fell under complete Magyar control about a century later. The population is a mixture of Hungarians, Germans, and Romanians. When Transylvania was independent, during the sixteenth and seventeenth centuries, many of the Hungarians and Germans became Calvinists, Lutherans, and Unitarians. This Protestantism survives in today's Catholic Hungary, where a quarter of the population still worships in Protestant churches.

Because of Austrian indifference and Transylvanian weakness, the Turks ruled central Hungary until the late 1600s. To protect themselves, the Hungarian peasants moved into rural fortified

Peasant Protestant cemetery in modern Hungary. *EPA*

A reminder of Ottoman occupation is this old Budapest building erected by the Turks. *EPA*

A Moslem minaret still survives in a Hungarian provincial city. Today it is surmounted by a tiny cross, symbolizing Christian expulsion of the Turks. *EPA*

towns which still exist. Even so, under Turkish tyranny the Magyar population was decimated by disease and famines. Somehow the Hungarian magnates survived, waiting to take control again when the Turks would decline and fall.

Turkey's Hungarian eclipse began outside of Hungary at the Battle of Vienna (1683), where a European international army crushed the Turkish besiegers. Three years later this army freed Budapest. By 1697 European forces under the command of Prince Eugene of Savoy chased the last Turks out of the south Hungarian plain.

But Hungary was not fated to be free. As the Turkish troops withdrew, the Austrian army invaded. Since Austria's emperor was king of West Hungary, he took title to the entire country. Under the able leadership of Transylvanian King Ferenc Rakoczi (1676–1735), north Hungary and Tran-

sylvania rose in revolt in 1703 against Austrian autocracy. But Austria won and in 1711 forced the Hungarian nobles to sign the Treaty of Szatmar, confirming the Austrian emperors as hereditary Hungarian kings. With rare tolerance Austria amnestied the rebellious Hungarian nobles, who were given much authority in their local regions.

"Era of national relapse" is the contemptuous name given by Hungarian historians to the next hundred years of Hungarian history. Slowly, painfully, the Magyars inched to recovery from the stagnation inherited from the unprogressive Turks. So depopulated was the Hungarian plain that hordes of Germans, Romanians, Serbs, and Croats were encouraged to settle vacant farmlands. By the late 1700s only two-fifths of Hungary's population was Hungarian.

As the eighteenth century merged into the

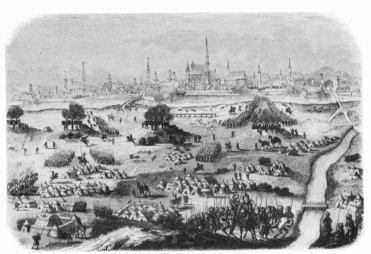

The Battle of Vienna in 1683, a fateful defeat of the Turks by an international European army which soon liberated Hungary from Ottoman misrule. *NYPL*

Three gentlemen of the many minorities who settled in sparsely populated regions of Hungary after the Turks left. *From left to right:* a Serb, a Croat, and a German. *NYPL*

◄ As the Turks were chased out of Hungary, Austria illegally took control. Transylvanian King Ferenc Rakoczi in 1703 aroused an anti-Austrian revolt, which was crushed by 1711. Rakoczi fled into exile, and eventually died in Turkey. *NYPL*

nineteenth, lucky Hungary suffered little from the Napoleonic Wars. Though Napoleon defeated Austria four times, his armies never invaded the Hungarian plain. By then Hungary was prospering, though still an agricultural colony of fast industrializing Austria.

After being amazed by a visit to industrial England, the "greatest Hungarian," Count Istvan Szechenyi (1791–1860), was convinced that the Magyars had to modernize. Lavishing his own magnate wealth and luring investment from home and abroad, the count founded factories, started steamships on the Danube River, laid down railways, created the Hungarian Academy of Sciences (1830), and built the first Danubian bridge linking Buda and Pest (1849). This "chain bridge" still stands, guarded by stone lions whose sculptor allegedly drowned himself in the Danube because Budapesters laughed at the lack of tongues in the open leonine mouths.

Politically Szechenyi was a moderate, believing that Hungary might prosper under Austrian rule. He was challenged by Lajos Kossuth (1802–94), a fiery intellectual, whose widely circulated writings demanded complete Hungarian autonomy. When a wave of democratic revolutions swept over Europe in 1848, Kossuth and his followers gained Hungarian autonomy from Austria. The first elective Hungarian cabinet included an almost unwilling Szechenyi, who soon after became insane.

Austrian Empress Maria Theresa (1740–80) addressing the Hungarian assembly of nobles, many of whom admired her. To gain sympathy, she often appeared in public carrying one of her younger children. *NYPL*

The first bridge built across the Danube to link Buda and Pest. Completed in 1849, this monumental project was the brainchild of the great Hungarian modernizer, Istvan Szechenyi. *EPA*

Besides bridge building, Count Szechenyi (1791–1860) constructed Hungary's first railways. This handsome station is in Budapest. *EPA*

Lajos Kossuth, the fiery intellectual who led the Hungarian revolution of 1848/49. *NYPL*

The Protestant cathedral in Debrecen where Kossuth in April 1849 proclaimed Hungarian independence from Austria. *EPA*

The "Greatest Hungarian" tried to drown himself in the Danube because of worry over Hungary's future. For Austria had no intention of letting the Magyars remain autonomous. In the four corners of Hungary, Vienna inspired the Serbs and Croats, Germans, Romanians, and Slovaks to rebel against Budapest. Austria's army also invaded Hungary to abolish the autonomy.

At a Protestant cathedral in the east Hungarian city of Debrecen, Kossuth on April 14, 1849, proclaimed Hungary an independent republic. His excellent generals, two of whom were Polish volunteers, at first repulsed the Austrians who were driven out of Budapest. Austria's emperor appealed for help from Russia's Tsar Nicholas I, a rabid reactionary who feared the Hungarian revolution might inspire revolt in Russian-ruled Poland. Happy to be the "gendarme of Europe," Nicholas sent into Hungary a 100,000-man Russian army which by August 1849 ended Magyar independence. Impressed by Hungarian courage, the tsar asked Austria not to punish the rebel leaders. But revengeful Vienna executed more than a dozen Magyar generals. Kossuth escaped death by fleeing abroad, where he spent the rest of his life vainly agitating for another Hungarian revolution.

Though 1848/49 were tragic years, some of the reforms of the autonomous Hungarian government proved permanent. Serfs were freed forever, and Magyar nobles had to pay the taxes they had long evaded. And Hungarians now knew that they could not be defeated by Austria alone.

The Magyar parliament which governed Hungary during the 1848/49 revolution. With Russian military aid, Austria finally regained control. *NYPL*

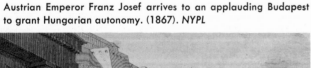

Austrian Emperor Franz Josef arrives to an applauding Budapest to grant Hungarian autonomy. (1867). *NYPL*

Ferenc Deak (1803—76), "sage of the fatherland," who convinced Austria to make Hungary a coruler of the Habsburg Empire.

Franz Josef announcing to the Hungarian parliament that Hungary will wield powers equal to Austria. *NYPL*

With Szechenyi insane and Kossuth in exile, Hungarian political leadership was inherited by the "Sage of the Fatherland"—Ferenc Deak (1803–76)—who had opposed the 1849 revolution. Biding his time, he waited until Austria was defeated in 1866 in a brief humiliating war with Prussia. Then he presented his program: complete Hungarian equality with Austria. Hungary would have its own parliament and cabinet ruling the eastern lands of the Austrian Empire. The Austrian emperor would be Hungary's king, and the two nations would share three joint ministries: foreign affairs, finance, and defense. Fearing another Hungarian revolution, Vienna accepted Deak's demands and on February 18, 1867, converted the Austrian Empire into Austria-Hungary.

Thus began Hungary's second "Golden Age"—the first complete freedom since the medieval Turkish invasion. Industry flourished, specializing in flour milling, textiles, and machine building. Several Magyars became world-famous writers and musicians, among them Franz Liszt (1811–86) whose fiery rhapsodies enchanted millions. In a burst of patriotism, Hungarian was decreed in 1879 as the official language of all schools for Hungary's many minorities.

Still, all was not well. So firmly did the magnates retain political power that only 6 percent of the population was permitted to vote. Half of Hungary consisted of giant estates, whose landlords were very rich and whose peasants were very poor. Since the landowning nobility abhorred crass com-

  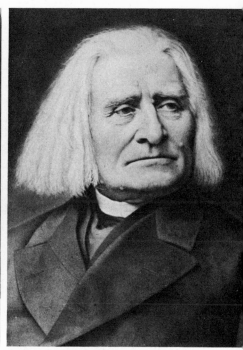

Labor conditions were not always ideal in nineteenth-century Hungary. These rope riders are descending in the dark to mine salt. *Photoworld*. Textile weaving was one of the earliest Hungarian industries. *EPA*. Franz Liszt (1811–86), the Hungarian composer whose fiery rhapsodies enjoy worldwide fame. *Photoworld*

Imre Madach, author in 1861 of the dramatic poem *Tragedy of Man*, which for many decades was a favorite play in the Hungarian national theatre.

Count Julius Andrassy (1823–90), first Hungarian premier after his country gained equal rights with Austria. Later he served long and well as foreign minister of Austria-Hungary. *Photoworld*

Monument to Istvan Tisza, Hungary's premier before and during World War I, which he opposed. *Photoworld*

June 28, 1914, the Bosnian student Gavrilo Princip being arrested in Sarajevo just after assassinating the Austrian archduke who was heir to the Austro-Hungarian throne. This murder was the cause of World War I. *UPI*

mercialism, many factories, stores, and banks came to be owned by the million Jewish refugees who were fleeing into Hungary from anti-Semitic Russia. Meanwhile Hungary remained an inferior economic partner of the more industrial Austria, which even insisted that German be the language of command in the Austro-Hungarian army.

With many misgivings, Hungary in 1914 began fighting World War I, which Austria had started by presenting an impossible ultimatum to Serbia after a Serb assassinated the Habsburg heir to the Austrian throne. As the war droned along, it became obvious that Austria-Hungary was losing.

In an attempt to disassociate Hungary from the disaster of Austrian defeat, Budapest in November 1918 announced the end of union with Austria and proclaimed Hungary an independent republic.

The attempt was in vain. Most of Hungary's national minorities seceded, their territories being grabbed by Czechoslovakia, Romania, and Yugoslavia. In early 1919, Hungary accepted a coalition Communist-socialist government that promised to restore former frontiers. Bela Kun, a Magyar Marxist who had been trained by Lenin in Russia, ousted the socialists from the coalition by March 1919 and created a Hungarian Soviet Republic.

Mass burial of Hungarian cavalrymen in Poland, where they died fighting the Russians during World War I. *Photoworld*

◄ Austrian Emperor Franz Josef (1848–1916), who started World War I by ordering the Austro-Hungarian army to invade Serbia. *Photoworld*

Hungarian motorcycle troops assembling in Budapest during World War I before leaving for the Italian front. *Photoworld*

Mass antiwar demonstrations in Budapest in the autumn of 1918 forced the Hungarian government to conclude peace in World War I. *Eastfoto*

Kun's four-month Communist regime was both incompetent and stupid. A welfare state was decreed without the money to pay such social-security benefits. Instead of pleasing the peasants by dividing the great estates into small private holdings, Kun converted the estates into state farms whose villagers became virtual state serfs. His political police have been widely condemned for their cruelty, yet often they spared the lives of nobles because Kun did not like to shed blood.

Lenin sent enthusiastic telegrams to the Hungarian Communists, but could not render military aid because of the Russian Civil War. Worried by both Magyar Marxism and nationalism, Romania

Communist dictator Bela Kun addressing a Budapest crowd in 1919 when he headed a short-lived "Hungarian Soviet Republic." *Eastfoto*

Hungarian railwaymen and the locomotive they hid in 1919, when the Romanian army occupied Budapest and overthrew the Hungarian Soviet Republic. Had the engine been found, the Romanians would have confiscated it. *UPI*

Admiral Nicholas Horthy, who as royal regent ruled the kingless kingdom of Hungary from 1920 to 1944. *UPI*

Horthy's troops restoring order in Budapest soon after he seized power. *Photoworld*

decided to intervene. The Romanian army occupied Budapest in August 1919, obliterating the Hungarian Soviet Republic. Kun fled to Russia, where he was eventually executed during a Stalinist purge.

Admiral Nicholas Horthy (1868–1957), the former chief of the Austro-Hungarian navy, took command of the Hungarian army and seized political power, proclaiming Hungary again a kingdom. But when the Habsburg heir to the throne tried to return to Budapest, Horthy unceremoniously sent him back into exile, for an Austrian king of Hungary could arouse suspicion from the victorious Western Allies of World War I. So until late in World War II, Hungary was a kingless kingdom ruled by an admiral without a navy.

Horthy could not prevent the dismemberment of Hungary, which by the Trianon Treaty of 1920 lost Slovakia and Ruthenia to Czechoslovakia, Transylvania and smaller territories to Romania, the Serbo-Croatian lands to Yugoslavia, and even a small border region to Austria. Thus the proud Magyars surrendered 71 percent of their territory, containing 56 percent of their industry and almost 64 percent of the total population. So poorly did the Western Allies define the new Hungarian frontiers that 3,000,000 Magyars fell under alien rule.

Not really a "simple sailor" as he described himself, Horthy established a mild dictatorship which he headed as royal regent. His government rigged the elections so parliament would be dominated by the conservative Magyar magnates. Yet he pleased the industrial workers by allowing them to form unions and have their own socialist political party. Communists he cruelly suppressed by long terms of imprisonment and sometimes by torture and execution. Himself a Protestant, Horthy tolerated Hungary's various religions. The country's basic weakness was that it remained mainly rural, with one-third of the farmland still owned by the unprogressive Magyar magnates.

Hungarian desire to regain its lost territories remained intense. Maps still showed the nation with its pre-Trianon frontiers, and schoolchildren were taught never to approve the Trianon decisions. Partly to oppose Czechoslovakia, Romania, and Yugoslavia, Horthy signed a treaty of friendship with Fascist Italy as early as 1927. When Hitler took power in Germany during 1933, Horthy did not wait long to become his friend. Though not himself a Nazi, the admiral knew that the Fascist Powers wanted to remake the map of Europe in their favor. In the remaking, Hungary might regain some of its lost territories.

Horthy's hopes were not in vain. After the Munich Conference ordered Czechoslovakia to cede the Sudetenland to Nazi Germany, it was obvious that Britain and France would not protect Czechoslovak territory. So Germany and Italy "arranged" in late 1938 for southern Slovakia to be returned to Hungary. During February 1939, Hungary allied with the Axis and was promptly repaid. A month

Former Austro-Hungarian Emperor Charles returning to Hungary from exile, assuming that the Hungarians wanted him as king. Horthy shipped him right back into exile. *UPI*

Ex-emperor Charles and his ex-empress living quietly in exile. He never regained the Hungarian throne. *UPI*

A common border scene in truncated Hungary just after World War I. As neighboring nations seized Hungarian territories, new frontier posts had to be established in open fields. *Photoworld*

A sad sight in Budapest after World War I. Refugees from Romanian-occupied Transylvania have posted their names on the wall to let out-of-touch relatives know that they have reached the Hungarian capital. *Photoworld*

A Budapest meeting protesting against the World War I treaties which gave 71 percent of Hungary's territory to neighboring nations. The banner proclaims: "Can it remain this way? No! No! Never!" *Photoworld*

Hungarian troops trying to hold a border town, which the World War I peace treaties ceded to Austria. *Photoworld*

A typical Hungarian border monument between World Wars I and II. The great poet Alexander Petofi (who died in the 1849 revolution) shows a modern soldier where to hurl a hand grenade against Yugoslavia. *Photoworld*

Hungarian magnates dominated the government and economy during the long regency of Admiral Horthy. At this lavish wedding, the groom and attendants wore ornate medieval costumes. *Photoworld*

From the late 1920s until World War II, Horthy's Hungary maintained close ties with Fascist Italy. Here the Italian air minister Balbo (*center*) is welcomed in Budapest. *Photoworld*

Girls welcoming Hungarian soldiers into south Slovakia, which Hitler gave to Hungary in late 1938. *Photoworld*

Hungarian troops in the winter of 1939 occupying Ruthenia after Nazi Germany dismembered Czechoslovakia. *Photoworld*

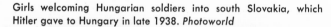

The 1939 Hungarian cabinet headed by Premier Paul Teleki (*seated, center*), who in 1940 annexed north Transylvania from Romania. But in 1941 he committed suicide in protest against the German invasion of Yugoslavia, which had a treaty of friendship with Hungary. *Photoworld*

later Nazi troops occupied most of Czechoslovakia, whose eastern territory—Ruthenia—was taken by Hungary. Another Axis gift came in August 1940, when Germany and Italy induced Romania to give to Hungary northern Transylvania, whose population was more Romanian than Magyar. Gratefully, Horthy allowed German troops to cross Hungary into Romania, which had requested Nazi protection from Russia. In early 1941, he permitted Hun-

gary to be the staging area for the German invasion of Yugoslavia. Hungary's reward was to occupy northern Serbia.

Though the Magyar Empire was fast expanding, Horthy was still not completely pro-Hitler. Only strong Axis pressure forced an unwilling Hungary to declare war on Russia in June 1941 and against the United States by December. At the end of 1941, Britain also declared war on Hungary.

Even before Hungary entered World War II, antiaircraft crews in Budapest prepared for future bombing. *Photoworld*

A German general inspecting Hungarian tank units on the Russian front during the Nazi-Soviet War. *Photoworld*

Hungarian troops in 1941 leaving for the Russian front after Hungary went to war against the USSR. *Photoworld*

An exhibit in Budapest of military equipment captured by Hungarian troops from Russia's Red Army. *Photoworld*

When Hungary tried to withdraw from World War II in 1944, German troops occupied Budapest, proudly renaming this square after Hitler. *Photoworld*

Budapest office of the Arrow Cross—the Hungarian fascist society which in 1944 became the puppet government of the Nazi German occupation. *Photoworld*

Members of the Arrow Cross giving the fascist salute. *Photoworld*

German troops mining one of the streets of Budapest, before surrendering the city to the approaching Russian army. *Photoworld*

What was left of Budapest's first Danubian bridge, after the Nazi Germans wrecked it before abandoning the city in early 1945. *Photoworld*

Since wartime Hungary was not directly fighting America and England, Horthy did not expect Allied air bombing and ordered Hungarian cities not to black out. In return, the Allied bombers spared Hungary, using its city lights as navigation signals for raids on Austria and Romania. A sizable Magyar army did invade Russia, at first performing police duties rather than front-line fighting. But in 1943, at the Battle of Voronezh southeast of Moscow, 200,000 Hungarian troops were crushed by Russia's immense Red Army. All Hungary was now sick of war, and Horthy began secret peace negotiations with the Western Allies. His peace offers were rejected because the Allies consulted Russia, which was disinterested.

Using the excuse that the German army was needed to defend Hungary against the Russian army, but really fearing Horthy's desire for peace, Hitler in March 1944 ordered the Nazi Wehrmacht to occupy the Hungarian plain. Though Magyar regent in name, the admiral was forced to become Hitler's puppet. Still, Protestant Horthy protected Hungary's 400,000 well-assimilated Jews, many of whom had married into Christian families. Under Axis pressure Hungary had passed laws barring Jews from high professional posts, but the admiral did not desire to doom his Jewish minority to Nazi death camps.

With Russia's Red Army invading a Hungary occupied by German troops, Horthy in October 1944 publicly proclaimed his nation's withdrawal from World War II. He was immediately arrested by the Germans, who imprisoned him in Germany. Freed by the Allied invasion of Hitler's Third Reich, Horthy was not considered by the Western Allies to be either a Fascist or a war criminal. His final years were spent in restful retirement at a Portuguese seaside resort.

As the angry German troops withdrew from Budapest, they spitefully beheaded famous Hungarian statues. *Photoworld*

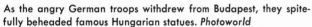

February 1945: Russian troops capture a badly battered Budapest. Here their antiaircraft crews are on the alert for Nazi air raids. *Eastfoto*

Corpses of Hungarian Jews slaughtered by the Nazis just before German withdrawal from Budapest. *Photoworld*

The human debris of battle: Hungarian war orphans being fed at a soup kitchen until better facilities are found for them. *Photoworld*

The Communist postwar mayor of Budapest, Zoltan Vas (*second from right, in shirt sleeves*), personally helping clean up the battle damage. *Photoworld*

Public hanging of an Arrow Cross official in Budapest for his mass murder of Jews. *Photoworld*

With lowered head a former Hungarian colonel (center) hears a war crimes court sentence him to death for anti-Jewish atrocities. *Photoworld*

Marshal Kliment Voroshilov (right, in uniform) headed the Soviet Control Commission in Hungary during the first years after World War II. *Photoworld*

Under pressure from the Soviet army of occupation, Hungary was forced to become Communist after World War II. Here is an "election rally," with Russian soldiers standing right in front of the Hungarian speaker. *Photoworld*

Matyas Rakosi (the bald man, front center) was the cruel Communist who ruled Hungary from 1948 to 1952. *Photoworld*

In taking control over Hungary, Rakosi in 1948 merged the Communist and Socialist parties to break socialist power. Here he (below) shakes hands with socialist leader Szakasits as the party merger was proclaimed. *Photoworld*

But back in 1944, Horthy was succeeded as Hungarian ruler by a fanatic Fascist—Ferenc Szalasi, leader of a Hitlerite political party called the "Arrow-Cross." Violently anti-Semitic, Szalasi tried to exterminate the Hungarian Jews whom Horthy had saved. Tens of thousands of Jews were arrested and marched off to Nazi death camps. Many others were executed in Hungarian prisons, drowned in the Danube, or simply shot on city streets. In four brutal months, the Arrow-Cross annihilated more than half of Hungarian Jewry.

Before the Russian army captured Budapest in February 1945, Szalasi was fleeing westward with the retreating Nazi Wehrmacht. After the war he was caught in Germany by the Western Allies, who returned him to Hungary, where he was executed as a war criminal.

Russia's Red Army conquered all Hungary in 1945, establishing a new Magyar republic with a coalition government consisting of local Communists, socialists, and peasant political leaders. This coalition had to accept the Allied peace terms, which were harsh: Northern Transylvania was returned to Romania; south Slovakia and Ruthenia to Czechoslovakia; and north Serbia to Yugoslavia. Again Hungary was reduced to its forlorn Trianon frontiers. Reparations totaling $300 million had to be paid to the USSR ($200 million), Yugoslavia ($70 million), and Czechoslovakia ($30 million). Much of Magyar industrial machinery was seized by the Red Army and removed to Russia.

When the war ended, some of the Soviet troops remained permanently to help Magyar Communists gain full control of the coalition government. The Hungarian Communist Party had little popular support, winning only 17 percent of the national vote in the 1945 elections, and 22 percent in 1947. But regardless of election results, Russia's army forced Hungary to become a Soviet satellite.

By 1948 the Magyars groaned under the iron fist of Matyas Rakosi—an old Communist who had served as cabinet minister in the 1919 Hungarian Soviet Republic and later served a fifteen-year sentence in Horthy's prisons. Rakosi's reign of terror, 1948–52, completed the nationalization of industry that the coalition government had started. By force he collectivized the small peasant farms, which the coalition government had created by dividing up the nobles' estates. Thus the peasants lost their land shortly after they had gained it. Atheist Rakosi confiscated church lands, closed convents and monasteries, persecuted the clergy, and imprisoned Cardinal Mindszenty, the head of the Hungarian Catholic Church. Savagely the old Communist even purged his own Communist Party to eliminate Marxists who resented Russian domination. The most prominent victim of the party purge was cabinet minister Laszlo Rajk, who was executed on false charges of treason.

After Soviet dictator Stalin died early in 1953, Stalinist Rakosi had to yield his Hungarian premiership to Imre Nagy, a kindly Communist who curbed police terror and tried to raise the low standard of living. By 1955 Rakosi returned to power, but was so unpopular that he resigned in mid-1956. His successor, Erno Gero, was soon overthrown by a new Hungarian revolution.

Ferenc Nagy, an agrarian party leader, was Hungarian premier during 1946/47 before the final Communist takeover. Then he was forced to flee, and is shown here with his family arriving as refugees in the United States. *Photoworld*

Emblem of the Hungarian Communist Party, which was to become all too familiar as Hungary suffered under Red rule. *Photoworld*

A Communist parade in Budapest, replete with portraits of Marx and Stalin. *Photoworld*

Hungarian Communist postage stamps urging better mining. The two stamp slogans say: "With more work shifts for peace," and "Produce more than yesterday." *Photoworld*

Symbols of Communist power adorn the gate of a Budapest stadium: pictures of Lenin and Stalin above Rakosi and another Hungarian leader. *Photoworld*

On the sacred Saint Gellert's hill in Budapest the Communist government lighted a huge red star and the sign: "Glory to Stalin!" The occasion was Stalin's seventieth birthday. *Photoworld*

Peasant women trudging to the village store on a Hungarian collective farm. *Photoworld*

To try to settle their frontier problem, Communist Czechoslovakia and Red Hungary exchanged their mutual minorities in the border area. These Slovaks are arriving in Slovakia after being deported from Hungary. *Photoworld*

This revolution of October-November 1956 was democratic, socialist, and spontaneous. Its goal was not to overthrow communism but to gain such reforms as free elections, freedom of press and speech, higher wages, more food, punishment of Stalinists, and end of Russian domination. These reforms were first demanded by a group of left-wing writers named the Petofi Circle in honor of poet Sandor Petofi, literary hero of the 1849 Hungarian Revolution. Soon the Circle attracted a wide student following.

In October 1956, when Poland defied Soviet leader Khrushchev and thus gained semi-independence from Russia, Budapest students became very excited. They decided to petition the Hungarian government to adopt the Petofi Circle reforms. Foolishly, on October 23, Hungarian political police fired upon a peaceful student demonstration. The students rose in revolt, and all Hungary rose with them.

The next two weeks were chaotic. The Hungarian army joined the revolution, which Soviet occupation troops in Hungary were unable to suppress. Gero yielded the Magyar premiership to popular Imre Nagy, who formed a coalition government, abolished the political police, released politi-

Cardinal Mindszenty (*left*), the head of the Hungarian Catholic Church, listening as a Communist court sentences him to life imprisonment in 1949. *Photoworld*

In 1951 a group of democratic Hungarians made this pathetic appeal to the United Nations for help against Communist tyranny. *Photoworld*

Laszlo Rajk, Hungary's Communist foreign minister, was executed in 1949 for allegedly conspiring with anti-Russian Yugoslavia. *Photoworld*

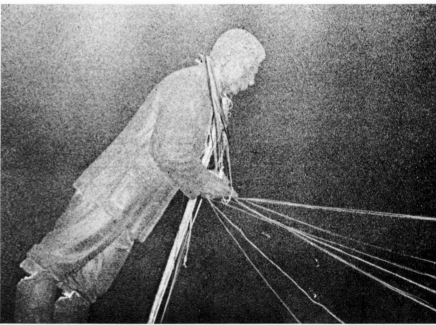

October 1956: the world is stunned by a lightning Hungarian revolt against Red tyranny and Russian domination. Down came this giant statue of Stalin in Budapest. *Wide World Photos*

Four young army officers chatting on a Budapest hill before the 1956 revolution began. Instead of suppressing the rebels, the Hungarian army supported them. *Wide World Photos*

Budapest students waving the old royal Hungarian flag over a Soviet tank they had just captured. *Wide World Photos*

Body of a Hungarian revolutionist slain by the Russians. The placard reads: "They did not die in vain!" *Eastfoto*

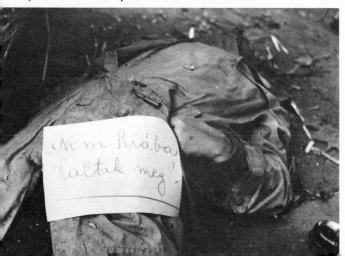

A Soviet tank sent into Budapest to restore order. *Eastfoto*

Freed by the Hungarian revolution, Cardinal Mindszenty had to seek asylum in the United States legation when the revolt was crushed. *UPI*

When the 1956 revolution failed, 200,000 Hungarians fled to Austria to escape Russian revenge. This Austrian border guard is helping a refugee family by carrying their one and only suitcase. *Photoworld*

Over 15,000 Hungarian refugees in 1956 sought safety in Yugoslavia, which received them kindly. These escapees await transport at a Yugoslav railway station. *Eastfoto*

Janos Kadar was the Hungarian Communist chosen by Russia to be puppet ruler after the 1956 revolution. At first he conducted a reign of terror, but later liberalized Hungarian Communism. *UPI*

The puppet and his master. Kadar (*center*) making humble explanations to stern Soviet Premier Kosygin. *UPI*

cal prisoners (including Cardinal Mindszenty), and obtained a USSR promise to send the Russian occupation troops back to Russia.

But the Kremlin promise proved worthless. A huge Soviet army moved from Russia into Hungary to defeat the revolution. Nagy then withdrew Hungary from the Soviet orbit and appealed for aid from the United Nations.

While the UN was debating the Hungarian request, the Soviet invasion army crushed the Hungarian revolt. Nagy was arrested, and was later ex-

ecuted in Russia. Mindszenty sought sanctuary in the US embassy, where he still remains. About 25,000 Magyars were dead, and 200,000 others fled to Austria to escape Russian revenge.

The USSR installed a Hungarian puppet ruler, Janos Kadar, who at first unleashed a reign of terror against the defeated rebels. Thousands of Magyar youths were freighted to prison camps in Russia. Other thousands were thrown into dungeons at home.

But as time passed, Kadar mellowed. His economic plans tried to create "goulash communism" (a better standard of living). The terror abated, allowing much freedom of speech, press, literature, and art. Most political prisoners were released from prison. Hungarians can travel abroad, and runaway rebels are invited to return. Only Soviet pressure forced Kadar in 1968 to use his troops to help suppress a Czechoslovak liberalism very similar to his own.

Thus today Kadar is almost popular in Hungary. Many Magyars say: "In the long run, we won our 1956 revolution."

Hungarian terminus of the "Friendship Pipeline" bringing Soviet petroleum into the Danubian plain. Most oil consumed in Communist Hungary comes from the USSR. *East Europe*

Present-day liberal Hungary: these cheerful girls (and everyone else on the street) ignore the wall posters which intone: "Peace for Vietnam." "We are with you, Vietnam." *Eastfoto*

The spirit of old Hungary still survives, as in this open-air concert at the majestic Fisher Bastion. *Eastfoto*

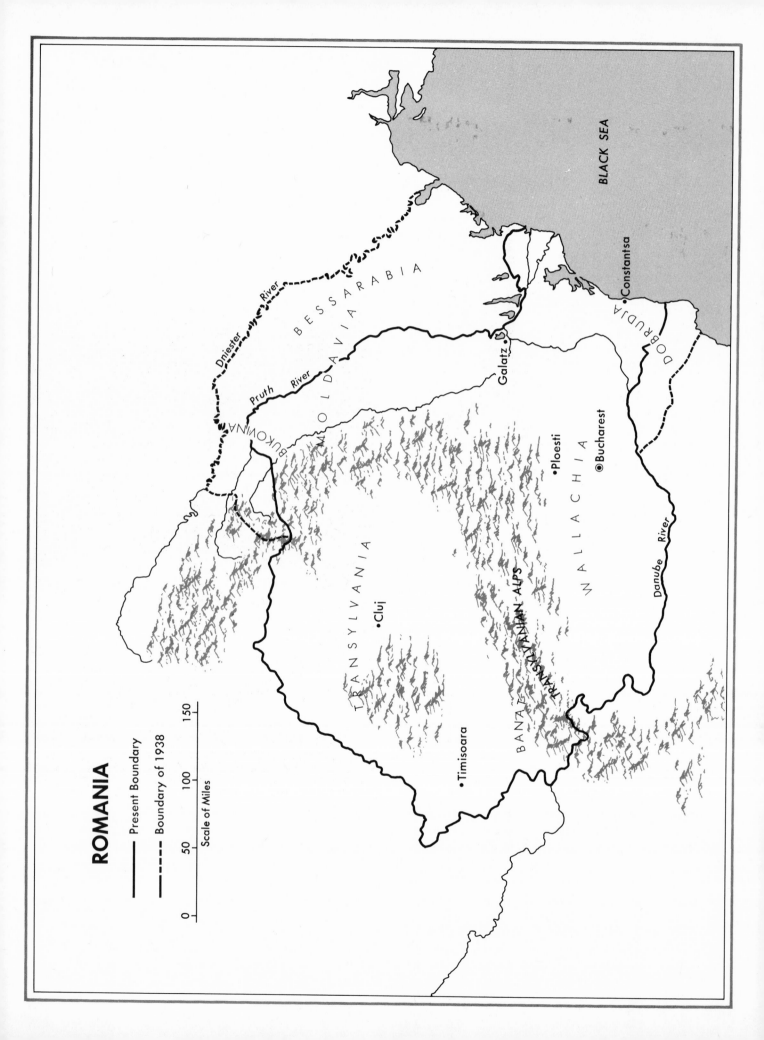

ROMANIA

— Present Boundary
--- Boundary of 1938

Scale of Miles

0 50 100 150

BLACK SEA

Dniester River

BESSARABIA

Pruth River

MOLDAVIA

BUKOVINA

Constantsa

DOBRUDJA

Galatz

TRANSYLVANIA

Cluj

BANAT

TRANSYLVANIAN ALPS

Ploesti

Bucharest

WALLACHIA

Danube River

Timisoara

Romania

"A LATIN ISLAND in a sea of Slavs" is how the gay Romanians describe their lush homeland. Of all East European nations, only Romania speaks a Romance language. The Romanians claim to be descendants of the ancient Romans, hence the name —Romania. Scholars are astonished to find modern Romanian speech closer than modern Italian to the Latin of ancient Rome. Because of this Latin heritage the Romanians consider themselves to be "Westerners"—superior to any neighboring East European nation.

"The Romanian never dies" is a proud proverb reflecting Romania's incredible will for survival. After a brief sojourn within the ancient Roman Empire, Romania for nine centuries was overwhelmed by countless conquests by Asian barbarians, who destroyed all written records. Yet after almost a thousand years of slavery, the Romanian nation reappeared, with its Latin language and culture miraculously intact. Hardly had Romania been reborn, when it fell for several more centuries under Hungarian, Polish, and then Turkish tyranny.

Again free in the late nineteenth century, Romania enjoyed independence less than seventy years. During World War II it was forced to become a Nazi protectorate, and at the war's end, a Soviet satellite. No other East European country was economically exploited by Red Russia more than Romania. After fifteen years of humble submission to Soviet domination, Romania quietly but firmly regained control of its own industry and resources. Romanian foreign policy began deviating from the Moscow party line. When the USSR occupied Czechoslovakia in 1968, Romania announced it would fight unto death any intrusion into its realm. The Soviets threatened invasion, but did not invade.

Defying mighty Russia took great courage, since Romania's north and northeast frontiers border the USSR. On the south is unfriendly Bulgaria, and west-northwest hovers hostile Hungary, both of whom joined the 1968 Russian invasion of Czechoslovakia. Romania's eastern border is the Black Sea, policed by a strong Soviet navy. The sole friendly frontier is southwest, bordering the independent Communist state of Yugoslavia.

Except for Yugoslavia, Romania is thus almost surrounded by unfriendly neighbors. And with its area of only 91,700 square miles (less than the state of Oregon), Romania is not a large country. There are great resources enticing invaders, and much of the Romanian landscape is easy to invade. Eastern Romania is the grain-growing plain of Moldavia, separated from the USSR by the Pruth River flowing south into the Danube estuary on the Black Sea. Southern Romania is another lowland— Wallachia, across the Danube River from Bulgaria and Yugoslavia. Besides growing huge crops of

169

Ruins in Romania of an ancient Roman amphitheatre, dating from the early Christian era. *Eastfoto*

Nazi troops building a pontoon bridge in Romania during World War II, when the country fell under German occupation. *Photoworld*

The swank Russian limousines of high Communist officials after World War II when Romania was under Soviet domination. *Photoworld*

Moldavian peasants with the one-horse cart which is the main means of rural transportation. In the background is a wooden religious shrine typical of the Romanian countryside. *EPA*

Romania today: the patriotic leaders headed by President Nicolae Ceausescu (*third from right*) who have changed Romania into an independent Communist country. *UPI*

Romania's greatest mineral wealth is oil, mined in fields like this forest of wells. *Photoworld*

A huge oil refinery in Moldavia. Petroleum processing is one of ▶ Romania's greatest industries. *UPI*

wheat and corn, Wallachia contains the largest oil deposits in Europe. Petroleum is a major Romanian export, and to attract tourists, foreigners traveling by automobile are given fifty gallons of gasoline free of charge.

Three vital corners of Romania have long been hotbeds of international intrigue. Northern Moldavia, called Bukovina, is a land of wooded hills whose ancient churches proudly display pictures of saints painted on their outside walls. On the Yugoslav frontier is the mountainous Banat, with farms growing grain and raising hogs, and an

industry mining coal and iron. Romania's sole section south of the Danube and bordering Bulgaria is Dobrudja, with beautiful Black Sea beaches melting into a hinterland granary of low fertile hills.

Of all Romanian regions, Transylvania is a

A fifteenth-century church in Bukovina, with elaborate religious frescoes on its outside walls. *Eastfoto*

The mountainous Banat region is famous for huge herds of fine hogs. *Eastfoto*

A gay folk dance by Banat peasants in native costumes. *EPA*

real natural fortress. As the Carpathian Mountains end their eastward trek into Russian Ruthenia, suddenly they turn south, becoming the East Carpathians or so-called Transylvanian Alps, dividing Romania into east and west halves. On the edge of the Wallachian plain the Alps turn again, westward into the Banat. Thus Transylvania, the Ro-

manian northwest, is a fertile plateau protected by high-rise barriers. Even on the west, more mountains divide the plateau from hostile Hungary.

The Transylvanian fortress is rich in upland cropland, mountain pastures, and underground minerals. Europe's largest deposits of gold and natural gas are unearthed from Transylvanian soil.

A fertile mountainside field in Transylvania near the Hungarian border. *EPA*

Miles of broad beach along the Black Sea in Dobrudja. *EPA*

Newly cut timber stacked for shipment in the Transylvanian Alps, where lumbering is a major industry. *Photoworld*

Bars of gold unearthed in the Transylvanian Alps, which contain Europe's largest deposits of this most precious metal. *Photoworld*

THE ROMANIAN NATION

	Pre-World War II	Post-World War II	Present
Area (square miles)	113,900	91,700	91,700
Population	19,900,000	15,900,000	19,700,000

In percent of total population

	Pre-World War II	Post-World War II	Present
Rate of Literacy	77%	77%	89%
Urban Populace	20%	23%	40.1%
Major Nationalities			
Romanians	85%	86%	88%
Magyars	7%	9%	8%
Germans	3%	2%	2%
Jews	3%	1%	1%
Main Religions			
Orthodox	81%	81%	90%
Uniate	9%	9%	0%
Catholic	7%	7%	7%

THE ROMANIAN ECONOMY

	Unit of Measurement	Pre-World War II	Post-World War II	Present
Industrial Production				
Oil	(metric tons)	5,200,000	4,600,000	13,200,000
Black and brown coal	" "	2,400,000	2,200,000	12,900,000
Iron ore	" "	140,000	100,000	2,800,000
Steel	" "	277,000	125,000	4,800,000
Agricultural Production				
Wheat	" "	3,000,000	1,245,000	5,800,000
Corn	" "	5,000,000	1,900,000	6,800,000
Communications				
Length of railways	(miles)	5,900	5,900	6,800
Number of Livestock				
Cattle		4,400,000	3,298,000	5,100,000
Swine		12,000,000	4,930,000	5,800,000
Sheep		14,000,000	7,039,000	14,300,000

Vast timberlands and huge salt mines are riches taken for granted. In ancient and early medieval centuries, when the Romanians had to hide from foreign conquerors, they sought safety in Transylvanian highlands.

All these Romanian regions are peopled by a population of only 20,000,000, just a few more residents than there are in California. Some 88 percent of the Romanian populace are Romanians, but coexisting are many minorities: Germans, Jews, Russians, Ukrainians, Poles, Yugoslavs, Czechs, Slovaks, Bulgarians, Armenians, Greeks, Turks, Tatars, and Gypsies. Most minorities are small and submissive to Romanian rule. Yet 8 percent of the population are Hungarians, living mainly in eastern Transylvania and forever longing to unite with their blood brothers in Hungary.

Despite intensive industrialization before and

A Transylvanian peasant sounding a six-foot homemade horn before a roadside religious shrine. *Photoworld*

during the Communist era, with mining, machine building, chemicals, and food processing the major industries, Romania is still mostly a rural nation. Three-fifths of the total population lives and works in quiet villages, where horse-drawn wagons must drive dirt roads to reach city civilization.

When a peasant wagon does go to town, it is usually to a city that is small or medium in size. Cluj, capital of Transylvania and a major railway junction, houses only 197,900 inhabitants. Biggest city of the Banat is Timisoara (202,200). Industrially important is Ploesti (213,700), a Wallachian town whose refineries handle petroleum products from the nearby largest oil field in Romania. To halt the flow of vital oil to Hitler's military machine, Ploesti during World War II was saturation-bombed by Allied long-range bombers. Of export importance is Constantsa (170,000), Dobrudja's biggest Black Sea port and the main gateway for shipping Romanian oil overseas. Near Constantsa are soft beaches, attracting more than a million East and West European tourists per year.

The Danube River estuary into the Black Sea is a borderland of Romania and Russia. Not far from the estuary is the Romanian city of Galatz (172,700), where oceangoing ships must stop because of shallow water, transferring their cargoes to Danubian riverboats. Despite Soviet objections that it was not necessary, a huge steel mill has risen in Galatz.

First founded by ancient Rome, then destroyed, and eventually rebuilt, Bucharest in Wal-

Hungarians are Romania's largest minority, living mostly in Transylvania. This adult literacy class for Hungarian peasants meets in a Romanian school using the Hungarian language. *Photoworld*

Gypsies are another of Romania's many minorities. Here they peddle flowers on a city street. *EPA*

A huge hydroelectric dam in the Transylvanian Alps, whose tremendous waterpower is just beginning to be harnessed. *Photoworld*

New railway tank cars produced by a big Bucharest factory. *UPI*

Huge oil refinery in Ploesti, a city in Wallachia near the greatest Romanian oil fields. *Photoworld*

City square in Timisoara, the largest city in the Banat. *Photoworld*

The busy harbor at Constantsa, Romania's main port on the Black Sea for export of oil. *EPA*

More than a million tourists per year visit Romania's Black Sea beaches, along which the government has built fine modern hotels. *EPA*

lachia north of the Danube is Romania's capital city and greatest center of industry, refining oil, manufacturing machines, and weaving colorful textiles. With its population of 1,457,800, Bucharest is the largest city in the Balkans. This "Paris of the East" has many buildings and monuments copied from France, even including an Arch of Triumph. Also imitated is Parisian glamour and gay living, with Romanian refinements. In 1944, when Russia's Red Army occupied Bucharest, *Pravda*

solemnly warned Soviet soldiers not to be distracted from duty by Romanian girls sporting painted heels.

Romania is rich in wheat-corn cropland, cattle, sheep, hogs, and many minerals (including uranium), all of which could be better marketed should transportation be improved. But the railway network is inadequate. Of all rivers, only the Danube and Pruth are deep enough for river shipping, but both are on frontiers instead of more helpfully

An old church surrounded by modern buildings in Bucharest, Romania's capital city. *EPA*

Because of its many buildings in French architectural style, Bucharest is called the "Paris of the East." This beautiful palace is the national library. *EPA*

Bucharest, the Balkan Paris, even has its own Arch of Triumph. *EPA*

Not a museum entrance, but a gracious gateway into a Bucharest bazaar. *UPI*

The "Iron Gates," where the Danube River becomes rocky rapids through mountains. Here the blue Danube is the border between Romania and Yugoslavia. *EPA*

Slow and smooth is the Danube, where it divides Wallachia from Dobrudja. *EPA*

inland. There are some oil pipelines oozing Ploesti petroleum into Danubian and Black Sea ports. In an attempt to become an international airline center, Bucharest in 1969 built a vast airport whose ultramodern terminal is adorned with stone arches seemingly floating in the air.

Remote ancestors of the Romanians were the Dacians, a Thracian people residing in Romania since prehistoric times. By the second century B.C., the Dacians united into a single state with well-established social and economic systems. At the dawn of the Christian era, Dacian King Decebalus was so powerful that he forced the Roman Empire to pay him tribute in exchange for frontier peace. But mighty Rome, unaccustomed to appeasing enemies, conquered Dacia by A.D. 106. Decebalus com-

Silver drinking cup of the ancient Dacians dating from the fourth century B.C. *Eastfoto*

Roman bas-relief showing the Romans (*left*) conquering the Dacians in the second century A.D. In the sky stands Jupiter, supporting the Roman soldiers. *Eastfoto*

Lack of water weakens the defenders of a Dacian fort besieged by the Romans. Here the Dacians divide the last precious drops. *Eastfoto*

Trajan (*third from right*) dedicates a bridge which he built across the Danube. *Eastfoto*

Roman Emperor Trajan (*standing in center*) supervises the construction of a castle in Dacia, which he annexed to the Roman Empire. *Eastfoto*

Ruins of an ancient Roman town on the bank of the Danube River. *UPI*

A Roman statue of the second or third century A.D. found fully intact in modern Constantsa. *Eastfoto*

After Roman withdrawal, the fierce Goths conquered the Romanian plains. Here they capture a town, slaying and enslaving its inhabitants. *NYPL*

To save themselves from slaughter by Gothic, Hun, Avar, and Bulgar invaders, the early Romanians withdrew into the Transylanian Alps, which served as a natural fortress. *EPA*

Nine centuries of barbarian conquest could not crush Romanian culture. This "modern" folk embroidery employs patterns surviving from Roman and pre-Roman times. *EPA*

A thirteenth-century battle between two of Romania's medieval conquerors—Hungarians and Mongols. Superior military skill brought victory to the Mongols, who occupied Romania and destroyed all written records. *NYPL*

mitted suicide to avoid being paraded in chains through Rome in the victory celebration. To commemorate Dacian defeat, Roman Emperor Trajan built in Rome an engraved stone column which still stands as proof of Romanian historical continuity. The Dacian costumes sculptured on the ancient pillar are the same as peasant ceremonial dress in modern Romania.

Rome ruled Romania little more than one and a half centuries, but in this short period Dacia was thoroughly Latinized. Countless Romans migrated into Dacia, intermarrying with the Dacians, who easily adopted Latin as a new language. This racial blend was so permanent that today Roman faces can be seen among Romanian peasants, and a modern Romanian looks much like a southern Italian.

Roman rule in Dacia was constantly threatened—not by the Latinized Dacians, but by endless barbarian attacks from the Ukrainian steppes. By A.D. 270, Rome decided Dacia was too difficult to defend. The Roman army withdrew south of the Danube so the river could be a natural military frontier. Also fleeing south across the Danube came some Romanized Dacians whose descendants

A fine old Orthodox cathedral in the Banat region. By the ninth century A.D. the previously pagan Romanians had been converted to Orthodox Christianity. *Eastfoto*

Moldavian church commemorating the first Metropolitan (fourteenth century) to be appointed as head of the Romanian Orthodox Church. *EPA*

Ruins of a Moldavian castle built during the fourteenth century, when Moldavia was briefly an independent Romanian principality. *Eastfoto*

Tall Transylvanian castle built by Hungarians in the fifteenth century, when Transylvania was under Magyar rule. *Eastfoto*

cians created the modern Romanian nationality—a handsome, healthy Roman-Dacian-Slavic blend.

Not so peaceful as the Slavs were the Asian Avars, who in the same sixth century crushed the Huns and took over the Hunnic empire. As the Avars weakened, the Mongoloid Bulgars occupied Romania in the seventh century, then moved south during the eighth. Quickly absorbed by Slavs in the land now called Bulgaria, the Bulgars adopted from Constantinople the Greek Orthodox religion to which by the ninth century Romania was also converted. Again the Romanian past has endured. Today 90 percent of Romania's population are Orthodox; about 7 percent, Roman Catholic; and the remaining 3 percent, Protestant, Moslem, and Jewish.

Just as Romania was becoming Christian it was invaded by the still-heathen Hungarians, who in turn were being driven westward by deadly Asian nomads named Pechenegs. To avoid the Pecheneg threat, the Hungarians (Magyars) crossed the Transylvania Alps and settled in the mid-Danubian plain now called Hungary. During the tenth and eleventh centuries, Romania's lowlands became Pecheneg camping grounds. Recovering its strength, Hungary began expanding eastward, seizing Transylvania in the eleventh century and Wallachia briefly during the twelfth.

Romania's last and most destructive invasion from the east came in 1241, when the Mongol Horde conquered the Romanian lowlands, then thundered across the Transylvanian highlands down into the Hungarian plain. All Romanian written records were destroyed, blanking out nine centuries of Romanian history. Having done their damage, the Mongols withdrew into Russia, and Hungary reconquered Transylvania.

Through all these centuries of turmoil, the Romanian nation survived mostly in Transylvanian mountain fastnesses. When Hungary ruled Transylvania, the Magyar magnates enserfed the Romanian peasants. With the Mongol danger gone, many Romanians longed for lands of their own beyond Transylvania.

Again records are sadly lacking. According to legend, Radu Negru (Ralph the Black) in 1290 led a Romanian migration from the Transylvanian mountains down into the Wallachian lowland, where he founded a semi-independent state. About the same time the legendary hero Dragos headed a Romanian trek from Transylvania into Moldavia,

can be found today far from home in northwest Yugoslavia and northern Greece. But instead of retreating with the Romans, most Dacians abandoned the Moldavian and Wallachian plains for safety in the Transylvanian Mountains.

For nine centuries cruel barbarian conquests devastated Romania's fertile lowlands. First came the Germanic Goths, who in the fourth century surged west and south out of Romania to loot the riches of the declining Roman Empire. On the heels of the Goths were the fierce, hideous Huns. They added Moldavia and Wallachia to a huge Hunnic empire stretching from Europe's Austrian Alps to Russia's Caucasus Mountains. During the sixth century, Romania was peaceably infiltrated by Slavs, whose intermarriage with the Latinized Da-

which became a second Romanian state separate from Wallachia.

Both new Romanian states were weak and usually dominated by powerful neighbors. Hungarian protection over Wallachia was accepted by Ralph the Black, rejected by Wallachian Prince Bassarab the Great (1330–52), only to be reaccepted by Prince Vladislav (1360–74). In 1372 Moldavia became a vassal of Hungary, but within a few decades switched to Polish protection.

Neither Hungary nor Poland could save Moldavia and Wallachia from the Moslem Turks, who surged north through the Balkans overwhelming every Christian nation in their path. After many heroic attempts to stem the Turkish tide, Prince Mircea the Old (1386–1418) in 1417 surrendered Wallachia to Turkish sovereignty. Moldavia fought off the Turks much longer. Its able prince Stephen the Great (1457–1504) won so many battles against the Turkish Moslems that all Europe honored him as the "Athlete of Christ." But soon after Stephen's death, Moldavia was forced to pay tribute to the Sultan.

At first Turkish control over the two Romanian principalities was threatened by many rebellions. The greatest Romanian revolt was led by Wallachian Prince Michael the Brave (1593–1601), who defeated the Turks, Poles, and even Transylvania's Hungarians. For the first time in history, Wallachia, Moldavia, and Transylvania were united under a single Romanian throne. But when Michael was assassinated by agents of jealous Austria, his Romanian empire died with him. Magyar princes regained control over Transylvania, while an angry Turkey reconquered Wallachia and Moldavia.

At first Turkey still entrusted the Romanian principalities to Romanian puppet princes, who gained and held their thrones by lavishly bribing the sultan. But even these puppets became unruly. So, in the late seventeenth century, Turkey put the Wallachian and Moldavian thrones up for auction in Constantinople to the highest bidders, who were usually wealthy Greeks. Thus began Romania's Phanariot tyranny, named after Constantinople's Phanar (lighthouse) district, a prosperous Greek ghetto. For almost 150 years, the alien Phanariots ruled Romania.

Some of these Greek princes were benevolent despots; others were famous for callous cruelty. All taxed Romania heavily to regain their auction outlay and to reap personal profit while paying im-

Moldavian Prince Stephen the Great (1457–1504) won so many battles against the Moslem Turks, that he was called the "Athlete of Christ."

A hermitage built by devoutly religious Stephen the Great. *Eastfoto*

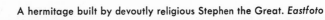

Triumphal entry of Prince Michael the Brave (1593–1601) into the Transylvanian city of Alba-Julia. By defeating the Turks, Poles, and Hungarians, he united Moldavia, Wallachia, and Transylvania into one large Romanian country. *NYPL*

Prince Michael's state seal with his title: "Michael of Hungro-Wallachia, Voevod of Transylvania and of the Moldavian Land."

An actor portraying one of the many Romanian guerrillas who harassed Turkish garrisons during the long centuries of Ottoman occupation. *Sovfoto*

mense annual tribute to Turkey. So mercenary were the Phanariot satraps that government jobs were bought and sold, and law courts gave judgments in favor of the highest briber. Romania was engulfed by a sea of corruption whose evil practices continued long after Greek governorship ended. Yet so rich were Romanian resources that Moldavia and Wallachia survived Phanariot looting.

At the dawn of the eighteenth century, Romania found a new outside protector—giant Russia, which had annexed the Ukrainian steppe while pushing south to reach the Black Sea. In tsarist eyes Romania's lowlands were the land gateway into the Balkans, which Moscow wanted to wrest from Turkish control.

Russia's first attempt to rescue Romania met with disaster. Tsar Peter the Great was defeated in 1711 at the Pruth River, leaving Romania to the mercy of the Turks. More successful was Empress Catherine the Great, whose troops occupied Moldavia and Wallachia in winning the Russo-Turkish War of 1768–74. By the peace treaty of Kuchuk Kainarji, Russia could protect Romanian interests as well as all Christians in the Turkish Empire.

City charter granted to the Transylvanian town of Oradea in 1600 by Austrian Emperor Rudolf II, when Austria controlled part of Transylvania. *Eastfoto*

The Moldavian national council debating whether Moldavia should join Wallachia to form a single Romanian state. The decision was for union, which occurred in 1859 when Moldavia and Wallachia accepted the same ruler: Prince Cuza. *Eastfoto*

Stern deputies of the Moldavian national council that agreed to union with Wallachia. *Eastfoto*

A huge fortress on the Dniester River in Bessarabia—a Romanian area annexed by Tsarist Russia in 1812. *Photoworld*

Taking advantage of this treaty, Moscow in 1802 forced the Sultan to give native nobles the right to control Romanian city, county, and village governments.

Making the mistake of allying with Napoleon, the sultan in 1812 lost another Russo-Turkish war, and in the Bucharest Peace Treaty promised home rule for both Wallachia and Moldavia. Romania's gratitude toward Russia turned to anger when Moscow annexed Bessarabia (eastern Moldavia), "land between the rivers"—a Romanian-inhabited plain east of the River Pruth.

Turkey simply ignored its promise for Romanian home rule, so Wallachia and Moldavia revolted against the Sultan in 1821. Though both rebellions failed, they frightened Turkey into ending the Phanariot regime in 1824. Thereafter Turkey appointed Romanian princes to rule the Romanian principalities. Soon came another Muscovite victory in the 1828/29 Russo-Turkish War, whose Adrianople Peace Treaty provided that Moldavia and Wallachia would be truly autonomous, electing Romanian princes for lifelong tenure of office. Russian troops remained in Romania till 1834, helping the principalities organize armies and police.

Moscow started the Crimean War (1853–56) by invading Moldavia, but the Russian troops soon withdrew because of threats from neutral Austria. When England, France, and Turkey won against Russia, they dictated their peace terms in the Treaty of Paris: all the Great European Powers guaranteed the autonomy of Wallachia and Moldavia, though both principalities continued to pay tribute to Turkey. Much against Tsarist desires, southern Bessarabia was returned to Moldavia.

Modern Romania was born in 1859 when Moldavia and Wallachia united by electing the same Romanian ruler: Alexandru Ioan Cuza (1859–66). A progressive prince who founded schools and freed the serfs, Cuza was so overly reformist that he was finally forced to abdicate. To quell internal rivalries, Romania elected a foreigner as its next prince—the Hohenzollern Charles, who reigned in Romania as Carol I (1866–1914). Proud to be prince, Carol ruled Romania wisely and well, developing democracy, education, industry, railways, and a strong army.

Romania's well-trained troops helped Russia defeat Turkey in the Russo-Turkish War of 1877/-78. As a reward, the Treaty of Berlin forced the sultan to free Romania, which triumphfully proclaimed itself a kingdom, crowning Prince Carol as king. But Russia again annexed fertile south Bessarabia, poorly compensating Romania with the gift of sandy north Dobrudja.

As the twentieth century started, by East European standards Romania was prosperous. Oil and grain were profitable exports, industry was increasing, and the Romanian court lived in lavish splendor. Yet there were grave problems, one being widespread anti-Semitism. Since most Romanian nobles preferred farming to crass commerce, most factories and banks were owned by Jews. In 1907 countless peasants rose in rebellion against Jewish rural moneylenders, then turned against the Romanian nobility whose estates still held half of all farmland. Peasants fought with guns, axes, and scythes to enlarge their dwarf farms by grabbing estate fields. Only with great bloodshed was this rural revolt suppressed.

Foreign relations were bad with several neighbors. Hungary still held Transylvania, most of whose population was Romanian. Russia retained south Bessarabia, and Austria clung to Bukovina, which had been under Viennese rule since 1775. After the 1913 Balkan War, in which Serbia, Greece, and Romania defeated Bulgaria, Romania embittered the Bulgarian nation by annexing south Dobrudja.

(Left) Prince Alexandru Ioan Cuza, first chief of state (1859–66) of newly united Romania. *Eastfoto.* (Center) Wise kindly Carol I, who ruled Romania first as prince (1866–81) and then as king 1881–1914. Under his rule Romania gained full independence from Turkey in 1878. *Photoworld.* Romania's second king, Ferdinand I (1914–27), who until 1916 kept Romania neutral in World War I. *Photoworld*

The outbreak of World War I so worried Romania's King Carol I that he died prematurely, leaving the throne to his nephew Ferdinand I (1914–27). Waiting to see which side was winning the war, Romania remained neutral till 1916, then attacked Austria-Hungary. German and Austrian troops quickly conquered Wallachia, forcing King Ferdinand to flee into Moldavia, where he made peace with the Central Powers.

When Russia disintegrated into civil war during 1918, Romania recovered Bessarabia. Later that year Austria-Hungary surrendered to the Western Allies. Ferdinand immediately annexed the Austro-Hungarian domains of Transylvania, Bukovina, and the Banat. Thus Romania emerged from World War I with twice as much territory as before the war.

The new enlarged Romania prospered and modernized. Machine building grew so fast that it became almost as big as the oil industry. A 1921 land reform placated the peasants by giving them four-fifths of the nobles' estates. Introduction of universal suffrage made the country more democratic. As protection against both Hungary and Soviet Russia, Romania allied with Czechoslovakia and Yugoslavia to form the Little Entente. Other alliances linked Romania with anti-Russian Poland (1921), Fascist Italy (1926), and democratic France (1926).

But there were signs of future trouble. Hungary's schools taught children that Transylvania must become Magyar. Soviet maps showed Bessarabia as Russian, and Bulgaria still desired Dobrudja. Partly because of this foreign danger, many Romanians turned fascist, banding together in the "Legion of Archangel Michael" or so-called Iron Guard. Violently nationalist, pro-peasant, and anti-Semitic, the Guardists wore green shirts, carried tiny bags of Romanian soil, and held mystic meetings in forest glens. As early as 1921, the Iron Guard assassinated the mayor of a Moldavian city. During the 1930s they even murdered two Romanian premiers.

Just when a stable monarchy was needed, Romania suffered dynastic difficulties. In 1925 Crown Prince Carol renounced his right to the Romanian throne, preferring to relax abroad with his mistress, Magda Lupescu. When King Ferdinand died in 1927, he was therefore succeeded by Carol's son, five-year-old Michael. Then in 1930 Carol returned to Romania and crowned himself king, sending young Michael back to school.

Coronation of King Ferdinand and Queen Marie. *Photoworld*

New recruits of the Romanian army as troops prepared for future fighting in World War I. *Photoworld*

King Ferdinand reviewing his troops, which he finally sent into battle against the Central Powers (Germany, Austria-Hungary, Bulgaria, and Turkey). *Photoworld*

A view of the Russian shore across the Dniester River from Bessarabia, which Romania regained at the close of World War I. *Photoworld*

Rugged mountains in Transylvania, which Romania took back from Hungary after World War I. *Photoworld*

Impoverished peasants in the 1920s attending a meeting to demand rural reforms. Though the weather is cold, some of the children are barefoot and clothed only in coats. *Photoworld*

By the late 1930s, King Carol became virtual dictator. To save Romania from the Iron Guards, who now had powerful outside support from Nazi Germany, fourteen Guard leaders were arrested and executed. Trade unions and freedom of the press were abolished.

As war clouds loomed over Europe in 1939, Romania requested and received a guarantee of protection from Britain and France. Meanwhile, unknown to Romania, the 1939 Nazi-Soviet Pact assigned Bessarabia to Russia's sphere of influence. In 1940 Germany conquered France and began bombing Britain, so the Anglo-French guarantee of Romania was worthless. Russia then demanded Bessarabia and northern Bukovina, and Romania surrendered both regions without daring to fight. Next Germany and Italy allowed Hungary to take north Transylvania, while Bulgaria grabbed south Dobrudja. In three months Romania thus lost one-third of its territory and 6,800,000 people, 3,700,000 of whom were Romanians.

Appalled by these losses, Romania forced Carol to abdicate in favor of his son Michael, who became a puppet king. Real power was held by General Ion Antonescu, whose governmental cabinet included Iron Guards. Romania joined the Axis alliance and admitted German troops as protection against Russia.

Once in power the Iron Guards ran wild, looting cities and massacring thousands of Romania's Jews. Shocked by Iron Guard brutality, Antonescu in 1941 ordered the Romanian army to subdue the Guardists, whose leaders fled to Germany. At long last the Legion of Archangel Michael became powerless. Nazi Germany did not protest, because Hitler needed Antonescu's army for invasion of Russia.

The invasion began in June 1941, with Romanian troops supporting the Nazi Wehrmacht against Russia's Red Army. So tough was the Romanian army that it soon conquered Bessarabia, northern Bukovina, and even the southwest Ukraine. All these territories were annexed by

A gathering of the "Iron Guard"—a powerful Romanian Fascist organization of the 1920s and 1930s. *Photoworld*

King Carol II (1930–40) who at first gave the throne to his son (1927–30), but then took power himself. Here Carol (*center*) negotiates with the president and foreign minister of Poland, an ally of Romania. *UPI*

State funeral in 1939 of antifascist premier Calinescu, who was assassinated by the Iron Guards. *Photoworld*

Mass meeting of the Iron Guards in the 1930s, waving Nazi swastika flags. *Photoworld*

Bucharest, bringing many Ukrainians under Romanian wartime rule.

Then the tide turned. By 1943 half a million Romanian troops had died in the USSR, and a reinvigorated Red Army was relentlessly battling westward toward Romania's eastern frontiers. When Soviet soldiers neared war-weary Romania in 1944, King Michael overthrew Antonescu and ordered the Romanian army to fight the Germans. So at the end of World War II, Romania joined the Allies fighting the Axis. Russia was so pleased that King Michael was awarded the Soviet medal of

191

Romanian sentries in early 1940 on guard near the Russian frontier. They were worried by Soviet troop concentrations near this border. *Photoworld*

Crude Soviet armored cars entering a city in Bessarabia, which Romania was forced to cede to Russia in June 1940. *Sovfoto*

Romanian troops on the eve of World War II parading past a statue of King Carol I. Though small, the Romanian army was one of the best in Europe. *Photoworld*

After the armored cars came masses of Red Army infantry, to keep Bessarabia quiet. *Sovfoto*

Soviet occupation of Bessarabia in 1940 included visits by military planes to peasant villages. This old biplane looks unfit for combat. *Sovfoto*

The Iron Guard taking power in Romania in 1940. This funeral is for a Guardist executed by the previous Romanian regime. *Photoworld*

Nazi soldiers teaching Romanian officers how to operate German antiaircraft artillery. By late 1940, Romania was allied to Hitler's Third Reich. *Photoworld*

German troops occupied Romania from 1940 to 1944. Here they man antiaircraft guns guarding a Romanian oil field. *Photoworld*

German and Romanian warplanes sharing a Romanian underground hangar during the Nazi-Soviet War. Romanian troops invaded the USSR in 1941, temporarily capturing Bessarabia and much of the western Ukraine. *Photoworld*

When Russia's Red Army invaded Romania in 1944, the Romanian army changed sides and helped the Soviets drive out the Germans. These Romanian soldiers and civilians are inspecting battle damage in Bucharest after the Nazis had been evicted. *Photoworld*

The last remnants of the Iron Guard—in Nazi Berlin after being chased out of Romania in 1944. In the front row are two former generals and two former cabinet ministers. *Photoworld*

King Michael (1940–47) and his mother Queen Helen. Though he allied Romania with the USSR in 1944, Russia forced him to abdicate three years later. *Photoworld*

"Order of Victory." The Allies forced Hungary to return northern Transylvania to Romania.

But Romania was still punished for having been Hitler's partner. Bessarabia and northern Bukovina were reannexed by the USSR. Russia demanded $300 million in reparations—a large sum for small Romania. Also, Moscow milked the entire economy by forming Soviet-Romanian joint companies controlling Romania's banks, insurance funds, airlines, shipping and shipbuilding, oil re-

fining, natural gas deposits, coal mines, uranium mining, metallurgy, tractor production, oil machinery manufacture, chemical industry, construction, lumbering, and even moviemaking. Romania was saddled with more of these "joint" businesses than any other Soviet satellite. Operation of these companies was the chore of the Romanian government, while Moscow relaxed and pocketed half the profits.

As if economic exploitation were not enough,

Gheorghe Gheorghiu-Dej, Romania's Red dictator from 1952 to 1965, at first was a mere Moscow puppet. Later he freed the Romanian economy from total Russian control. *UPI*

Romania's large timber industry was taken over by a Soviet-dominated "joint-stock" company in the first years after World War II. Similar companies ruled other key industries. *Photoworld*

North Koreans sent by Russia into Romania as laborers during the period of extreme Soviet control. These Asian workers look annoyed by the laughter of the Romanian women. *Photoworld*

the Russian army of occupation also helped Romanian Communists take over the government. King Michael became a prisoner in his own palace, powerless to halt Communization of his country. By 1947 he was forced to abdicate and fled into foreign exile. Then Romania was proclaimed a "People's Republic" and signed a twenty-year military alliance with the USSR. Agriculture was collectivized, and all industry nationalized. Communist strongman Gheorghe Gheorghiu-Dej emerged as the ruler, ruthlessly purging all opposition.

After Romania was completely Communized, Russia was less cruel. Half of the remaining repara-tions were canceled in 1948, saving Romania about $73 million. Russia in 1953 sold to Romania the Soviet share in the joint companies. And the Russian army of occupation departed in 1958.

Until the 1960s, Romania seemed the most docile of all Soviet satellites, staunchly Stalinist even after Stalin's death. Then came a major change. Soviet Premier Khrushchev ordered the member countries of CEMA (East Europe's Communist common market) to specialize in producing what they could best produce. Other goods could be imported from other CEMA nations. Romania's place in this master plan was to grow grain and

As Communist Romania became semi-independent, Soviet leader Nikita Khrushchev tried to woo Bucharest back into subordination. Here he clasps hands in 1962 with Romanian Premier Ion Maurer and President Gheorghiu-Dej. *UPI*

Youthful Nicolae Ceausescu (*right*), Romanian president since 1965, negotiating with Britain's foreign minister (*left*). During Ceausescu's presidency, Romania's trade with West Europe has sharply increased. *UPI*

A large Romanian steel mill. Romania is expanding its metallurgical industry to free itself from imports of Soviet steel. *UPI*

Ceausescu (*left*) and Romanian Premier Maurer (*right*) enjoying a conversation with Premier Chou En-lai of Communist China. Romania has remained strictly neutral in the bitter Sino-Soviet dispute. *UPI*

Post-Khrushchev leaders of the USSR examining the model of a new Romanian electric train. *In front from right to left (omitting the stooping man)*: Party Secretary Suslov, Soviet Premier Kosygin, and Communist Party Chief Brezhnev. Suslov seems to be impressed by Romanian technique, which is sometimes better than Soviet. *UPI*

produce oil, but not develop manufacturing.

Angrily Romania replied that it would not be a mere "gas station and grocery store" for the Soviet orbit. Against Moscow desires, Bucharest began building a big heavy industry. When Russia suggested joint Soviet-Romanian improvement of their adjacent borderlands, Bucharest bluntly refused. Then Romania started joint construction of Danubian power plants with the Communist heretic —Yugoslavia. In 1958, 51 percent of Romania's foreign trade was with the USSR; by 1968, only 27 percent. Increasingly, Romania traded with the capitalist West, hiring West European firms to build new Romanian industries.

Meanwhile Romania de-Russified. All streets, towns, institutions, factories, and farms with Soviet names were given Romanian titles. Russian-language courses were no longer compulsory in schools and colleges. Bucharest even reminded Russia that Marx and Engels, the founders of Communist ideology, had said that Bessarabia should belong to Romania. Dictator Gheorghiu-Dej's death in 1965 caused no change in policy. He was succeeded by youthful President Nicolae Ceausescu, who was even more anti-Russian.

Romanian foreign policy in the 1960s strayed from the Soviet line. Instead of supporting Moscow in the Sino-Soviet dispute, Bucharest remained neutral. When Red China exploded its first nuclear bomb, Romania sent congratulations. After the 1967 Near Eastern war, Romania refused to join Russia in breaking diplomatic relations with Israel.

Instead, Israeli-Romanian trade increased. During 1968/69, Bucharest gaily entertained French President de Gaulle and US President Nixon, much to Moscow's displeasure.

When Russia, Bulgaria, East Germany, Hungary, and Poland occupied Czechoslovakia in 1968, Ceausescu angrily condemned the invasion. Announcing Romania's readiness to fight aggression from abroad, he ordered all Romanian young people—girls and boys—to take military training. Moscow massed troops on the Romanian frontier, then pulled them back.

Thus Bucharest dares defy mighty Moscow, whose armed forces outnumber the Romanian army eighteen to one. But Russia is plagued by quarrels with other communist heretics—Albania, Yugoslavia, Czechoslovakia, and giant China. At least at present, the Kremlin prefers not to battle with brave Romania. So the old slogan holds true:

"The Romanian never dies."

Angrily Ceausescu tells the Romanian parliament that "nothing can justify" the 1968 Soviet invasion of Czechoslovakia. He added that, if Russia invades Romania, the Romanian army will fight. *UPI*

Romania's small but strong army, now training to fight any Soviet invasion. *Eastfoto*

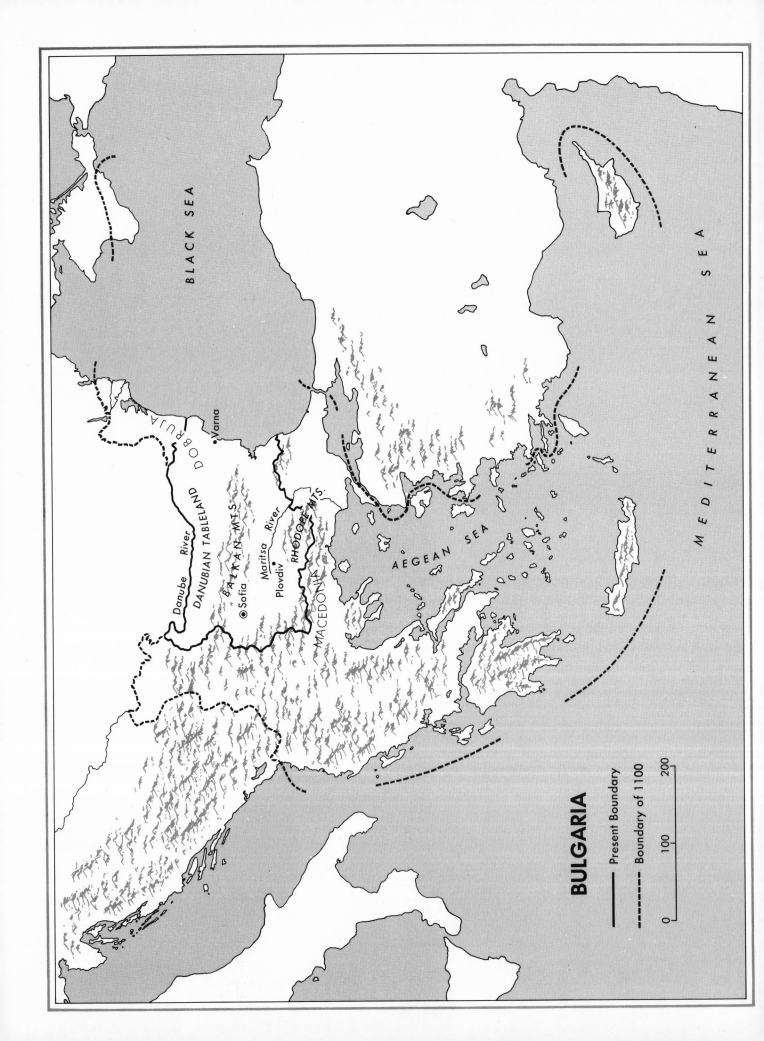

BLACK SEA

MEDITERRANEAN SEA

DOBRUJA

• Varna

DANUBIAN TABLELAND

Danube River

BALKAN MTS.

Maritsa River

◉ Sofia • Plovdiv

RHODOPE MTS.

MACEDONIA

AEGEAN SEA

BULGARIA

—— Present Boundary
---- Boundary of 1100

0   100   200

Bulgaria

"He who falls in battle, fighting for freedom,
He does not die."

THESE FIERY WORDS from a Bulgarian poem symbolize the hard-fought history of the brave Bulgarian people. Countless Bulgarians have willingly sacrificed their lives to free their mountainous homeland from foreign oppression. During five centuries of Turkish tyranny, Bulgarian brigands roamed the hills like Robin Hood, robbing the Turkish rich to aid the Bulgarian poor. In the evening, at the fireside of peasant homes, legends are told and retold immortalizing these bold brigands and many other heroes who through the centuries have died so Bulgaria might live.

The dark-haired, dark-eyed Bulgarians appear to be a placid people. They work hard, save money, tirelessly learn skills, and seem earnest rather than emotional. If left in peace, the Bulgarians are a quiet nation. But when attacked, they fight to kill. Woe to the Bulgarian statesman who leads his country astray! Often his punishment is exile, imprisonment, torture, or death.

This land of extremes is small, its area of 42,800 square miles being just a little larger than that of Ohio. The population numbers 8,500,000, not much more than the city of New York. Almost nine-tenths of the people are Bulgarians, a south Slavic nationality named after the Mongoloid Bulgars who in medieval times were the first royal rulers. Turks are the sole sizable minority, and they are decreasing in number because of mass deportations to Turkey. There are tiny colonies of other ethnic groups: Serbs, Greeks, Romanians, Macedonians, Jews, and even descendants of the ancient Pechenegs. About 2 percent of the population are nomadic Gypsies who are now being forced to settle down.

Bulgaria has the misfortune of having some unfriendly neighbors. To the north lies Romania, which in the past has quarreled with Bulgaria over Dobrudja. In the south are tough Turkey and forever-hostile Greece. Across the west frontier sits Yugoslavia, ruling Macedonians whom Bulgaria considers to be Bulgarians. And on the east is the Black Sea, dominated by a big Russian navy.

With such surroundings, every area of Bulgaria is drenched with the blood of brutal past wars. Northern Bulgaria (the ancient Moesia) is a plateau gently descending northward down to the Danube River. This Danubian tableland has cold winters, so most villages lie in valleys cut deep by tributaries of the Danube. From these sunken villages peasants climb to the plateau to travel for miles to till their high-level fields. Sometimes called the "Balkan foreland," the tableland grows large crops of wheat and corn. Along the Black Sea coast the northern plateau is named Dobrudja, a land of inland hills lowering to lush coastal beaches. There are no minerals in the tableland, except a little oil in Dobrudja.

Bulgarian girls in richly embroidered native costumes. *BTO*

In the Danubian tableland many villages lie in deep river valleys to escape the full force of chill winter winds. *BTO*

"Golden sands" along the Black Sea coast of Dobrudja. *BTO*

The wooded slopes of the Balkan Mountains, which divide Bulgaria into northern and southern territories. *EPA*

Harvesting the rose crop in southern Bulgaria. Rose oil, (for perfume), has long been a major Bulgarian export. *BTO*

The romantic Rhodope Mountains along Bulgaria's southern frontier. *BTO*

Crowded marketplace of a peasant village in the Danubian tableland. *Photoworld*

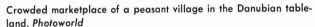

South of the Danubian tableland rise the Balkan Mountains, running west to east and separating Bulgaria into northern and southern halves. With rounded summits and wooded slopes, the Balkans are low mountains easy to cross. Here small deposits of coal, oil, copper, lead, zinc, and uranium are mined. Much livestock grazes on high-hill pastures, and much timber is cut along the mountainsides. Hardy grains like rye and barley grow wherever land is level.

South of the Balkan Mountains lies the valley of the historic Maritsa River, which first flows east, then turns south out of Bulgaria to drain into the Aegean Sea. This area is the ancient Thrace and modern Rumelia. Sheltered by the Balkan Mountains, the Maritsa basin is warm, and here are raised such subtropical crops as grapes, tobacco, and roses. Wine, cigarettes, and rose oil (for perfume) have long been major Bulgarian exports.

Still farther south are the Rhodope Mountains, dividing Rumelia from Greece and southeast Yugoslavia. These uplands, with rocky peaks and forested slopes, yield much timber and brown coal and a little manganese and chrome. Grapes and tobacco thrive in the valleys, while huge herds roam the mountain pastures. Tucked into the valleys are ancient monasteries of Orthodox Christianity—Bulgaria's main religion. Yet this holy land also houses a Bulgarian Moslem minority, whom the Turks converted to Islam.

West of the Rhodope Mountains and beyond present Bulgarian borders is the mountainous plateau of Macedonia—a frontierland of mixed Greek, Yugoslav, and Macedonian population. In the past, Macedonia was part of Bulgaria, which still claims it because the Macedonian and Bulgarian languages are closely akin. Macedonia has few resources, but its strategic mountain passes link much of the Balkan peninsula to the ports of the Aegean Sea.

Despite intensive industrialization during the communist era, Bulgaria remains a predominantly rural nation with three-fifths of the population living in peasant villages. Cities are few and usually small. Largest and most beautiful of the cities is Sofia, Bulgaria's capital, with a population of 825,000. Founded in the first century A.D. by the Romans, the original city was burned down four centuries later by the Huns, so few Roman buildings survive today. Painstakingly rebuilt by the Bulgarians, the city later assumed an Oriental appearance during five hundred years of Turkish rule. There are many mosques, now mostly converted into public or business buildings. Rising from a high plateau in the west Balkan Mountains,

Sofia—Bulgaria's capital and largest city. *BTO*

The Alexander Nevski church built in Sofia to honor the Tsarist Russian armies that liberated Bulgaria from Turkish misrule. *EPA*

Sofia is the main Bulgarian railway junction, with tracks radiating in all directions to Yugoslavia, Central Europe, Turkey, the Danube River, and the Black Sea. Also Bulgaria's biggest industrial center, the city manufactures a wide range of products from radios, telephones, machinery, and armament to cigarettes, flour, and cosmetics. One of the several cathedrals is named Alexander Nevski in gratitude to Russia for freeing Bulgaria from the Turks.

In the Maritsa basin lies Bulgaria's second largest city, Plovdiv, in ancient times the Macedonian capital Philippopolis, from which Alexander the Great sallied forth in the fourth century B.C. to conquer Greece, the Near East, Egypt, and even south Central Asia. Modern Plovdiv, with a population of 226,000, is a charming city of gardens and chief center of the Bulgarian tobacco industry.

In the Dobrudja on the Black Sea coast is Varna (population 184,000), eastern terminus of the Bulgarian railway system and Bulgaria's largest port. Founded by Greeks in the sixth century B.C., the city later became a huge medieval fortress besieged in many battles. Though busy loading, unloading, and building ships, Varna is also a lush resort luring many tourists to its beautiful beaches.

Bulgaria, crossroads between Europe and Asia Minor, operates a small but very strategic network of railways. Highways are well built and easy to ride. Riverboats ply the Danube, and oceangoing ships from all corners of the world visit Black Sea

THE BULGARIAN NATION

	Pre-World War II	Post-World War II	Present
Area (square miles)	39,800	42,800	42,800
Population	6,100,000	7,000,000	8,500,000

In percent of total population

	Pre-World War II	Post-World War II	Present
Rate of Literacy	69%	69%	85%
Urban Populace	20%	24%	41%
Major Nationalities			
Bulgarians	87%	87%	86%
Turks	10%	10%	9%
Gypsies	1%	1%	2%
Main Religions			
Orthodox	84%	85%	85%
Moslem	13%	13%	10%

THE BULGARIAN ECONOMY

	Unit of Measurement	Pre-World War II	Post-World War II	Present
Industrial Production				
Black coal	(metric tons)	219,000	93,000	500,000
Brown coal	" "	3,800,000	4,000,000	26,700,000
Oil	" "	0	0	500,000
Steel	" "	0	0	1,500,000
Agricultural Production				
Wheat	" "	2,000,000	1,500,000	2,500,000
Corn	" "	900,000	890,000	2,100,000
Barley	" "	400,000	249,000	1,100,000
Number of Livestock				
Sheep		9,900,000	8,800,000	10,000,000
Communications				
Length of railways	(miles)	2,200	2,100	2,400
Length of highways	"	13,900	13,900	17,700

Varna—Bulgaria's biggest port on the Black Sea coast. *BTO*

At the dawn of human history the Bulgarian lands were inhabited by Thracians. This fine fresco decorates a Thracian tomb which still stands amid the Balkan Mountains. *BTO*

Plovdiv—the biggest city in south Bulgaria. *BTO*

An Oriental-type street in the old section of Plovdiv. *BTO*

The Thracians were fine architects, as shown in the walls and arches of this ancient mausoleum, which was built in the third century B.C. *EPA*

ports. But Bulgaria still longs for the Aegean Sea ports it owned before World War I, from which ships could bypass the Black Sea and sail straight into the Mediterranean.

At the dawn of human civilization in the eighth century B.C., Bulgaria was inhabited by the Thracians, an Indo-European people related to the Illyrians on the west and the Greeks to the south. Lacking a central government, the early Thracians lived in disorganized tribes. During the seventh century B.C., Greeks founded trading colonies on the Black Sea coast, bestowing some Hellenic civilization on the primitive Thracians. Mighty Macedonia conquered Thrace in the fourth century B.C., only to lose control a century later. The Thracians resumed their pastoral tribal way of life until overwhelmed by the great Roman army in A.D. 46.

Roman rule lasted five hundred years, creating vast changes. Beautiful cities were built and joined together by fine paved roads. Commerce and agriculture flourished, schools were started, and a strong colonial government maintained strict law and order. When the Roman Empire split into two realms late in the fourth century A.D., Bulgaria became part of the East Roman Empire ruled from nearby Byzantium (Constantinople).

Migrating slowly south from their original homeland in east Poland, Slavs invaded the Danubian tableland toward the close of the fifth century. At first they raided, robbed, and retreated. But a hundred years later they came to stay, subduing and settling all Bulgaria. The Thracians disappeared forever, completely absorbed by a sea of Slavs. Today Thracians are only a distant memory, recalled by stone statues and gold, silver, and bronze ornaments found in excavations.

The Slavs were primitive pagans living in

Early Greeks founded trading colonies along the Thracian seacoast. This skillful Greek sculpture dates from the fifth century B.C. *EPA*

From the first century A.D., Rome ruled Thrace for 500 years. Still standing in Sofia is this Roman church built in the fourth century A.D. *EPA*

A marble bas-relief sculptured by ancient Thracian artists. *BTO*

tribes, but their tribal alliance was strong enough to oust the Danubian tableland from Byzantine rule. But Slavic autonomy was short lived. Not Byzantium but the Bulgars conquered the tableland in the year 680.

Distant Central Asia was the original home of the Bulgars, who were Turkic nomads with veiled women and turbaned men. Both sexes wore loose-fitting trousers so they could ride horses fast and long. Driven from Asia by drought during the second century A.D., the Bulgars migrated into the grasslands of the north Caucasian plain, where they were soon enslaved by the Huns.

In the fifth century the Hunnic Empire disintegrated, so the Bulgars gained a precarious freedom lasting two hundred years. Then a new danger arose from the east—the Turkic Khazars who seized control of the north Caucasus in 660. Some Bulgars fled north, founding a kingdom which survived for six centuries in the upper Volga valley. Others rode west across the Ukrainian steppes to the Danube River. In 680, under the leadership of Khan Asparouh, these horsemen invaded and conquered the Danubian tableland. So warlike were the Bulgars that Byzantium paid tribute to Asparouh. Thus began the First Bulgarian Empire, which lasted three hundred years despite almost constant wars with Constantinople.

By hard-won battles the early khans greatly expanded their empire. Asparouh was succeeded by Khan Tervel (701–18), who annexed part of Rumelia. Khan Krum (803–14), one of Bulgaria's most famous heroes, won Transylvania and east Hungary from the Avars plus the rest of Rumelia from Byzantium. In a brilliant battle he routed the Byzantine army and killed the East Roman emperor. Krum lined the emperor's skull with silver and enjoyed using it as a drinking cup.

Krum's successor, Omourtag (814–31), seized northeast Yugoslavia, and Khan Pressian (836–52) conquered most of Macedonia. These vast domains were consolidated by the next ruler, Boris (852–89), Bulgaria's first great statesman who titled himself "prince" instead of khan.

Ancient Roman wall in the modern town of Khisar. *BTO*

Ancestral wedding costume of a Bulgarian peasant girl. The trousers are for horseback-riding, which all peasant children learn at an early age. *Photoworld*

Khan Omourtag (*holding his son*) in the ninth century added Serbia to the First Bulgarian Empire. *BTO*

Byzantium had justified its wars against pagan Bulgaria as Christian crusades, so Boris desired to end this holy excuse. Also, the Orthodox Church of the Byzantine Empire taught the populace to obey the Byzantine emperor. A similar church in Bulgaria could become a pillar of the Bulgarian state. In 865 Boris was baptized an Orthodox Christian, ordering his nation to follow suit. This Christian conversion proved so permanent that more than 80 percent of today's Bulgarians belong to the Orthodox Church.

Two Greek monks who were brothers, Saints Cyril and Methodius, helped Prince Boris convert his nation to Christianity. Since Bulgaria lacked a written language, the brothers modified Greek letters to fit Slavic sounds, creating the Cyrillic alphabet now used in Russia and Serbia as well as Bulgaria. By creating a written language, Cyril and Methodius founded Bulgarian culture. Modern Bul-

garia reveres them, and it celebrates an annual holiday in their memory.

Boris was succeeded by his son Simeon (893–927), who took the title of tsar—Bulgarian version of the Roman word "caesar." By annexing more of Macedonia, part of Albania, and all Serbia, Tsar Simeon ruled the biggest Bulgaria in history. From the Carpathian Mountains in the north, his empire spread south across the Balkan peninsula to the shores of the Black, Aegean, and Adriatic seas. His word was law in half of Hungary, most of Yugoslavia and Romania, and even part of Greece.

When he took the title of tsar, Simeon dreamed of conquering Constantinople and becoming Byzantine emperor. But disavowal of the Turkic term "khan" meant much more. By this time the never numerous Bulgars, like the Thracians before them, had been absorbed in a sea of Slavs. The Asian Bulgars had simply disappeared, leaving their traditions and name to a south Slav nation. So completely Slavic is modern Bulgaria that the language contains very few Bulgar words.

After Simeon came the decline and fall of the First Bulgarian Empire. Tsar Peter (927–69) lost Hungary and Transylvania to the Magyars. Byzantium seized all of Bulgaria proper by defeating Tsar Boris II (969–71). For a few brief decades Macedonia clung to precarious freedom under Bulgarian rule. Then in 1014 the Byzantine army conquered and captured 14,000 Bulgarian warriors. Of every 100 Bulgarian captives, 99 were blinded, while the hundredth was left one eye so that he could see to lead his helpless companions home. When this defaced horde stumbled back into Macedonia, Tsar Samuel was so shocked by their misery that he died on the spot of a broken heart. Quickly and easily Macedonia was annexed by Byzantium, which converted all Bulgaria into a mere East Roman province.

Byzantium was strong enough to control Bulgaria, but too weak to prevent raids into the Danubian tableland by the Asian Pechenegs and Magyars, or to halt looting of Bulgaria by the West European armies of the First and Second Crusades marching toward the Holy Land. Tired of incompetent Byzantine tyranny, two north Bulgarian nobles—the brothers Assen and Peter—led a successful revolt that in 1187 freed the Danubian tableland from East Roman rule. Thus began the Second Bulgarian Empire; it endured for two hundred years.

Saints Cyril and Methodius, who in the ninth century devised the Cyrillic alphabet to give Bulgaria a written language. An annual holiday is still celebrated in their memory. *BTO*

A Danubian town in 969 besieged by a Russian army, which tried and failed to conquer the First Bulgarian Empire. *NYPL* ►

A leonine bas-relief sculptured during the reign of Tsar Simeon. *EPA*

The Bachkovo monastery, founded in the eleventh century when all of Bulgaria was ruled by Byzantium. *BTO*

The devil seizes the soul of the dying Tsar Ivan Assen II (1218–41), who added Albania, Macedonia, and Rumelia to the Second Bulgarian Empire. *BTO*

From the very start Bulgaria's second empire was plagued by power struggles between the tsars and the landowning nobility. Both Assen and Peter became tsars, and both were assassinated. So was their brother, Tsar Kaloyan (1197–1207), who annexed much of Macedonia to the Bulgarian realm.

Fortunately for Bulgaria, the weak Byzantine Empire was conquered by the Catholic knights of the Fourth Crusade who created an equally weak "Latin Empire." Taking advantage of this confusion in Constantinople, Tsar Ivan Assen II (1218–41), son of Assen, annexed Albania, all Macedonia, and Rumelia. Again Bulgaria bordered the Black, Aegean, and Adriatic seas.

By the end of the thirteenth century, Bulgaria was again on the decline. The Byzantine Greeks overthrew the Latin Empire, regained control of Constantinople, and again attacked Bulgarian lands. Much more dangerous was the constant raiding of the Danubian tableland by the fierce Hungarians and deadly Mongols. Tsars rose and fell in rapid succession, often being killed by foreign invaders or Bulgarian rebel nobles. The short-lived Tsar Chaka (1298–1300) was even a Mongol.

By the mid-fourteenth century most of Bulgaria's second empire had been lost, with only the Danubian tableland remaining under Bulgarian rule. So constant were the civil wars that the tableland divided into three separate Bulgarian states in the west, east, and Dobrudja.

Meanwhile Asia Minor produced a terrible new threat—the Ottoman Turks, who crossed the Aegean Sea, bypassed Byzantium, and commenced a relentless conquest of the Balkan peninsula. By 1382 Turkish troops had occupied Rumelia and Sofia and were invading the Danubian tableland. The hero tsar Ivan Shishman briefly stemmed the Turkish tide in northwest Bulgaria. But by 1396 the Turks had killed Shishman and seized the entire tableland.

This was the beginning of five hundred years of Bulgarian agony under the Ottoman yoke. The native nobility was exterminated and replaced by Turkish military aristocracy. Bulgaria became a nation of peasant serfs toiling on Ottoman-owned estates. After Byzantium fell to the Turks (1453), the Greek Orthodox Patriarch of Constantinople supported the Turkish Sultanate, which responded by subordinating the Bulgarian Orthodox Church to his control. Bulgaria's bishops were therefore

Tsar Ivan Alexander of the mid-fourteenth century, when the Second Bulgarian Empire was declining and controlled only the Danubian tableland.

The old section of Turnovo—capital of the Second Bulgarian Empire which in the late fourteenth century was conquered by the Turks. *BTO*

Greeks little interested in preserving Bulgarian culture. Neither the Turkish administrators nor the Greek high priests tried to develop industry or commerce. Worst of all was the "blood tax" by which thousands of Bulgarian boys each year were torn from their homes, taken to Turkey proper, converted to Islam, and forced to become high-class slaves in the Ottoman army or government. A few of the slaves became court officials, but most spent their lives as Janissaries—the sultan's shock troops who preferred to die in battle rather than retreat. Bulgaria's occasional revolts against Turkish tyranny were often suppressed by these fanatic Janissaries, many of whom were Bulgarian by birth.

Hope for liberation rose in 1444, when a combined Polish-Hungarian-Serbian army drove south into the Balkans in a Christian crusade to crush the Moslem Turks. But the Turks crushed the crusade in a gigantic battle near the Bulgarian city of Varna. Again Bulgaria relapsed into despair.

Bulgarian émigrés in neighboring countries tried to keep Bulgarian culture alive. In 1508 the first book printed in the Bulgarian language, a church liturgy, was published in Romania and circulated in Bulgaria., Romanian publication was necessary because Bulgaria had no printing presses.

Early in the seventeenth century the lot of the Bulgarian peasants improved, when the hated "blood tax" was abolished, not as a result of Turkish kindness but because the sultans had trouble controlling the fierce Janissaries. Late in the same century well-armed Turkish troops annihilated small groups of poorly armed Bulgarians who rose in revolt in Macedonia and the Danubian tableland.

Real revival of Bulgarian culture commenced in 1762, when the monk Paissi of Hilendar (1722–93) completed his massive *History of the Slav-Bulgarian Peoples, Tsars and Saints,* which was widely read in manuscript because Bulgaria still had no printing presses. For the first time in several centuries, Bulgarians realized they were a true nation with a glorious past. Paissi inspired many historical works by other Bulgarian scholars, both at home and abroad. Never completely under Greek ecclesiastical control, Bulgaria's mountain monasteries now became great centers of medieval culture.

Most political émigrés went to Russia, which welcomed them as Slavic brothers. Since the Bulgarian and Russian languages are closely akin, young Bulgarians had little linguistic difficulty in

Under Turkish tyranny Bulgaria hated the "blood tax," which took countless Christian boys to Turkey to be converted to Islam and trained for service in Ottoman elite troops called Janissaries. Here is the Sultan *(in pavilion)* surrounded by his Janissary bodyguard. *NYPL*

Courtyard of the Rila monastery, a great center of Bulgarian culture during the five centuries of Turkish misrule. *BTO*

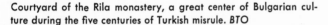

Commemorating Tsarist Russian troops, this monument in the Balkan Mountains stands at Shipka Pass, where great battles were fought during 1877/78 in the Russo-Turkish war which liberated northern Bulgaria from Ottoman rule. *BTO*

studying at Russian universities. Bulgarian priests were among the refugees, some rising to high positions in the Russian Orthodox Church. All these émigrés begged Moscow to free Bulgaria from Turkish misrule.

Moscow responded with a series of Russo-Turkish wars which at first brought no benefit to Bulgaria. The war of 1768–74 sent Russian troops into the Danubian tableland, where they were welcomed as liberators. But the troops withdrew, and the peace treaty gave Moscow some territory in the distant Ukraine.

Russian armies crossed all of Bulgaria during the Russo-Turkish War of 1828/29, forcing the sultan to grant autonomy to Serbia and Romania. But Bulgaria was returned to Turkish tyranny.

Then came the sad Crimean War of 1853–56, with Russia badly defeated by an alliance of Turkey, England, and France. Angrily Bulgarians watched British and French troopships sail from Varna to invade Russia's Crimean coast. A small Bulgarian revolt was crushed by Turkish troops, who massacred anyone openly pro-Russian.

Again and again in 1862, 1867, 1868, 1875, and 1876 Bulgaria rebelled against Turkish torment. All Europe was horrified by the brutality with which the revolts were crushed. Finally Russia came to the rescue with a new Russo-Turkish War (1877/78), which Moscow easily won.

The peace treaty of San Stefano gave autonomy to a big Bulgaria whose vast domains included the Danubian tableland, Rumelia, Macedonia, and a coastline on the Aegean Sea. Bulgarians were overcome with pride and joy, celebrating in a festival of wine, song, and dance.

But happiness was short lived. Austria, England, France, and Germany feared Russian influence in the Balkans; they believed the big Bulgaria would be a huge Moscow puppet. So they forced Russia to cancel the San Stefano pact and sign a new Treaty of Berlin (1878), which returned Macedonia to direct Turkish control. Rumelia became semiautonomous under the rule of a Christian prince appointed by the sultan. Complete autonomy was granted to the Danubian tableland, which could elect its own ruler. Big Bulgaria was thus sliced into three small territories, each governed in a different way.

The tableland declared itself "Princedom of Bulgaria," and chose as prince a German nobleman Alexander of Battenberg (1879–86). Fearfully, many Turks fled to Turkey proper, abandoning estates that Alexander divided into small farms for the Bulgarian peasants. Overnight the tableland changed from a land of Turkish aristocracy and Bulgarian serfs to a country of native free farmers.

At first the country's government was dominated by Russian "advisors" who drafted the constitution, trained the army, and even served as ministers in the Bulgarian cabinet. But the Bul-

Throughout Bulgaria hundreds of monuments honor the Tsarist Russian armies that defeated the Turks. This monument crowns the "Hill of Liberators" at Plovdiv. *Photoworld*

garians, though grateful for Russian aid, had no intention of becoming vassals of Moscow. Their goal was real freedom from both sultan and tsar. Bitterly disappointed, Russia gradually withdrew its advisors and quarreled with Bulgaria's Prince Alexander.

Russia's disapproval became intense in 1885 when Rumelia elected as its boss Prince Alexander, who promptly annexed Rumelia to the Bulgarian princedom. Also mad was Serbia, fearing that its future expansion might be blocked by the bigger Bulgaria. Serbia attacked, expecting easy victory over a Bulgarian army whose Russian officers had gone home. But Bulgaria easily defeated Serbia and retained Rumelia. Wrathful Russia in 1886 forced Alexander to abdicate, then severed diplomatic relations with the Bulgarian princedom.

For a new prince Bulgaria chose another German noble, Ferdinand of Saxe-Coburg (1887–1918), who after ten years finally succeeded in restoring relations with Russia. When Turkey was weakened by internal revolution in 1908, Ferdinand with Russian blessing proclaimed the Bulgarians a completely independent nation. For the first time in over five hundred years, Bulgaria was again a sovereign kingdom.

Banding together in a "Balkan League," Greece, Serbia, Montenegro, and Bulgaria invaded Turkey in 1912, quickly winning the first Balkan War. But the victors quarreled over who should inherit Macedonia. So in 1913 there was a Second Balkan War with Bulgaria battling Greece, Monte-

negro, Serbia, Romania, and even Turkey. Hopelessly outgunned, Bulgaria had to surrender. Romania seized south Dobrudja, while most of Macedonia was divided between Serbia and Greece. All that Bulgaria gained and retained was a small coastline along the Aegean Sea.

Naturally Bulgaria was bitter and longed for revenge. When Greece, Serbia, and Romania took the Allied side in World War I, Bulgaria joined the Central Powers (Germany, Austria, and Turkey). Entering the war in 1915, the Bulgarian army invaded the territory of its Serb, Greek, and Romanian neighbors.

But the Allies won World War I, with Bul-

Ready to return home in 1912 are these Bulgarian army officers after being trained at a tsarist military academy in Saint Petersburg, Russia. *Photoworld*

On a visit to Berlin before World War I, Bulgaria's King Ferdinand (*center*) is greeted by German Chancellor Bethmann-Hollweg. Bulgaria entered the war on the German side. *Photoworld*

Bulgarian infantry campaigning against the Turks during the First Balkan War of 1912/13. *Photoworld*

Bulgarian troops firing across the Turkish frontier during the First Balkan War, which ended in Ottoman surrender. *Photoworld*

World War I: Bulgarian infantry leaving Sofia to invade Serbia. *Photoworld*

garia defeated by a combined British-French-Serb-Greek army. Serbia's successor state, Yugoslavia, annexed a strip of Bulgarian borderland. Bulgaria's Aegean seacoast was lost to Greece. So disgraced was King Ferdinand that he abdicated the Bulgarian throne to his son Boris (1918–43). The members of the governmental cabinet, which had lured Bulgaria into war, were imprisoned.

The humiliation of defeat encouraged political extremists. A large Communist movement arose, believing that Marxism might solve Bulgaria's problems. Macedonian émigré terrorists tried to assassinate any government leaders who didn't care to free Macedonia from Yugoslavia and Greece. For a few years some semblance of order was maintained by able Premier Alexander Stambolisky

A 1916 meeting of the German Kaiser *(left, facing sideways)* and Bulgarian King Ferdinand *(right, bearded)* in Serbia which they had jointly conquered. *UPI*

A mass of mourning by Bulgarian troops when their country surrendered to the Allies at the end of World War I. *Photoworld*

A Communist revolutionary *(second from right)* under arrest in the early 1920s for rebelling against the royal government. *Photoworld*

(1879–1923), a liberal agrarian who encouraged trade unions and aided the peasant farmers. But his efforts to befriend Yugoslavia were unpopular, and his government was toppled in 1923 by a right-wing coup. Stambolisky was forced to dig his own grave. Then the executioners cut off his right arm, because it had signed the peace treaty of World War I. After these preliminaries, he was beheaded.

Next year the Communists swung into action with a rebellion that failed. Still trying, Communist agents in 1925 blew up a Sofia cathedral in an attempt to kill King Boris during church service. Boris was unharmed, but 128 other worshipers died in the bomb explosion.

The right-wing government lasted until 1931, when a national election installed a more democratic regime. But democracy survived only three years before an army coup established a military dictatorship. Tired of coups, King Boris in 1935 overthrew the military junta and made himself the dictator. For the next eight years Boris was undisputed boss of Bulgaria.

Though the king signed a friendship treaty with Yugoslavia in 1937, his sympathies were with Nazi Germany and Fascist Italy. By the time World War II started in 1939, Germany and Italy took more than half of Bulgaria's foreign trade. To Boris the war was a golden opportunity to recover lost Bulgarian territories, if he joined the Axis Powers. So he joined.

When Romania was occupied by German troops in 1940, Romania agreed to return south Dobrudja to Bulgaria, and the two countries exchanged their mutual minorities. A year later Boris joined the Axis alliance, declared war against England and America, and let German troops use Bulgaria as a base for invasion of Greece and Yugoslavia. Also, Russian ships on the Black Sea were attacked by German warships operating from Bulgarian harbors. After Hitler's Wehrmacht conquered Greece and Yugoslavia, Bulgaria occupied Macedonia and its old Aegean coastline.

Boris was succeeded by his six-year-old son Simeon (1943–46), who played with his toys while a three-man regency governed the country. Neither Boris nor the regency really liked Hitler. The Bulgarian army never fought actively on the Axis side. Care was taken not to declare war against nearby Russia. When Hitler asked Bulgaria to ship its Jews to his death camps, the Bulgarian government refused.

Todor Alexandrov—leader of the Macedonian terrorists who in the early 1920s tried to overthrow the Bulgarian government. *Photoworld*

Bulgaria's King Boris III (1918–43) chatting with England's King Edward VIII (*left*). *UPI*

The 1923 right-wing coup: soldiers questioning a servant of liberal Premier Stambolisky, who was soon arrested and beheaded. *Photoworld*

Ceremony at the reopening of Sofia's Saint Nedelia cathedral, rebuilt after being destroyed in 1925 by a Communist bomb. *Photoworld*

A Sofia demonstration of 1932 against the 1919 peace treaty that ceded some Bulgarian territory to Greece and Yugoslavia. For many Bulgarians this treaty was an act of shame requiring revenge. *Photoworld*

Sofia mounted police in 1934 dispersing another violent demonstration against the peace treaty of World War I. *Photoworld*

King Boris in 1941 let German troops cross Bulgaria to invade Yugoslavia and Greece. Nazi troops built this boat bridge over the Danube to ride from Romania into Bulgaria. *UPI*

German motorcycle troops entering Bulgaria from the Danubian boat bridge. *Photoworld*

Bulgaria joining the Axis in 1941, hoping to regain Macedonia and Thrace. *Seated from right to left*: German foreign minister Von Ribbentrop, Bulgarian Premier Bogdan Filov, and a Japanese diplomat. *Photoworld*

German tanks rolling down the streets of Sofia in 1941. *Photoworld*

King Boris reviewing his troops, who occupied Macedonia and Thrace after Hitler defeated Yugoslavia and Greece. *UPI*

A World War II parade of Bulgarian fascists, a small but noisy political group. *Photoworld*

Public funeral for King Boris, who died suddenly and strangely in 1943 after visiting Hitler. The girls with flowers represent Bulgarian fascist youth. *Photoworld*

Top military men from Nazi Germany in Sofia for the funeral of King Boris. Heading the delegation was Marshal Keitel (*center, with raised baton*). *UPI*

After Boris's death, his six-year-old son Simeon inherited the Bulgarian throne (1943—46). Here soldiers help him operate a toy tank. *UPI*

Simeon, the world's youngest king, reviews his troops. *UPI*

Taking the oath of office are the three regents chosen to rule Bulgaria during King Simeon's childhood. *From left to right:* Premier Filov, Prince Cyril, and General Mihov. *Photoworld*

Driving westward in 1944, the Soviet armed forces occupied Bulgaria which did not resist, left the Axis, and allied with Russia. These Soviet marines are marching in Sofia. *Photoworld*

Russian officers and Bulgarian officials inspecting fifteen trucks donated by the Soviet army to Sofia's city government. By such gestures, the USSR tried to gain goodwill. *Photoworld*

Bulgaria under Soviet occupation: standing under a Stalinist placard proclaiming Slavic unity, Bulgaria's three regents look worried. They were soon arrested and executed for having been pro-Axis. *Photoworld*

All this did not help Bulgaria in 1944 when Russia's victorious Red Army approached the Danubian tableland. Hurriedly Bulgaria made peace with Britain and America and declared war against Nazi Germany. Russia promptly declared war on Bulgaria, which the Red Army invaded. Bulgaria did not resist the invasion, but sent the Bulgarian army north to help Russian troops defeat the retreating Germans.

The first postregency Bulgarian cabinet—a coalition of liberals, agrarians, socialists, and communists. Trying to please all Allies, the posters include portraits of Tito (*left*), Truman, and Stalin (*center*). *Photoworld*

Stalin and George Dimitrov, who became Communist boss of Bulgaria during 1946–49. This picture was taken in the mid-1930s, when Dimitrov was a Bulgarian exile working in Moscow. *UPI*

Giant poster ridiculing Bulgaria's former kings when the country became a republic in 1946. King Ferdinand supports King Boris, who is topped by child king Simeon. *UPI*

While Bulgaria was joining the Allies in 1944, its regency was overthrown by the "Fatherland Front"—an anti-Fascist coalition of Bulgarian liberals, agrarians, Socialists, and Communists. Quickly the Front executed 2,000 prominent people who had been too pro-Axis. Among the victims were 68 members of parliament, 22 former cabinet ministers, and all three regents. Bulgaria became a republic, dethroning child King Simeon, who was allowed to leave the country.

Under constant pressure from the Soviet army of occupation, the Fatherland Front government was soon dominated by the Communist Party. In 1946 the new premier was George Dimitrov (1882–1949)—former secretary-general of Communist International headquarters in Moscow. This veteran Communist nationalized industry and banking, forced the peasants into collective farms, persecuted the Orthodox Church, and gave Bulgaria a Soviet-style constitution. Ruthlessly he purged not only Fascists and rightists, but also the liberal, agrarian, and Socialist leaders of the Fatherland Front. Nikola Petkov, popular chief of the Peasant Party, was arrested in 1947 at a meeting of parliament, imprisoned, and hanged. After Yugoslavia's quarrel with Moscow in 1948, the purge hit the Communist Party itself, liquidating all Marxists not completely obedient to Moscow. Executed in this slaughter was Traicho Kostov—Communist vice-premier.

Dimitrov died in 1949 while visiting Moscow

Dictator Dimitrov began his reign with a mass purge of all political opposition. Here a Sofia parade shows anticommunist prisoners marching handcuffed under heavy guard. *UPI*

High-ranking army officers on trial for alleged anticommunist conspiracy. They received prison sentences ranging from one to fifteen years. *Photoworld*

Communist influence on the annual celebration honoring Saints Cyril and Methodius. Portraits of Stalin and Dimitrov hang between pictures of the two medieval saints. *UPI*

Two Balkan Communist dictators, Yugoslavia's Tito (*left*) and Bulgaria's Dimitrov, in 1947 when they were still friends. A year later they were bitter enemies. *UPI*

Nikola Petkov, leader of the democratic Agrarian Party, defending himself in 1947 before a Communist court which sentenced him to death. His last words were: "I will die, but Bulgaria will be free!" *Bulgarian National Committee*

Dimitrov died in 1949 during a visit to Moscow. Before his body was returned to Bulgaria, this honor guard of Soviet leaders stood by his coffin. *From left to right:* police chief Beria, party secretary Malenkov, Marshal Voroshilov, and Generalissimo Stalin. *UPI*

A quartet of Communist leaders including Vulko Chervenkov (*second from left*), Bulgaria's dictator from 1949 to 1956. *Photo-world*

Bulgaria in 1950 began expelling part of its large Turkish minority. This ship at Varna is taking Bulgarian Turks and their livestock to a new life in Turkey. *Photoworld*

and was succeeded as premier by his relative Vulko Chervenkov, who antagonized the United States into breaking diplomatic relations with Bulgaria for ten years. His policy of favoring consumer-goods industry finally angered Russia, which forced him to resign in 1956. He was replaced by Todor Zhivkov, the present premier, who expanded heavy industry.

Great changes have been wrought in Bulgaria's economy by this Communist industrialization. Huge factories dot landscapes where only farm fields were seen before. Machine building is now the largest industry, surpassing food processing,

Todor Zhivkov, Communist dictator of Bulgaria since 1956. *BTO*

wine making, and the manufacture of cigarettes. Before World War II, tobacco, eggs, and wheat comprised the biggest Bulgarian exports. Today one-fourth of all exports are machines, mostly shipped to the USSR.

Bulgaria's Communist regime is Moscow's most obedient satellite. Soviet occupation troops withdrew as early as 1947. Russia in 1948 objected to a proposed Yugoslav-Bulgar federation, so Bulgaria dropped the idea and quarreled with Belgrade. Later when the Sino-Soviet dispute erupted, Sofia immediately backed the USSR. And in 1968 Bulgarian airborne troops helped Russia invade Czechoslovakia.

Despite this Soviet domination over Sofia, fifty new factories are being built in Bulgaria by West European firms. Foreign tourists are welcome, and tens of thousands enjoy lush Black Sea beaches each year. As time goes by, Bulgaria has traded more and more with the West.

In 1965 an anti-Soviet group of high Bulgarian officials and army officers tried and failed to overthrow their pro-Soviet government. Thus the spirit of freedom is still alive and may erupt again.

Nearly 2,000,000 foreign tourists per year visit Bulgaria's Black Sea beaches. *BTO*

Communist Bulgaria is forever faithful to the Warsaw Pact military alliance linking Russia with the East European satellites. In this group of Warsaw Pact generals, the Bulgarian representative stands fourth from left. *UPI*

Yugoslav shipyards build merchant vessels for many nations. *Photo-world*

A new governmental building in modern Belgrade. *EPA*

Belgrade, the "white city," is capital of both Serbia and Yugoslavia. *EPA*

Belgrade's old Palace of Parliament has been the scene of much political intrigue and violence. *EPA*

Zagreb—Croatia's capital city. *EPA*

A fine old church in the city of Zagreb. *EPA*

Skoplje, the capital of Macedonia. *EPA*

cient aqueduct still supplies water, the city is divided by the river into old Turkish and modern Macedonian quarters. Poppies grow in the surrounding fields, so opium is one of the city's indus-

tries. Another is the processing of minerals from nearby mountain mines. Largely destroyed by an immense earthquake in 1963, Skopje was rebuilt with much foreign aid.

The oriental bazaar in Sarajevo, the capital city of Bosnia-Hercegovina. *Photoworld*

The Morava River, whose valley is a gateway from central Europe to the Near East. *EPA*

gateway from powerful Austria into agrarian Pannonia. Today, with a population exceeding 138,-000, Ljubljana is the fourth largest Yugoslav city, with large factories specializing in metal, machines, textiles, and paper. Trade and transport are big business along the roads and railways to the nearby Austrian frontier.

Tucked away in the valley of the small Miljacka River in central Yugoslavia rests Sarajevo, the capital of Bosnia-Hercegovina. With a population above 143,000, this quiet provincial city is the fifth largest in Yugoslavia. Founded in the thirteenth century by the then-ruling Hungarians, Sarajevo later acquired a Moslem appearance during long centuries under Turkish domination. One hundred mosques, red-tile roofs, and an Oriental bazaar remind visitors that they are viewing the shrine of south Slav Moslems. On a house wall near the riverbank hangs a plaque with the simple inscription: "Here in this historic place Gavrilo Princip was the initiator of liberty on Saint Vitus Day, June 28, 1914." On this side street Serbian student Princip fired the shots assassinating the Archduke and Archduchess of Austria, whose deaths triggered World War I.

At first glance mountainous Yugoslavia would seem tortuous for travel through the Balkans. But there is one easy route from Austria or Hungary across the Pannonian plain, then south along the Morava-Vardar river valleys into Greece. The Serbian River Morava flows north along the Bulgarian border, eventually joining the Danube east of Belgrade. Near the Morava headwaters is the Macedonian River Vardar, running south to the Greek coast of the Adriatic Sea. Once the historic trail for Turkish invasion of Europe, the Morava-Vardar gap is now the main railway route from Central Europe to the Near East. To attract tourists, Communist Yugoslavia has built the 770-mile "Continental Highway" from the Austrian border through Slovenia, across Pannonia, and down the Morava-Vardar gorges to the Greek frontier.

Also Communist constructed is another great road—the 650-mile "Adriatic Highway" from the Italian border down the Dalmatian coast to Montenegro. Few of the world's expressways enjoy such spectacular scenery, with rocky mountains towering over the clear blue sea.

Aside from the Continental and Adriatic highways, most Yugoslav roads are gravel or dirt. Railways are also inadequate, not reaching many

Like almost all Slovenian cities, with a castle on a hill and the town below, Ljubljana—capital of Slovenia—is a reminder of medieval glories. Founded by the Romans just before the birth of Christ, this clean-cut city for centuries was the

Much of present Yugoslavia was once under Roman rule. This well-preserved Roman arch still survives in the Dalmatian city of Pula. *EPA*

This ancient wall was once part of the huge palace of Roman Emperor Diocletian (A.D. 284–305). Most of the modern city of Split lies within the old palace grounds. *EPA*

Dating from the tenth century A.D. are these Bosnian tombs of the Bogomils, who were early Protestants opposing the Orthodox religion. *Foto-Tanjug* ▶

mountainous regions. A problem is Bosnia-Hercegovina, where all rail lines were built narrow gauge by former Austrian rulers so the area would be isolated from the broad-guage railways of Serbia. Like everything else in Yugoslavia, even the rail network reflects past political disputes.

With its many Adriatic seaports, small Yugoslavia operates a large merchant navy. There is also a Yugoslav airline, formerly Russian-controlled, which connects Belgrade with West and East Europe, Moscow, and even the Near East.

At the dawn of recorded human history, Yugoslavia was inhabited by a primitive Indo-European people called Illyrians. Early Greek historians write that the tattooed Illyrians lived in tribes, sacrificed human beings to pagan gods, and were forever fighting tribal civil wars. As early as the seventh century B.C., Greek colonies were founded along the Dalmatian coast, but the colonists were afraid to move inland. To repulse a Celtic invasion of north Illyria during the fourth century B.C., the Illyrian tribes finally united into a single state. By the second century B.C., Roman settlements had replaced the Greek coastal colonies, and Illyrian pirates waxed rich robbing Roman ships on the Adriatic Sea. To stop this piracy Illyria was invaded by Roman legions, who after many defeats finally conquered the country in the year A.D. 9.

Under Roman occupation, Illyria was quickly Latinized. Beautiful cities were built, fine roads connected the various regions, and mines produced a wealth of gold, silver, and copper. So tough were the Illyrians that Rome was delighted to recruit them as soldiers for the imperial army. Many Illyrians rose to the rank of general, and five became

A medieval bridge in Bosnia, which was the center of a medieval kingdom. *Photoworld*

Roman Emperors. Most famous of these imperial Illyrians was the Emperor Diocletian (A.D. 284–305), Rome's first absolute monarch who built his palace on his native Dalmatian coast. So huge was this royal residence that most of the modern city of Split lies within the old palace walls.

Diocletian divided his vast domains into a West Roman Empire ruled from Rome and an East Roman Empire governed by Byzantium (Constantinople). Inland Illyria fell under Byzantine control, while Dalmatia remained West Roman. But neither Byzantium nor Rome was strong enough to protect the Balkans from barbarian raids during the fifth century A.D., when Illyria was invaded and sacked by the Visigoths, Ostrogoths, and Huns. Fortunately for Illyria, all these invaders soon left for Italy to attack Rome itself. Byzantium regained Illyria, and about 535 also seized the Dalmatian coast.

Almost immediately new barbarians—the Asian Avars—conquered and devastated both Illyria and Dalmatia, then withdrew northward into the Hungarian plain. There the Avars displaced huge numbers of Slavs, who saved themselves by migrating south into all Illyrian areas. These Slavs were divided into three main groups—Serbs, Croats, and Slovenes—each of which settled in a different Illyrian region. Hopelessly outnumbered, most Illyrians by the late seventh century had been absorbed by south Slavs. Even the name "Illyria" disappeared. Only in the southwest coastal mountains did some Illyrians survive, calling themselves "Albanians."

The south Slavs lived in primitive pagan tribes, which slowly began uniting to form small feudal states. First of the south Slav states was Slovenia, which during 630 became the southern part of a kingdom founded by the Frankish merchant Samoe. After the kingdom of Samoe was overthrown by the Avars in 659, Slovenia maintained a precarious independence till the late eighth century, when it was conquered by Frankish Emperor Charlemagne the Great. For the next 1,100 years Slovenia remained under Germanic rule, first as part of the Holy Roman Empire and later as an Austrian province.

A century after the fall of Slovenia another South Slav state arose—the "Duchy of Croatia" in Dalmatia. From its very start, this dukedom was embroiled in constant wars against Constantinople, which still controlled much of the Dalmatian coast. Despite many defeats, Croatia managed to exist and expand. Duke Tomislav, who reigned over both Dalmatia and Pannonia, proudly raised his rank to

Croatian "prince" in 910 and then "king" by 925. A later ruler, Petar Kresimir (1058–74), lengthened the royal title to "King of Croatia and Dalmatia."

The next king, Dimitri Zvonimir (1076–89), died in battle, leaving no heir. His greedy brother-in-law, the King of Hungary, promptly claimed the right of inheritance to the Croatian throne. Rising in revolt against Hungarian overlordship, the Croatian nobility fought for several years to keep their country free. But Hungary won and annexed Pannonia and Dalmatia in 1102. Croatia thus fell under alien rule, which lasted for the next eight hundred years.

After conquering Croatia, Hungary struck south and seized Bosnia in 1137. But the tough Bosnian mountaineers refused to remain vassals of the Hungarian horsemen. Under the leadership of the capable Kulin (1180–1204), Bosnia rebelled and regained freedom. By war and intrigue, Hungary was victorious once more in 1254. This triumph proved temporary since Bosnia was again liberated by Stephen Kotromanic (1322–53) who also took Hercegovina. He was succeeded by his nephew Stephen Turtko (1353–91) who, after annexing part of Dalmatia, proudly proclaimed himself "King of the Serbs, Bosnia, and the Coast." Bosnia's kingdom survived till the mid-fifteenth century, when it was overwhelmed by the Turks.

Meanwhile foreign invaders long prevented the Serbs from forming their own south Slav state. During the entire ninth and tenth centuries, Serbia was the hapless battleground for wars between Byzantium and Bulgaria. Whoever won became the master of Serbia, which then was forced to be a colony of either Sofia or Constantinople.

Only by hard fighting in the mid-eleventh century did the Serbs win the freedom so long desired and denied. A series of strong rulers culminated in Stevan Nemanja (1168–96), who conquered the Morava-Vardar valleys, annexed Montenegro, and sired a dynasty that ruled Serbia for the next two hundred years. His youngest son Rastko (1174–1235) never took the throne, but as an archbishop freed the Serbian Orthodox Church from control by despotic Constantinople. Today he is still revered as a Serbian saint.

Greatest of the medieval Serb rulers was Stevan Dusan (1331–55), who created an empire including Albania, Macedonia, and even northern Greece. Dusan, whose law code was a model of medieval chivalry, proclaimed himself "Emperor of the Serbs and the Greeks."

His son Stevan Uros V (1355–71) was the last of the Nemanja dynasty and the loser of the Serbian Empire, which under his weak rule simply fell apart. Bosnia's kingdom now became the strongest of the south Slav states. But both Chris-

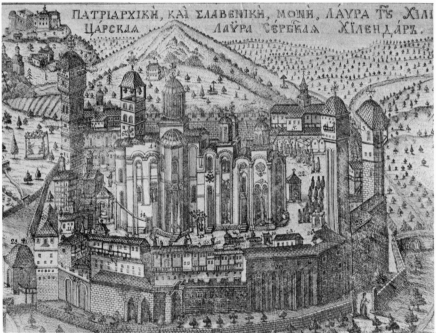

On Mount Athos in Greece the deeply religious Stevan Nemanja built this huge fortified monastery. *Foto-Tanjug*

Great among early Serbian rulers was Stevan Nemanja (1168–96), who founded a dynasty which ruled Serbia for 200 years. As shown in this painting, he became a monk shortly before his death. *Foto-Tanjug*

Coronation of Stevan Dusan (1331—55), "Emperor of the Serbs and the Greeks," whose domains included Serbia, Albania, Macedonia, and northern Greece. *Foto-Tanjug*

Pages from the law code issued by Stevan Dusan, who was Serbia's greatest medieval legislator. *Foto-Tanjug*

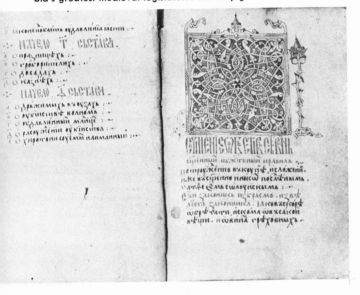

Stevan Dusan elevated the Orthodox archbishop of Serbia to the rank of Patriarch, whose residence was this medieval church in the city of Pec. *Foto-Tanjug*

tian countries were soon threatened by a new danger—the fierce Moslem Turks.

Like a plague the Turkish army advanced northward into south Serbia. An international army of Bosnians, Bulgarians, and Serbs was hastily assembled by Serbian Prince Lazar (1374–89), who on June 28, 1389, gave battle at Kosovo ("field of blackbirds"). Like most European medieval knights, the Slav horsemen wore heavy suits of armor. Turkish cavalry wielded lances with hooks, which easily pulled the Slavs off their steeds. Once grounded, the Slavic knights could not rise because of weight of armor and were slaughtered by Turkish infantry. Today the field of blackbirds has strange scattered scarlet poppies, and legend says each flower grows over the grave of a knight who perished in 1389.

Prince Lazar was captured and killed at Kosovo, and his henchman assassinated the enemy Turkish sultan. But the Turks were victorious, and the Balkans could no longer halt the Moslem menace. For a while the south Slavs remained free, because Turkey decided to conquer Bulgaria first.

In 1420, during these troubled times, the strong Venetian navy seized most of the Dalmatian coast. Thereafter, for almost four hundred years, Dalmatia was under Italian rule.

But Venice could never conquer one south Slav port, the Republic of Ragusa (now Dubrovnik), whose high sea walls could not be scaled. Ragusa also repulsed the Turks, and for centuries it was the intellectual center of Yugoslav national-

The Battle of Kosovo (1389), where Serbian Prince Lazar and his international army were overwhelmed by the Turks. Lazar *(left, hatless)*, already wounded, is being removed from his horse. He died in this battle. *Foto-Tanjug*

One of the last monasteries built in Serbia before the entire country was conquered by the Turks. *Foto-Tanjug*

In 1420 Venice conquered most of the Dalmatian coast, which remained under Venetian rule for nearly 400 years. Dalmatian architecture still reflects the conquest, like this building in the town of Koper. *EPA*

Never conquered by the Venetians or Turks, the Dalmatian seaport of Ragusa (Dubrovnik) survived as an independent city-state until the Napoleonic Wars. *EPA*

ism, welcoming artists and writers from all the Yugoslav lands. Prosperous from trade and powerful in warships, Ragusa stayed free until the start of the nineteenth century, when it was finally stormed by the armies of French Emperor Napoleon.

Ragusa long was fortunate, but inland Yugoslavia was not. After overwhelming Bulgaria, Turkey seized Serbia in 1459, Bosnia in 1463, and Hercegovina by 1483. After humbling Hungary, the Turks in 1526 also conquered Croatia. Down over most of Yugoslavia descended harsh Turkish tyranny, which was to continue for four hundred years. Almost all south Slav nobles were wiped out, except in Bosnia, where the aristocracy saved itself by becoming Moslem.

Somehow Turkey knew how to conquer and control, but not how to promote prosperity. Yugoslav mines shut down, trade decreased, and peasants were taxed into wretched poverty. Even worse than the heavy levies in money or crops was the brutal "blood tax" that each year conscripted thousands of south Slav boys into the Janissary shock troops of the Turkish army. Sons were torn from

Belgrade under Turkish rule. Crescents have replaced the crosses on steeples and towers. *Foto-Tanjug*

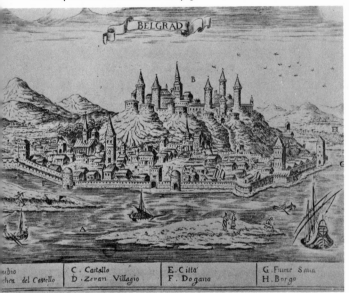

A modern building reflecting the Turkish influence on Yugoslav architecture. *Photoworld*

A mosque built by the Turks in the Kosmet region of Serbia. *EPA*

During the dark ages of Turkish tyranny, monasteries like this kept Yugoslav culture alive. *Foto-Tanjug*

Croat peasants battling Turkish cavalry in an unsuccessful uprising of 1573. *Foto-Tanjug*

The Austrian army in 1688 capturing Belgrade from the Turks, who later reconquered the Serbian capital. *Foto-Tanjug*

Throughout the Turkish tyranny over Yugoslavia, Montenegro remained free under the rule of bishop-princes. At right is Bishop Petar Petrovic Njegos, Prince of Montenegro (1813– 51) and a faithful friend of Tsarist Russia. *Foto-Tanjug*

their parents, converted to Islam, and never again seen at home except as Moslem suppressors of local Christian rebellions.

Mostly the south Slavs did not rebel but learned how to survive as peasant serfs of harsh Turkish landlords. Hogs were raised in huge herds because they would not be seized by the Moslem bosses, whom Islam forbade to eat pork. Left relatively undisturbed by the Turks, the huge Orthodox and Catholic monasteries kept Yugoslav culture alive. Learned bards wandered from village to village, reciting epic poems about past Slav glories, like the Empire of Dusan. Many bold men became brigands in the woods and mountains, where they robbed and killed Turkish travelers but left Yugoslavs unharmed.

Meanwhile, like the port of Ragusa, one small inland area always remained free. Never could the Turks conquer tiny Montenegro, whose rocky mountains and rugged mountaineers repulsed all invasions. After failing many times to subdue the "Black Mountain," Turkey once sent an army large enough to cover all of Montenegro's tiny territory. This huge force promptly starved to death, unable to find food amid the barren cliffs and crags.

The last royal family of Montenegro, before this princedom joined the Yugoslav state in 1918. King Nicholas, his wife, and two of his six daughters. *Photoworld*

Peasants enjoying a cockfight in Turkish-occupied Serbia of the eighteenth century. *Foto-Tanjug*

Life was primitive in Serbia during Turkish misrule. These human draft animals are towing a boat past Belgrade. *Foto-Tanjug*

When Turkey conquered the rest of inland Yugoslavia, Montenegro was a free principality ruled not by a prince but by the local Orthodox bishop. Because religious custom forbade bishops to marry, each bishop upon his death was succeeded by another high priest, who for almost two hundred years was chosen by free election. Then Bishop Danilo I (1696–1737) started a church dynasty by decreeing that each priest-prince be succeeded by a relative, usually a nephew.

This strange system of succession was successful, and the Danilo dynasty survived until 1918, when Montenegro became part of Yugoslavia. But the last prince—Nicholas I (1860–1918)—was no longer a bishop, therefore married, and sired six beautiful daughters who married into the royal families of four other nations. Thus he won fame as the "father-in-law of Europe."

From its very start, the Danilo dynasty maintained warm friendship with the Romanov rulers of Russia. Bishop Danilo personally visited the tsarist court, where he obtained large gifts of Russian money. Each of his successors did the same. At a time when the Montenegrins numbered less than 500,000, Prince Nicholas boasted: "We and the Russians are a hundred million strong!"

Besides financing free Montenegro, Slavic Russia longed to liberate the other Yugoslav lands which were still Turkish colonies. But Russia was far away from the west Balkans, so Germanic Austria became the first rescuer of the southern Slavs. By defeating Turkey in war, Austria annexed Croatia in 1699. Thus Croatia changed masters, but Austria's European-type rule proved to be much more tolerant than Turkish Oriental despotism. Almost a century later in 1797, Austria took Dalmatia from Venice.

Then came a strange interlude during the Napoleonic Wars, when France conquered and annexed the entire Adriatic coast. To arouse Yugoslav nationalism against Austria, Napoleon in 1809 combined Slovenia, western Croatia, Dalmatia, and Ragusa into the so-called Illyrian Provinces of his far-flung French Empire. When Napoleon fell a few years later in 1814, so did Illyria, all of which (including Ragusa) was absorbed by Austria. But Yugoslav nationalism had been aroused, never to quiet down again.

Meanwhile, Serbia was seething. Under the able leadership of George Petrovic (1752–1817), a wealthy pig farmer who called himself Kara-

Left to right: Filip Visnjic (1765–1835), the great bard who composed epic poems about Serbian heriosm. *Foto-Tanjug.* Dositej Obradovic (1742–1811) whose popular writings called for unity of all South Slavs, thus creating a Yugoslav "national conscience." *Foto-Tanjug.* Vuk Karadzic (1787–1864) who tried to combine the various South Slav dialects into a common Yugoslav language. *Foto-Tanjug*

Left to right: Franz Presern (1800–1849), the best of Slovenia's patriotic poets. *Foto-Tanjug.* August Senoa (1838–81), famous author of Croatian historical novels. *Foto-Tanjug.* George Petrovic (Karageorge), the wealthy farmer who in 1804 started a rebellion which temporarily freed much of Serbia from the Turks. *Foto-Tanjug*

george (Black George), the Serbs in 1804 rose in a revolt that soon freed most cities from the Turks. In the 1812 Treaty of Bucharest, ending a Russo-Turkish war, Russia forced Turkey to promise Serbian autonomy. But Turkey broke its promise, crushed the Serb revolt in 1813, and chased Karageorge into Austrian exile.

A new rebellion erupted in 1815 under a new leader—a peasant intellectual named Milos Obrenovich. So fierce was this revolt that by 1817 Turkey was forced to grant some home rule to Serbia, which immediately abolished serfdom. Karageorge hurried home and was promptly assassinated, probably by Milos's accomplices.

Another Russo-Turkish war ended in the 1829 Treaty of Adrianople, which gave Serbia almost full autonomy. Turkey still collected tribute and maintained city garrisons, but otherwise Serbia was free. So in 1830 Serbia proclaimed itself a principality with Milos Obrenovich as its first royal ruler.

Then came a parade of princes. So autocratic was Milos that in 1839 he was forced to abdicate in favor of his sixteen-year-old son Michael, who in turn was overthrown and exiled by 1842. Tired of the Obrenovich dynasty, the Serbs gave their crown to Alexander Karageorgevich, son of the dead Karageorge. Alexander proved to be so weak that he had to be removed in 1859. Back to the throne came the aged Milos Obrenovich, who soon died, in 1860. For the second time he was succeeded by his son Michael, who ruled wisely and well, but was assassinated in 1868 by friends of the Karageorge family.

Next to be prince was Milos's nephew Milan (1868–89), a playboy preferring affairs with women to affairs of state. Yet his long reign produced some political victories.

To aid an anti-Turkish revolt in Hercegovina, Serbia attacked Turkey in 1876. Then Russia helped by fighting and defeating Turkey. The 1878 peace treaty of Berlin gave Serbia full independence and some additional southern territory. Four years later Milan proudly raised his rank from prince to "king."

These successes were soured by the same Treaty of Berlin, which let Austria administer the still-Turkish territories of Bosnia-Hercegovina. Serbia had hoped to annex Bosnia-Hercegovina and thus gain an outlet to the Adriatic Sea.

Another worry was neighboring unfriendly

Karageorge's rebel army in 1806 besieging Turkish-occupied Belgrade. *Foto-Tanjug*

Milos Obrenovich, leader of the anti-Turkish rebellion of 1815–17; Prince of Serbia during 1830–39 and again in 1859–60. *Foto-Tanjug*

Milos Obrenovich (center) in 1815 arousing Serbian peasants to rebel against the Turks. *Foto-Tanjug*

Michael Obrenovich, Prince of Serbia 1839–42 and again from 1860 to 1868. *Foto-Tanjug*

Turkish commandant of Belgrade yielding the keys of the city fortress to Prince Michael in 1867, when the European Great Powers forced all Turkish garrisons to withdraw from Serbia. *Foto-Tanjug*

Prince Milan (*on center balcony*) in 1876 reviewing Serbian troops before sending them into war against Turkey. *Foto-Tanjug*

Silvije Strahimir Kranjcevic (1865–1908), Bosnia's patriotic poet and editor of the literary magazine *Hope* in Sarajevo. *Foto-Tanjug*

Serbian soldiers leaving the Belgrade fortress in 1876 to fight the Turks. *Foto-Tanjug*

Bulgaria, which enlarged itself by seizing Rumelia in 1885. Feeling threatened, Serbia immediately attacked Bulgaria and was immediately defeated. Milan's prestige sunk, his amorous adventures were already a scandal, so he was forced to abdicate in 1889.

He was succeeded by his son Alexander I, the most hated of all Serbian rulers. Besides being a tyrant, Alexander disgraced his country by marrying his aged mistress, who was a commoner of dubious reputation. Both were killed in 1903 when the Serbian "Black Hand," a secret military society, hurled them out an upper-story palace window. So ended the Obrenovich dynasty.

The fall of the Obrenoviches was a boon to their Karageorge rivals. Joyously the legislature gave the throne to Peter I (1903–21), son of Prince Alexander Karageorgevich and grandson of Black George. Under Peter's democratic regime, Serbia achieved its greatest triumph—unification of all south Slavs.

But at first, there was more sorrow than success. In 1908 Austria annexed Bosnia-Hercegovina —an area which Serbia had long desired to acquire. Then in 1912–13 came the First Balkan War, with Moslem Turkey defeated by a Christian alliance of Serbia, Bulgaria, Montenegro, and Greece. Among the fruits of victory, landlocked Serbia expected to gain a coastline on the Adriatic Sea. By creating a new country, Albania, Austria blocked Serbia from the seashore.

The division of Macedonia was the main cause of the Second Balkan War (1913), with Bulgaria overwhelmed by Romania, Turkey, Greece, and Serbia. Though northern Macedonia was taken by the Serbs, they still longed to liberate all south Slavs from Austrian autocracy. So Belgrade began encouraging Bosnian students to assassinate Viennese officials.

In 1914 several of these students visited Serbia, where they were armed by the Black Hand secret military society. Returning to the Bosnian capital of Sarajevo, they awaited the state visit of Archduke Francis Ferdinand (1863–1914), the heir to the Austrian throne. When he arrived on June 28 (the anniversary of the medieval Battle of Kosovo), the students were ready to greet him with bullets and bombs. They spread out along his parade route, so if one assassin missed, another might succeed. A bomb was thrown at the archduke's automobile, but exploded harmlessly. Later

Nadezda Petrovic (1873–1915), the great Serbian painter, in a pensive mood. *Foto-Tanjug*

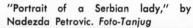

"Portrait of a Serbian lady," by Nadezda Petrovic. *Foto-Tanjug*

A 1912 scene of the First Bakan War: Serbian infantry going into battle against the Turks. *Foto-Tanjug*

The allied Montenegrin and Serbian armies join forces in south Serbia during the First Balkan War. *Foto-Tanjug*

Serbia's King Peter I (*with plumed hat*) chats with friendly Tsar Nicholas II of Russia on the eve of World War I. *Photoworld*

when the car slowly turned a corner, nineteen-year-old Gavrilo Princip shot and killed both Francis Ferdinand and his wife.

Austria was furious. Princip was thrown into prison (where he died in 1918), but Vienna considered him a mere pawn of Belgrade. So Serbia received an Austrian ultimatum demanding that Austrian police be permitted to conduct an investigation on Serb soil. With Russian backing, Belgrade refused. Austria's army promptly invaded Serbia, thus starting World War I.

At first the small Serb army drove back the Austrian invaders. But in 1915 a combined German-Austrian-Bulgarian offensive conquered all Serbia, whose government and surviving soldiers escaped to Greece. There King Peter and a committee of Yugoslav exiles from Austria decided to unify all south Slavs when the war was won. After a combined British-French-Greek-Serb force liberated Serbia in 1918, Peter was proclaimed "King of the Serbs, Croats, and Slovenes." Boundaries fixed by the Paris Peace Conference gave to the kingdom Serbia, Croatia, Slovenia, Dalmatia, Bosnia-Hercegovina, Macedonia, and Vojvodina. Montenegro voluntarily joined the new realm. For the first time in history, all Yugoslavs were united under their own ruler.

But the Kingdom of the Serbs, Croats, and Slovenes was immediately plagued by grave internal problems. Serbia formed a centralized Yugoslav government dominated by Belgrade. Croat politicians protested that Croatia had been promised autonomy. In the first national election the new

Communist Party (founded 1919) won one-sixth of the popular vote. When the Communists in 1920 called for Soviet-style revolution, their party was outlawed.

Amid this turmoil King Peter died and was succeeded by his son Alexander (1921–34), who tried to restore peace and quiet. But at a 1928 meeting of parliament a Montenegrin deputy shot and killed Stepan Radic (1871–1928), the chief Croatian political leader. So angry was Croatia that it was ready to secede.

To save this situation, King Alexander proclaimed himself dictator in 1929 and ruled with an iron hand. Trying hard to unify his country, he even changed its name to Yugoslavia (land of the south Slavs), so Serbs and Croats would feel akin.

Yet Croatia still demanded autonomy. Much more dangerous for Alexander's throne, many Croats became Fascist. Führer of these Fascists was Ante Pavelic (1889–1959), leading a widespread organization named Ustashi (rebels) which quickly found a friend in the Italian dictator Mussolini. Instead of autonomy, the Ustashi called for complete Croatian independence.

In 1934, on a state visit to France, King Alexander was assassinated on the streets of Marseilles by a Macedonian terrorist who was an agent of both Croatian and Italian fascism. Alexander was succeeded by his eleven-year-old son Peter II (1934–45), but the real power behind the throne was his older cousin, the regent Prince Paul.

When World War II erupted in 1939, Yugoslavia tried to stay neutral. But in the spring of

Aged King Peter I leaving his automobile to mount a horse during World War I, when the Serbian army retreated across Albania to sail to Greece from Albanian Adriatic ports. *Foto-Tanjug*

Frontier quarrels plagued the new state of Yugoslavia after World War I. This roadblock by irregular Italian troops was created at Fiume, a disputed Adriatic port on the Italo-Yugoslav border. *Photoworld*

Wedding of Yugoslav King Alexander II (1921–34) to Princess Marie of Romania. *Photoworld*

Queen Mother Marie and her eleven-year-old son Peter, who became King of Yugoslavia after Alexander II was assassinated. *Photoworld*

French police in 1934 seizing the fascist terrorist who had just assassinated King Alexander II (*dead in car*) on the streets of Marseilles, France. *Photoworld*

Solemn Orthodox priests in Belgrade mourning the death of King Alexander II. *Photoworld*

Taking the oath of allegiance in 1934 are the three regents chosen to rule Yugoslavia until young King Peter came of age. On the right is Prince Paul, who dominated the regency until 1941. *Photoworld*

German Foreign Minister Von Neurath (*with raised hand*) in 1937 arriving in Belgrade on a state visit. Walking with him is Yugoslav Premier Milan Stovadinovic, who was pro-Axis. *UPI*

1941, Hitler demanded that his Wehrmacht be permitted to use Yugoslav roads and railways for the Nazi conquest of Greece. Fearfully Prince Paul agreed, and Yugoslavia allied with the Rome-Berlin Axis on March 25. Two days later the Yugoslav army overthrew Paul and swore allegiance to the eighteen-year-old King Peter II. Happy crowds demonstrated in city streets, shouting anti-Axis slogans. In revenge the German army on April 6 invaded a Yugoslavia that was still technically an Axis ally.

The small Yugoslav armed forces were no match for Hitler's mighty Wehrmacht, which was aided by the Bulgarian, Hungarian, and Italian armies. In ten days Yugoslavia was conquered, then totally dismembered. Italy seized Dalmatia, Montenegro, and west Slovenia, while Germany occupied Serbia and east Slovenia. Vojvodina was annexed by Hungary, Macedonia by Bulgaria, and the Kosmet by Albania. Croatia (including Bosnia-Hercegovina) became a Fascist puppet state ruled by Ante Pavelic, whose Ustashi swiftly slaughtered 600,000 men, women, and children who were Serbs or Jews.

In true Yugoslav tradition, guerrilla resistance movements began harassing both the foreign occupiers and native Ustashi. Unfortunately, the guerrillas soon divided into two quarreling camps who hated each other.

Weaker of the two guerrilla movements were the Chetniks, headed by Colonel Draza Mihailovic (1890–1946) of the royal Yugoslav army. The Chetniks were a national guard who kept their weapons in their peasant homes. Loosely organized and poorly armed, they started sabotaging Nazi supply lines and ambushing German garrisons. So impressed was King Peter II, who headed the Yugoslav exile government in London, that in 1942 he made Mihailovic both a general and his minister of war. But the war minister soon stopped active

Chetnik operations, because they aroused savage German reprisals against Chetnik villages. Mihailovic then held his forces in reserve until the German occupiers weakened.

This policy of Chetnik caution aided the growth of the other guerrilla army—Tito's Communist Partisans. Joseph Broz Tito (1892–) was the son of a Slovenian peasant mother and a Croatian father who was the village blacksmith. Drafted into the Austrian cavalry during World War I, Joseph was taken prisoner by the Russians, witnessed the 1917 Bolshevik Revolution, and was an officer of Lenin's Red Army in the Russian Civil War of 1918–20. During the 1920s and 1930s he became a Communist Party organizer, operating both in Yugoslavia and elsewhere in Europe. By 1937 he was secretary-general of the Yugoslav Communist Party, which he molded into a tight-knit revolutionary force.

Using his 12,000-man party of 1941 as a nucleus, Tito welcomed into his Partisans anyone willing to fight the foreign occupiers. Unlike the Chetniks, the Partisans withdrew from their native villages into mountain fastnesses, where the enemy could not catch them. From these hideouts they made swift raids, blowing up bridges, wrecking trains, sabotaging supply depots, and ambushing enemy troops. Then like ghosts, the raiders would vanish into mountain mists.

Trying to help, Britain and the United States at first sent arms, ammunition, and other supplies to the Chetniks. But it soon became obvious that Mihailovic was waiting while Tito was fighting. So in 1943 British-American aid was transferred to the Partisans who were now battling Germans, Italians, Ustashi, and even the Chetniks.

Russia never sent supplies, but in 1944 its Red Army rolled into Yugoslavia and helped the Partisans defeat Nazis, Fascists, and Chetniks. After putting Tito into power, the Red Army left to conquer Austria. By 1945 the war was over, all south Slav lands had been reunited, but Yugoslavia lay in ruins. One-seventh of the entire population was missing. Other war losses included three-fifths of all horses, and half of the cattle, hogs, and sheep.

Tito wasted no time Communizing his devasted country. King Peter was dethroned, and Yugoslavia became a "People's Republic." The army and police executed no less than 200,000 anticommunists, including Chetnik leader Mihailo-

vic, who was accused of treason. Churches were persecuted, industry was nationalized, and peasants began to be forced into collective farms. In foreign relations Yugoslavia allied with the USSR and proved its toughness by shooting down two unarmed American transport planes. South Slavland seemed to be the most faithful of all Soviet satellites.

Suddenly in 1948 the Communist Information Bureau (Cominform—a league of European Communist parties) expelled Yugoslavia from the Soviet orbit of nations. Adding insult to injury, the expulsion came on June 28—a date revered by Yugoslavs as the anniversary of both the Battle of Kosovo and Princip's assassination of the Archduke of Austria. Yugoslavia was accused of being undemocratic, anti-Soviet, procapitalist, and much too nationalistic. The Cominform also complained that Soviet specialists working in Yugoslavia had been ridiculed and even shadowed by police spies. Tito was told to reform or be removed from power.

A Yugoslav political rally of 1948 in the huge Adriatic port of Trieste, which both Italy and Yugoslavia wanted to annex and eventually agreed to divide. *Photoworld*

Tito replied direct to the USSR, reminding Russia how hard his wartime Partisans had fought without Soviet supplies. He denied all Cominform accusations, said the Soviet specialists had been caught spying, and thundered: "No matter how much each of us loves the USSR, he can in no case love his country less."

Obviously the quarrel concerned who should rule Yugoslavia, Tito or Stalin. But Tito neither reformed nor was overthrown. Most of his people, party, and army supported him, preferring their own dictator to Russian domination. The few Yugoslav Stalinists were swiftly rounded up by Tito's efficient police. A war of words erupted between Belgrade and Moscow, whose press called Tito a Judas, Fascist, snake, and mad dog.

But there was more than a war of words. Russia in 1949 broke the Soviet-Yugoslav alliance, ceased all technical aid to Tito, and ordered all Communist nations to stop trading with the south Slavs. Tito struck back by stopping supplies to the Greek Communists, who were fighting a civil war against the Greek capitalist government. Without Yugoslav supplies, the Greek Communists soon had to surrender.

To break the Communist economic blockade, Tito traded with the West and in 1950 began re-

ceiving American aid—first in goods and then also in armaments. By 1953 Yugoslavia allied with Greece and Turkey, both of whom already belonged to the Western military alliance—NATO. Toughly Tito declared that, if Russia attacked his country, Yugoslavia would fight.

Meanwhile to keep popular support at home, the Yugoslav Communist government moderated its internal policies. Churches were less restricted, factory workers were given some control over their plants, private stores were encouraged, and farm collectivization was stopped. Life became more free than in any other Communist country.

After Stalin's death in 1953, Russia awkwardly tried to end its quarrel with Yugoslavia. Trade re-

Farm machines ready for shipment from a factory built in the Communist era. *EPA*

One of the few Yugoslav collective farms. Most cropland is still tilled by private owners. *EPA*

Freighter on the Danube near Belgrade. Before Tito quarreled with Stalin, Russia controlled Yugoslav river shipping. *EPA*

After Yugoslavia was expelled from the Soviet orbit, other Communist countries tried to subvert the Yugoslav nation. This army captain and his civilian accomplices are on trial in 1951 for betraying Yugoslav military secrets to Hungarian army intelligence. *Photoworld*

Another treason trial—of a Yugoslav naval officer and his accomplices who spied for the Czechoslovak government. *Photoworld*

Yugoslav President Tito (*right*) and Polish leader Gomulka in 1957 when Yugoslavia again temporarily had good relations with the Soviet orbit. *Wide World Photos*

Tito in a relaxed mood at his country villa, entertaining the royal family of Greece. *UPI*

sumed in 1954, Soviet leader Khrushchev visited Belgrade in 1955, and by 1956 the USSR promised Yugoslavia a technical-aid credit worth $285 million. Tito was told he was forgiven and could rejoin the Soviet orbit.

Yugoslavia gratefully accepted USSR trade and aid, but refused to reenter the orbit. Then Tito angered Russia by condemning Soviet suppression of the 1956 Hungarian revolution. Russia retaliated by promptly suspending its aid to Yugoslavia. So started the second Soviet-Yugoslav dispute, which burst into the open by 1958, when a congress of the Yugoslav Communist Party criticized the USSR for dominating small Communist nations by force, exploiting satellite economies, and unnecessarily dividing the world by cold war.

Not as long or strong as the first Soviet-Yugoslav dispute, the second was ended by Russia in 1961, when the USSR sought world Communist support for its quarrel with Red China. A third Soviet-Yugoslav dispute broke out in 1968, because Tito denounced the Soviet invasion of Czechoslovakia. Though this argument calmed down, Yugoslavia in 1970 was still training its people for guerrilla warfare against possible attack from the USSR.

So Yugoslavia goes its independent way, free from both East and West. It seems strange that there is a Communist country where one-fourth of all stores and nine-tenths of the farmland are privately owned and operated. There is no Iron Curtain: Western tourists are welcome, and half a million Yugoslavs are permitted to live abroad as workers in West Europe. And, for once, the south Slav nationalities are living together in some peace and harmony.

But Yugoslavia faces an uncertain future. Tough tolerant Tito is very old, and there seems to be no suitable successor. Only time will tell whether south Slav unity and freedom will survive after Tito is gone.

Monument in Zagreb honoring the antifascist resistance movement of World War II. Today the whole Yugoslav nation is training to resist any future Soviet invasion. *EPA*

Yugoslavia jealously guards its independence amid its natural fortresses—mighty mountains. *Photoworld*

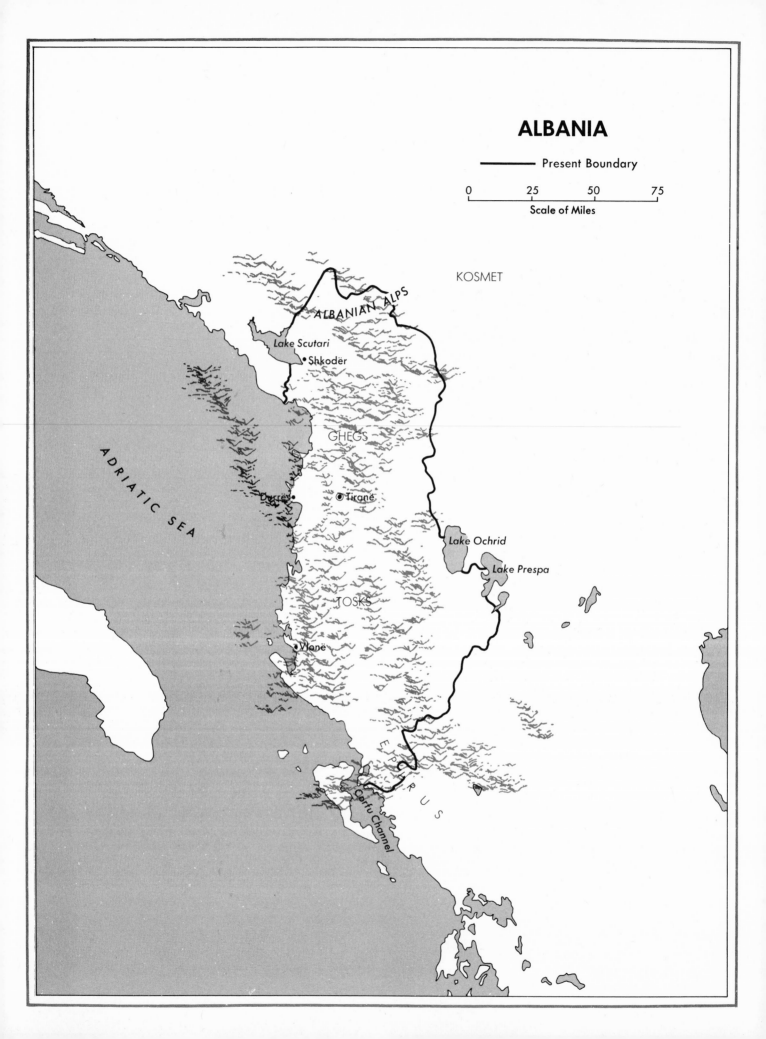

ALBANIA

—— Present Boundary

Scale of Miles
0   25   50   75

KOSMET

ALBANIAN ALPS

Lake Scutari

• Shkodër

GHEGS

ADRIATIC SEA

Durrës •   ◉ Tiranë

Lake Ochrid

Lake Prespa

TOSKS

• Vlonë

EPIRUS

Corfu Channel

Albania

IN THE ALBANIAN émigré districts of New York City, mugging is dangerous—for the mugger, who is usually killed on the spot by a crowd of angry Albanians. Welfare workers also avoid this district, because even the poorest residents resent relief. Albanians despise beggars, and mere acceptance of charity is considered begging.

These proud tough émigrés come from a tiny Balkan homeland poor in property but rich in valor and honor. Blood vendetta still survives in remote mountain villages, where even accidental murder must be avenged by the victim's relatives, who try to kill either the killer or some male from the murderer's family. Yet revenge is done decently. The murderer can visit his victim's household and as a guest be perfectly safe, because traditionally a host must safeguard any visitor. But when the killer leaves, his protection ends, and he may be murdered just outside his host's farm.

"Sons of the Eagle" (Shqiptar) is the native name for Albanians, who by legend are descendants of these huge mountain hawks. Actually these tall, dark-haired people are the last of the ancient Illyrians, who inhabited the whole northwest of the Balkan peninsula at the dawn of human history. Eventually most Illyrians were conquered and absorbed by invading Slavs, but the Albanians survived in almost impassable mountains along the Adriatic coast. Today they still speak a language akin to Illyrian and are proud to be the oldest nationality in the Balkans.

Smallest in area of all East European countries, Albania rules a territory of only 11,100 square miles, about the same size as the state of Maryland. Squeezed between Yugoslavia on the north and east, Greece on the southeast, and the Adriatic Sea to the west, Albania is only 215 miles long north to south, and 50 to 90 miles wide east-west. Yet this tiny Albanian territory contains five massive mountain ranges running north-south parallel to the Adriatic. In the north these "Albanian Alps" from afar resemble raw rock, seemingly devoid of human habitation, but southern slopes are green with grass and lush forests. Less than one-fifth of the country is fit for farming, with most fields cultivated in mountain valleys and on the coastal plain whose former marshes have now been drained.

Geography tends to isolate Albania from the outside world. Many Sons of the Eagle live amid mountains, away from the sea that is the easiest route to other Mediterranean nations. Though the majority of rivers flow into the Adriatic, they are usually unnavigable, silting seaports with their sludge. Land frontiers are mountain crags crossed by no railways and few roads. There are three large frontier lakes—Scutari (Shkodër) in the north and Ochrid to the east, both bordering Yugoslavia, and Lake Prespa in the southeast with shores on Yugoslavia and Greece. Of the three,

Albanian mountaineers often carry arms, so the Communist regime had little trouble forming a "home guard," shown here at a celebration in Tiranë. *Eastfoto*

Three young Albanians in old native costumes. *SAM*

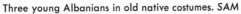

The mighty mountains that rise over most of Albania. *Photoworld*

The hotly contested Albanian-Greek frontier. Greece is in the foreground, with Albania over the first hill. *Photoworld*

Lake Scutari on the troubled Albanian-Yugoslav frontier. *EPA*

A water vendor filling his barrels on the shore of Lake Ochrid, which borders both Albania and Yugoslavia. *Photoworld*

Mechanized grain harvesting on an Albanian collective farm. *Eastfoto*

Tobacco is a major Albanian crop in southern valleys and along the seacoast. *SAM*

Despite some mechanization, most collective farm work is still done by hand. *SAM*

Sheep outnumber all other Albanian livestock taken together. This herd is grazing on a hillside pasture. *Photoworld*

only Lake Scutari is connected by a navigable river to the Adriatic Sea.

Because of geographic isolation Albania's population of 2,000,000 is still 97 percent Albanian. The sole sizable minority are Greeks living mostly in south Albania (Northern Epirus), which Greece has long tried to annex. Though small, the Albanian population is multiplying faster than any other nation in Europe. There are twice as many Sons of the Eagle today as during World War II.

Despite intensive industrialization since the Communist takeover in 1944, two-thirds of the Albanians still are peasants tilling lowland soil or tending herds on highland pastures. Corn and wheat are basic grains of the north, while the warm southern valleys and seacoast cultivate subtropical crops like rice, cotton, tobacco, olives, and grapes. Since one-third of the land is suitable for grazing, there are large numbers of livestock, especially sheep and goats. Agriculture provides important exports in the form of cotton cloth, tobacco, and cigarettes. But homegrown food is insufficient for the booming population, so Albania must import grain in order to survive.

Nobody knows the true mineral wealth of the Albanian Alps, because they have never been fully prospected. Oil, chrome, asphalt, and brown coal were mined in small amounts before World War II. Production of these minerals expanded enormously under the Communist regime, which also began unearthing copper, nickel, and iron. Mining and mineral refining have grown into Albania's biggest industries, with ores, oil, and coal comprising three-fifths of annual exports. Other industries are still small, mostly processing farm produce into cloth, cigarettes, flour, bread, cheese, and olive oil.

Most of Albania's mines, factories, cities and seaports lie in the center and south of the country, which also contains fertile soil. This fortunate area is mainly the home of the Tosks—a group of tribes who in modern times prefer to work in farm fields and factories rather than herd sheep and goats. Before World War II, the Tosk countryside was tilled by great estates owned by feudal nobles called "beys." Rural villages look like forts, since each house usually hides behind high stone walls. Cities seem Oriental, with narrow streets, sidewalk bazaars, and skylines dominated by tall slender minarets. The many mosques show that most Albanians are Moslems, though southern Tosks worship in the Orthodox Christian faith.

Tosk country contains only one-third of Albania's total population, with the rest living farther north amid barren mountains where the tribes are named Ghegs. More warlike than the Tosks, most Ghegs fight frequent duels and are shepherds. Until World War II, the Ghegs still lived in tribes and clans headed by fierce native chiefs. Islam is the main religion, but there is a minority of Roman Catholics. The Gheg villages are breathtaking,

A huge new coke plant built by the Communists at "Stalin City." SAM

Textile weaving is a major Albanian manufacture. *Eastfoto*

Walled Albanian houses, resembling little forts. The loopholes were for rifle fire by houses' defenders. *SAM*

Devout peasant woman wearing the traditional Moslem veil. The sheepskin hanging from the shoulder board is for winter warmth. *Photoworld*

Though most Albanians are Moslems, there are good-sized Christian minorities. This Orthodox priest stands behind an ancient archway. *Photoworld*

Private baptism of a Christian child in a small village church. *Photoworld*

Lonely village amid the northern mountains. *Eastfoto*

Stark beauty of a mountain lake. *Eastfoto*

clinging precariously to steep mountain slopes. Cities are few and far between. Like the American hillbillies, most Ghegs are impoverished rural inhabitants of unproductive mountains.

All Albanian cities are small, the biggest being Tiranë (Tirana) with a population of 161,000. Lying in a plain amid the wooded hills of west-central Albania, Tiranë is the country's capital and a town of vivid contrasts. The government district is laced by broad boulevards lined by big bureaucratic buildings, often with arched windows of Oriental style. Outside this city center the broad boulevards become narrow lanes twisting between rows of small shops and low weatherworn houses. There is little traffic, because Albania has few automobiles. Founded in the seventeenth century by the Turks, Tiranë today is an industrial town with factories specializing in cement, textiles, and processed food.

West of Tiranë on the Adriatic coast sits Durrës (Durazzo), Albania's largest seaport. Founded by Greeks in 627 B.C., Durrës is one of the most ancient Albanian cities. Here most buildings rise in tiers along the slope of a seaside hill near ruins of a Byzantine citadel. Alcohol, cigarettes, flour, and soap are the primary products of local industry. There are many mosques, and most of the 64,000 townsfolk are Moslems.

Even older is the city of Shkodër (Scutari) on

Albania's only university, in the capital city of Tiranë. *Eastfoto*

the southeast shore of Lake Scutari. Spreading over a lowland semicircled by high mountains, Shkodër was the capital of an ancient Illyrian kingdom before the rise of the Roman Empire, which with difficulty conquered the city during the second century B.C. Atop a hill overlooking the town is a huge fortress built by the Venetians and later long garrisoned by the Turks. Town industry concentrates on textiles, cigarettes, and copper wire. An ornate Catholic cathedral reminds visitors that more than

Oriental-type street in the old section of Tiranë, Albania's largest city. *Sovfoto*

A quiet side street in Durrës. *Photoworld*

The city of Shkodër on Lake Scutari was the residence of ancient Illyrian kings. *UPI*

The shoreline of Durrës, Albania's biggest port on the Adriatic Sea. *UPI*

Poor transportation is a grave Albanian problem. This covered wagon is a "city bus" in modern Durrës. *Photoworld*

half of the 48,000 townspeople are devout Roman Catholics.

Safest of all Albanian harbors is the port of Vlonë (Vlore Valona), a city of 49,000 in Albania's southwest. Nearby oil fields pipe petroleum into the city, where the "black gold" is refined for export in tankers. Besides oil refining, local factories distill alcohol, mix cement, tan leather, and can fish.

Poverty of communications is a grave Albanian problem. The sole railway—110 miles of track—links Durrës with Tiranë and other neighboring towns. To serve the whole country there are two newspapers, one experimental television station, six radio stations, and five thousand telephones. Most foreign trade must be carried on foreign vessels, because Albania's merchant marine comprises a grand total of eight ships. Aside from three big highways, roads are bad, and many mountain villages can be reached only by pack animals climbing steep, narrow trails.

At the dawn of recorded human history Albania was inhabited by fierce Illyrian tribes, who tirelessly battled each other and the Greeks to the south. As early as the seventh century B.C., Greek merchant sailors founded trading colonies on the Illyrian coast but dared not move inland. During the third century B.C., these ports were annexed by the rising Roman Empire, which at first also clung close to the coast. So troublesome became Illyrian raids against the Adriatic seaports that Rome in self-defense decided to annex all of Illyria, which fought hard but finally surrendered in the second century B.C.

Because of Albania's many mountains and sparse farmland, few Romans became permanent settlers. Some new towns and forts arose, and a great Roman road was built from Durrës past Lake Ochrid all the way to Constantinople. Modern Albania rebuilt this road, which today is one of the country's three highways.

When the Roman realm divided into two states during the fourth century A.D., most of Illyria became part of the East Roman Empire ruled from Byzantium (Constantinople). By the fourth century the pagan Illyrians had become Roman Catholic, ruled politically by Byzantium but spiritually from Rome.

During the next thousand years the Byzantine Empire became too weak to defend Illyria, which

A station on Albania's one and only railway. SAM

fell prey to many foreign invaders. Goths overran the Land of the Eagles in 399, only to leave in a march on Rome. Slavs seized northern Albania in 640, holding this Gheg territory until the ninth century, when Bulgaria conquered much of Albania. Back came the Byzantines in the eleventh century, while Normans occupied part of the Adriatic coast. During the thirteenth century the Albanian north was governed by Serbia, the center by Naples, the south by Greece, and Durrës by Venice. In the following century all Albania was ruled by a Serb empire that soon disintegrated, leaving the coast to Venice and the Albanian Alps under the rule of Albanian native chiefs. All these foreign conquests altered the Albanian language, whose basic Illyrian was enriched by adding many Latin, Greek, Slavic, and Italian words.

Unpleasant as these Christian foreign conquerors had been, they were mild compared to the Moslem Ottoman Turks who in 1415 overwhelmed the Albanian chiefdoms. But the Sons of the Eagle

Ruins of an ancient Greek city
on the Albanian Adriatic coast.
Eastfoto

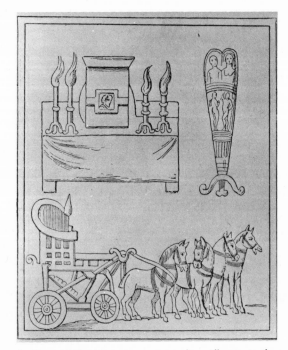

Emblems of the Roman governor ruling Albania in the
fourth century A.D. *NYPL*

Serbian King Dusan in the fourteenth century annexed Albania
to his Slavic empire. *Foto-Tanjug*

refused to accept defeat, soon rising in a revolt led by a military genius named Scanderbeg (1405–68).

His real name was George Castrioti, and he was born into Gheg nobility. As a boy, George was taken hostage by the Turks, sent to Turkey, converted to Islam, renamed "Iskander," and trained to be an Ottoman army officer. While commanding some Turkish cavalry in Yugoslavia during 1443, he took advantage of battle confusion to defect to his native Albania. Racing home, he became a Roman Catholic and a leader of Albanian rebels who called him Scanderbeg—a modification of "Iskander Bey." So well had the Turks trained Scanderbeg that he defeated them, freeing much of Albania. All Europe rejoiced, proclaiming him the "Athlete of Christendom."

With the support of the Pope of Rome, Scanderbeg prepared an international crusade to liberate more Christian Balkan countries from Moslem Ottoman oppression. But the Pope died, and his successor sent few foreign troops to aid the Albanian crusaders. When Scanderbeg died undefeated in 1468, Albania again fell under Turkish tyranny. It continued for the next 450 years.

The mighty Venetian navy kept control of some Adriatic ports till 1571, when these towns were also taken by the Turks. A century later Venice captured Vlonë, but held it only two years

Mohammed II (1451–81), the Turkish Sultan who conquered most of Albania after Scanderbeg's death. *NYPL*

Scanderbeg, Albania's greatest hero, who in the fifteenth century won every battle he fought against the Turks. *Eastfoto*

Scanderbeg's sharp sword and goat helmet. *Eastfoto*

THE ALBANIAN NATION

	Pre-World War II	Post-World War II	Present
Area (square miles)	11,100	11,100	11,100
Population	1,000,000	1,200,000	2,000,000

In percent of total population

Rate of Literacy	20%	20%	71%
Urban Populace	10%	20%	33%
Major Nationalities			
Albanians	92%	92%	97%
Greeks	5%	5%	3%
Main Religions			
Moslem	69%	70%	65%
Orthodox	21%	20%	20%
Catholic	10%	10%	10%

THE ALBANIAN ECONOMY

	Unit of Measurement	Pre-World War II	Post-World War II	Present
Industrial Production				
Oil	(metric tons)	130,000	120,000	1,100,000
Brown coal	" "	4,000	28,000	340,000
Chrome	" "	7,000	52,000	327,000
Cement	" "	9,000	15,000	139,000
Agricultural Production				
Wheat	" "	41,000	85,000	126,000
Corn	" "	129,000	108,000	165,000
Number of Livestock				
Sheep		1,574,000	1,000,000	1,682,000
Swine		15,000	10,000	147,000
Communications				
Length of railways	(miles)	0	0	110
Length of highways	"	2,000	1,766	2,800

against continuous Ottoman assaults. All Albania thus fell under Turkish misrule.

To improve their status, most Albanians abandoned Christianity and embraced Islam. By becoming Moslem they rose from second-class to first-class citizens of the Ottoman Empire, ranking almost equal to the Turks. So part of the Albanian aristocracy survived, with many beys and tribal chiefs serving with high rank in the Ottoman army and administration.

Still the Sons of the Eagle longed for liberty, and there were many local revolts. In the late eighteenth century, first the Ghegs and then the Tosks rebelled, winning some home rule. But during 1822–32 this Albanian autonomy was crushed by many Turkish massacres.

The Italian city-state of Venice in 1498, when its fleet controlled ports on the Albanian coast. *NYPL*

Ali Pasha (1744–1822), perhaps the cruelest of all Turkish governors of Albania.

A sixteenth-century battle showing the Venetian army (*right*) and navy defeating the Turks on the Balkan coast. *EPA*

An eighteenth-century church built in Albania during the Turkish occupation. *Eastfoto*

Monument of Ismail Qemal, the first premier when Albania in 1912 became an independent country. *Eastfoto*

The proud Albanians refused to remain quiet. Anti-Ottoman revolts erupted in all or part of Albania during 1833, 1836, 1842/43, 1847, and 1872. None succeeded.

An astonishing about-face came in 1878, when Albanian leaders formed a pro-Turkish league. They feared Slavic Serbia, Montenegro, and Bulgaria, whose domains Russia was adding to after Tsarist victory in a Russo-Turkish war. Albania preferred to remain temporarily under Turkey rather than risk rule by Slavs. Fortunately the European Great Powers blocked Russia's plans, so the Land of the Eagles was briefly secure. The Albanian League then turned against Turkey, which destroyed it in 1881.

By 1908 a group of Ottoman army officers called the "Young Turks" forced the sultan to grant widespread Turkish reforms. A newborn Albanian movement supported the Young Turks, who promised that Albania's schools and press could use the Albanian language instead of the previously compulsory Greek or Turkish. Within a year this promise was broken.

Taking advantage of Turkey's defeat by Bulgaria, Greece, Montenegro, and Serbia in the First Balkan War, the Albanians in November 1912 declared the Land of the Eagles to be a free nation. This angered landlocked Serbia, which wanted to annex Albania to gain a coastline on the Adriatic. But Austria and Italy opposed a Serb seashore and backed Albanian independence; it was guaranteed in 1913 by all European Great Powers. After a revolt by the Greeks of southeast Albania, the Great Powers forced Albania to make these Greeks semiautonomous.

Albania proclaimed itself "Principality of the Eagles," inviting a German noble, William of Wied, to be prince. William's reign set a record for

Soldiers of free Albania's first army, which during World War I was too poorly armed to prevent occupation of their homeland by Austrian, Italian, Yugoslav, and French forces. *UPI*

Armed Albanian mountaineers of the early 1920s, when their young country had difficulty forming a stable government. *Photoworld*

Ahmed Bey Zogu, president from 1925 to 1928, when he crowned himself as Zog I, King of the Albanians. *UPI*

shortness. Arriving in Albania in 1914 just before the outbreak of the First World War, he fled back to Germany when the war began.

The princeless princedom of Albania tried to be a wartime neutral, but by 1915 was an unwilling battleground for neighboring belligerent nations. First came the defeated Serbian army, retreating across Albania to be evacuated by Allied ships from Adriatic ports. Chasing the Serbs were the Austrians, who occupied northern and central Albania while Italy seized the south and coast. By the war's conclusion in 1918, the Austrians had been expelled, but south and central Albania were held by Italy, the northeast by newly formed Yugoslavia, and the southeast by troops from distant France. The French left voluntarily but the Alba-

nian army had to fight three years to oust the Yugoslavs and Italians, who left only in 1920/21. Meanwhile, Greece asked for south Albania, but was overruled by the Paris Peace Conference, which restored Albania's prewar frontiers.

During the next two decades the Land of the Eagles lived in peace under the benevolent dictatorship of a noble named Ahmed Bey Zogu, who became premier of the princeless principality in 1922. After a brief fall from power, he recovered his premiership by force in 1924, and next year proclaimed Albania a republic with himself as president. Seeking greater glory, Zogu in 1928 converted Albania into a kingdom, crowning himself Zog I, "King of the Albanians."

A man of simple tastes, Zog lived modestly

The royal bodyguard taking down the republic flag in 1928, when Albania became a kingdom. *Photoworld*

A peasant parade celebrating the coronation of popular King Zog. *Photoworld*

Though King Zog tried to modernize Albania, shortage of funds prevented fast progress. Old ways of life still survived, like selling water by the glass at the Tiranë market. *UPI*

King Zog on the balcony of his "palace," which is merely a large house. *UPI*

Reviewing Albanian troops are *(from right to left)* King Zog, his chief of staff, and an Italian military advisor sent by Mussolini to help modernize the Albanian army. *UPI*

and enjoyed playing cards with foreign diplomats. To overcome the backwardness Albania had inherited from centuries of Turkish mismanagement, he built several roads, mills, hospitals, and schools. Since there were no Albanian colleges, he sent several hundred students abroad to study in west European universities. But his funds were limited, so as early as 1927, Zog allied with Fascist Italy, which was invited to develop Albanian resources.

Italy did much to aid Albania, improving seaports, constructing factories and highways, digging mines, and even retraining the army. The entire Albanian oil industry (wells, pipelines, and refineries) was built by Italian firms. Many Albanians resented this Italian infiltration and considered King Zog to be too friendly with Mussolini.

Despite aid from Italy, Albania remained the most underdeveloped country in Europe. Four of every five Sons of the Eagle were illiterate. The Italian companies concentrated mainly on Albanian export trade, dredging ports, building coastal roads, and producing goods for sale abroad. Still desperately needed were inland mountain highways, urban improvement, scientific farming, and industries serving the home market.

To make matters worse, Mussolini proved to be a false friend. In April 1939, before World War II began, the Italian army suddenly landed on the Albanian coast, then slammed inland, conquering the entire country. Zog fled into exile, unable to save his beloved kingdom from becoming a mere Italian province.

Italy seized Albania to gain a base for future attack upon Greece. During the autumn of 1940, the Italian army crossed the Greek frontier, was defeated, and had to retreat back into southern Albania, which Greece now invaded. To the Italian rescue rushed Hitler's Wehrmacht, crushing both

The Italian military occupation of Albania in 1939: Italian officers (*in uniform*) announcing the takeover to a Tiranë crowd. *UPI*

Albanian troops retreating into the mountains in 1939 after being defeated by the mechanized might of the Italian invaders. *UPI*

A sad King Zog in exile, after fleeing Albania to avoid Italian capture. With him are his queen (*right*) and his royal sister. *UPI*

Greek troops receiving battle orders in southern Albania, where in 1940 they were fighting the Italians. *Photoworld*

World War II: one of the many Albanian guerrillas harrassing the Italian army of occupation. *UPI*

The Albanian bodyguard for the British wartime military mission, which supplied Allied arms to the Albanian guerrillas. *UPI*

Left: Enver Hoxha, Communist wartime guerrilla leader who after World War II became dictator of Albania. *UPI. Right:* Another Albanian guerrilla chief, Mehmet Shehu, who eventually was appointed Communist premier.

Postwar victory parade of Communist guerrillas, after they defeated all democratic opposition. *Eastfoto*

Albania under Communist rule: a sports parade showing huge portraits *(from left to right)* of Marx, Engels, Lenin, and Stalin. *Eastfoto*

Yugoslavia and Greece during the spring of 1941. At this point Albanian respect for Italy was almost zero.

To win some support, the Axis gave to Albania the Yugoslav territories of Kosmet and Western Macedonia, which taken together were the home of 1,000,000 Albanians. Albania was pleased, but still longed for freedom from Italian control.

By 1942 the Italian army of occupation was harassed by two groups of Albanian guerrillas: a democratic "National Front," and a "National Liberation Movement" of the Albanian Communist Party, which had just been formed with Yugoslav Communist help.

Italy surrendered to the Allies during 1943, so German troops occupied the Land of the Eagles. A Nazi offer to recognize Albanian statehood was accepted by an Albanian anticommunist government and partly by the National Front, both of which lost prestige by collaborating with the Germans. Posing as true patriots, the Communists conducted guerrilla warfare against the National Front.

Fearful of being trapped by Allied troops, Hitler's Wehrmacht withdrew from Albania during 1944, abandoning the country to a civil war that was won by the National Liberation Movement. These left-wing victors in 1944 formed a government headed by Premier Enver Hoxha, the First Secretary of the Albanian Communist Party. He inherited a devastated country whose losses were said to include one-fifth of all houses, one-third of the livestock, every bridge, and 7 percent of the human population.

In usual Communist fashion, Hoxha abolished the kingdom, proclaimed a "People's Republic," massacred anticommunists, persecuted religion, nationalized industry and commerce, and collectivized the peasantry. His foreign relations were highly unusual:

Albania's Communists showed no interest in good relations with the West. In 1946, when two British destroyers were sunk in the Corfu Channel by Communist mines, Tiranë refused to pay damages or even express regrets. Albania's American vocational school was forced to close despite its long distinguished record of training Albanian intellectuals and technicians. After constant harassment of their missions, both Britain and the United States broke diplomatic relations with Albania during 1946/47. Neither Western journalists nor tourists were welcome in the Land of the Eagles, which became a hermit country sealed off from the non-Communist world.

Meanwhile Albania was the only East European Communist country not a Soviet satellite. Instead, Albania was the puppet of neighboring Yugoslavia, which took back Kosmet and Western Macedonia. Albania and Yugoslavia allied, formed a customs union, coordinated their economic plans, and formed joint companies to aid Albanian railway construction, industry, mining, merchant shipping, and banking. When the Communist parties of Russia and East Europe formed a joint Communist Information Bureau (Cominform) during 1947, Albania was not invited to join because the Land of the Eagles was considered to be a mere Yugoslav colony. Early in 1948 Stalin told Yugoslavia it could "swallow" Albania anytime.

Then like a bolt of lightning in mid-1948 came the Soviet-Yugoslav dispute, with Albania immediately forced to choose sides. If it stayed with Yugoslavia, the future was annexation by Belgrade. But by supporting Stalin, Albania would stay free and receive Soviet aid.

Quickly Albania aligned with Russia. The Land of the Eagles dissolved all Albanian-Yugoslav joint companies, broke its alliance with Yugoslavia, and canceled its debt of $32 million to Belgrade. Soviet advisers and submarines fled from Yugoslavia to safety in Albania. Ruthlessly Hoxha massacred pro-Yugoslav Albanians, the most prominent purge victim being Koci Xoxe—former chief of secret police.

During the next decade, Russia, East Germany, and Czechoslovakia did much to develop Albania, expanding industry and mining, building roads and bridges, beautifying Tiranë, and partly mechanizing collectivized agriculture. Movie production started, and Albania's first university opened at Tiranë. No longer was Albania the outcast of the Soviet orbit. The Land of the Eagles was one of the original members of the Russo-East European "Council of Economic Mutual Assistance" (CEMA) in 1949 and of the Warsaw Pact military alliance in 1955.

Mehmet Shehu, a cruel Communist, known as the "Butcher of Tiranë," became premier in the mid-1950s, replacing Hoxha who remained First Secretary of the Communist Party. Both were shocked in 1955 when the Russian leader Khrushchev ended the Soviet-Yugoslav dispute by be-

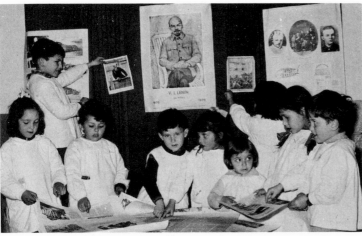

Even infants are indoctrinated in Communism. These kindergarten children are putting up pictures of Lenin. *Eastfoto*

Communist Albania's cropland has been greatly increased by draining swamps and irrigating dry fields. This huge canal bed will carry mountain lake water down to arid valleys. *Eastfoto*

Albania's Premier Shehu (*left*) and Russia's Premier Bulganin signing a 1957 agreement canceling a $100,000,000 Albanian debt owed to the USSR. *Sovfoto*

A Soviet-Albanian friendship meeting in 1957, when Moscow and Tiranë worked in close cooperation. Standing at the speaker's table are (*from left to right*): USSR Premier Bulganin, Albanian Premier Shehu, Albania's dictator Hoxha, and Soviet leader Khrushchev. *Sovfoto*

USSR Premier Khrushchev (*waving hat*) in 1959 gaily visiting an Albanian collective farm. A year later, Albania and Russia became bitter enemies. *Sovfoto*

When Moscow in 1961 broke relations with Tiranë, Albania be-friended giant Communist China. Here Enver Hoxha (*right*) warmly embraces Chinese Premier Chou En-lai. *Eastfoto*

China worship in Albania: The Tiranë ballet company performs a Chinese dramatic dance. *Eastfoto*

Puzzled Albanians view an exhibit of Chinese "proletarian art." *Eastfoto*

Young Albanians absorbing a Chinese propaganda magazine. *Eastfoto*

friending Tito. Again Albania feared that it might become Moscow's gift to Belgrade.

Meanwhile Communist China showed sympathy by giving small loans to the Land of the Eagles. Tiny Albania had found a new giant friend. As the Sino-Soviet dispute deepened, Hoxha crudely criticized Khrushchev at a 1960 international Communist conference in Moscow.

Russia retaliated in 1961 by ending trade and aid to Albania, breaking diplomatic relations and trying to take the Soviet submarines out of Vlonë harbor. Albania seized the subs, and canceled its $200 million debt to Moscow. To Albania's rescue rushed China with grain, advisers, technical aid,

and a $124-million loan. Chinese experts even trained Albanians to sail the Soviet submarines.

Thus Albania became the sole European satellite of Communist China. Back in the 1950s, 60 percent of Albanian foreign commerce was with the USSR. Today there is no Russian trade, and the 60 percent goes to China. Depending heavily on Albanian chrome, most of East Europe still trades with the Land of the Eagles, which, however, is not invited to CEMA meetings. During 1968 Tiranë angrily withdrew from the Warsaw Pact in protest against the Soviet invasion of Czechoslovakia.

So small Albania survives, still free, boldly defying both Belgrade and Moscow. It would not be surprising if the Sons of the Eagle eventually quarrel with Peking.

Albania arms feverishly to repel any future invasion from Yugoslavia, Greece, or the USSR. These antiaircraft rockets are proudly displayed in a Tiranë parade. *Eastfoto*

Girls in Albania's home guard, which is trained for tough guerrilla warfare. *Eastfoto*

PART 3

THE SOVIET REPUBLICS

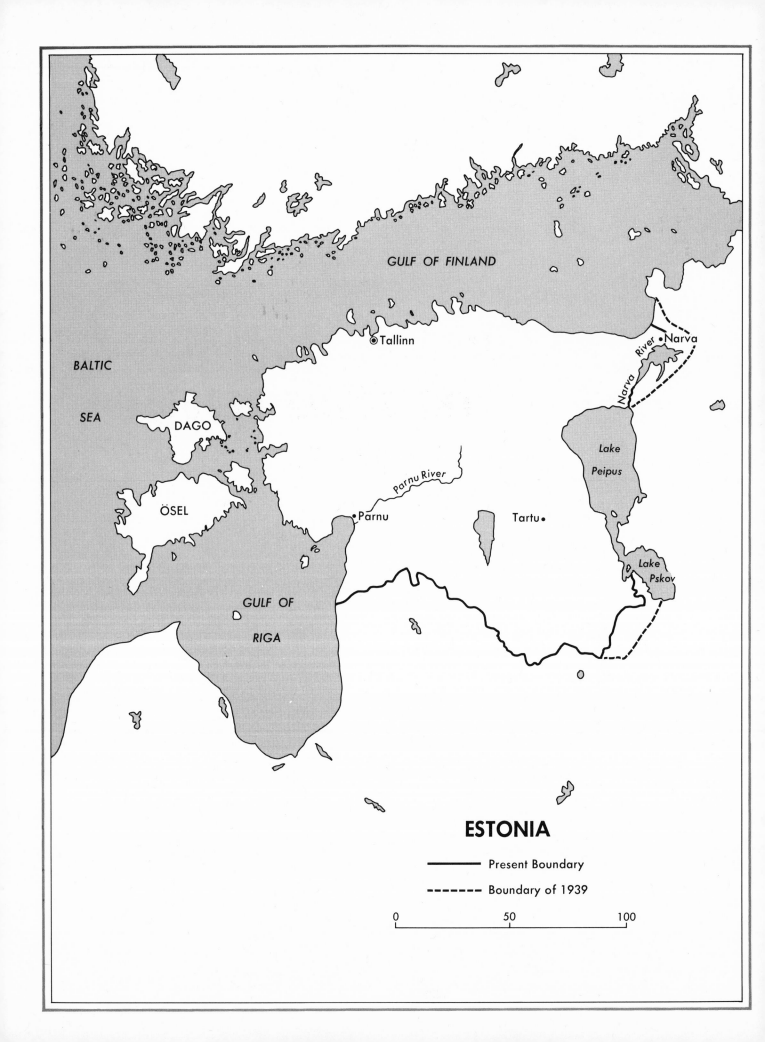

BALTIC

SEA

GULF OF FINLAND

⊙ Tallinn

Narva River

• Narva

DAGO

Lake
Peipus

ÖSEL

Parnu River

• Parnu

Tartu •

Lake
Pskov

GULF OF

RIGA

ESTONIA

———— Present Boundary

- - - - - Boundary of 1939

0   50   100

Estonia

"I believe in my free Estonian homeland.
I believe in her resurrection.
I believe in her eternal existence!"

WRITTEN ON THE cell wall of a Soviet jail, these brave words of an unknown prisoner are the creed of all Estonians. Conquered and reconquered by Danes, Germans, Swedes, Poles, and Russians, Estonia has been an independent nation only twenty-two years during the past seven and a half centuries. Today it is forced to be a Soviet republic within the USSR. But the tall blond Estonians hate alien rule, often rebel, and never lose hope for future freedom.

At first glance, one might wonder why Estonia has attracted foreign conquerors. Its area is only 17,000 square miles—about the same as the little states of New Hampshire and Vermont taken together. Estonia's inhabitants number a mere 1,-300,000—less than half the population of the nearby Russian city of Leningrad. By any measurement, Estonia is one of the smallest nations of East Europe.

Nor is Estonian soil fertile. The countryside is a rolling plain, with many woods, briars, and swamps. One-third of the land is good only for pasture. A mere one-fifth can be farmed, with plowing often hampered by stony soil. Though rye, vegetables, flax, and other northerly crops are grown, Estonia does not feed itself and must import grain to survive.

But tiny land-poor Estonia has a fantastically strategic location. Bounded on the north by the Finnish Gulf, on the west by the Baltic Sea and Gulf of Riga, on the south by Latvia, and to the east by the USSR, Estonia is the gateway from Scandinavia and Central Europe into north European Russia. Even in ancient times Estonia was a crossroads of commerce, and during medieval centuries several Estonian towns joined the merchant empire of the Hanseatic League. Aiding trade are the largely ice-free harbors along the country's jagged Baltic coast.

Estonia's fifteen ports and eight hundred islands are also natural naval bases. Osel (Saaremaa), the biggest island, almost blocks off the Gulf of Riga. Dago (Hiiumaa), the next largest, commands the entrance from the Baltic Sea to the Finnish Gulf. Ever since the USSR seized Estonia in 1944, both islands bristle with Soviet coastal artillery, rocket pads, bomber bases, and submarine pens. The Soviet Baltic fleet spends much time in Estonian ports, especially in winter, when Leningrad harbor fills with ice.

Of the three Baltic states (Estonia, Latvia, and Lithuania), Estonia alone has mineral wealth. There are vast bogs of peat, which is burned for fuel in power stations and peasant homes. Mineral

Formerly in Tallinn, this heroic statue commemorated Estonian teachers and students who sacrificed their lives to free their country from Soviet Russia during the independence war of 1918–20. When the USSR occupied Estonia in 1944, the Russians removed the statue. *ECG*

Shipbuilding has been an Estonian skill and industry since Viking times. This shipyard is on Osel (Saaremaa), Estonia's biggest Baltic island. *LC*

The north coast of Estonia beetles over the Finnish Gulf in sheer cliffs sometimes 180 feet high. These are called the "glint." *LC*

This Estonian cotton mill, on an island in the fast-flowing Narva River, is one of the largest in all Europe. *LC*

Medieval merchant ships of the Hanseatic League leaving Germany for Estonian ports, which were already thriving centers of commerce. *NYPL*

A bulldozer digging up oil-bearing shale—the "magic stones" which are Estonia's main mineral. Shale fuels the Estonian nation, and plentiful shale gas is even piped to the Russian city of Leningrad. *Sovfoto*

Giant sulphate-cellulose factory at Kehra. More than fishing or farming, industry is the main Estonian occupation. *Photo by Artur Kalm*

A secondary school in a fishing village. Estonia has a better school system than most other Soviet republics. *Sovfoto*

Medieval buildings adorn the old section of Tallinn, Estonia's capital city. *Sovfoto*

building-materials are found everywhere, the most important being fine sand for cement. Large phosphate deposits on the north coast provide ample fertilizer for the poor farm soil. Overshadowing all these resources are deposits containing billions of tons of oil-bearing shale. In a part of Europe lacking oil fields, Estonia has oil to spare. The shale is also burned as locomotive fuel and converted into gas flowing by pipeline to both Estonian cities and Russia's Leningrad.

Though small in number, the Estonians are great in skill. Some of Tsarist Russia's first industries arose in Estonia, including what was then the largest textile mill in the world. Since crop-raising is difficult, Estonia's peasants concentrate on livestock, producing huge quantities of butter, bacon, other meat, and eggs.

By hard work and skill, the Estonians even prosper under alien rule. Among the fifteen Soviet republics of the USSR, present-day Estonia is the most urbanized and spends the most money per capita on education. In production per capita, Estonia also is first in farm products, mineral fertilizer, cement, and electric power. All Soviet sources agree that Estonia has the highest standard of living in the USSR.

These capable Estonians were originally a Finnish nationality, and their language is closely related to that of Finland. Racially, the Estonians are a mixture, since throughout history they have assimilated many immigrants from neighboring nations. These immigrants were particularly numerous after great wars, which killed so many Estonians that empty land lay open for foreign settlement.

The busy docks at Tallinn, which is Estonia's biggest Baltic port. *Sovfoto*

Though two-thirds of the Estonian nation are urbanites, there are no big cities. Tallinn (Revel), with 363,000 inhabitants, is the largest and is the Estonian capital. Located in the northwest of the country, Tallinn is the main seaport and contains half of Estonian industry. There are huge shipyards, many precision-machinery factories, and large textile mills.

Other important cities include Tartu (Dorpat) in southeast Estonia. It is the national cultural center, with a famed old university and the largest library in the Baltic states. On the Gulf of Riga in southwest Estonia is Parnu (Pernau, Pernov), the country's second largest port. In the Estonian

Fishing boats in the harbor of Pärnu, Estonia's second largest port. *Sovfoto*

A nineteenth-century etching of the frontier city of Narva, with former Swedish (*right*) and Russian (*left*) forts facing each other across the Narva River. *LC*

THE ESTONIAN NATION

	Pre-World War II	Present
Area (square miles)	18,370	17,000
Population	1,100,000	1,357,000

In percent of total population

	Pre-World War II	Present
Rate of Literacy	96%	100%
Urban Populace	34%	68%
Major Nationalities		
Estonians	88%	75%
Russians	8%	22%
Main Religions		
Lutheran	78%	70%
Orthodox	19%	25%

THE ESTONIAN ECONOMY

	Unit of Measurement	Pre-World War II	Present
Industrial Production			
Electricity	(kilowatt-hours)	190,000,000	9,200,000,000
Shale gas	(cubic meters)	1,700,000	564,000,000
Oil-bearing shale	(metric tons)	1,900,000	16,400,000
Steel	" "	—	7,000
Cement	" "	71,000	942,000
Cotton cloth	(meters)	22,800,000	197,400,000
Agricultural Production			
Grain	(metric tons)	702,000	740,000
Potatoes	" "	1,200,000	1,500,000
Flax	" "	7,000	1,000
Number of Livestock			
Cattle		528,000	653,000
Swine		319,000	556,000
Communications			
Length of railways	(miles)	860	800
Length of roads	"	13,800	14,300

northeast is Narva, on the fast-flowing Narva River which drains Lakes Peipus and Pskov into the Gulf of Finland. Here are two giant power stations, one hydroelectric and the other burning shale. Both supply much electricity to Estonian cities and Leningrad.

All four cities were founded during the eleventh to thirteenth centuries, have quaint medieval Gothic and baroque buildings, and played major roles in Estonian history.

The Estonians are a very ancient people, first known in antiquity as Finno-Ugrian nomads roaming Central Asia. About 3000 B.C. these desert people are believed to have migrated northwest into the area between the Volga River and the Ural Mountains. Then they inched westward across the Russian plain and, by the first century A.D., finally settled in their present homeland along the north Baltic coast. Soon they were trading by sea with the Goths of the south Baltic shore. Instead of remaining mere hunters, trappers, and fishermen, the Estonians began prospering from agriculture and trade.

There was no unified Estonian state. Each region was a petty kingdom ruled by a hereditary "elder." His nobility were called "betters," and the peasants were "freemen." At the bottom of this feudal society were slaves—foreigners captured in battle from neighboring nations. To win the numerous foreign wars, elders allied with each other and at times formed a confederation of Estonian kingdoms.

Estonia's recorded history began in the ninth century, when Viking traders and raiders arrived by sea from Scandinavia. To combat these Norsemen the Estonians themselves became Vikings, making many successful raids into Denmark and Scandinavia during the eleventh and twelfth centuries.

Meanwhile fierce wars were fought against Novgorod, the Slavic city-state ruling all north European Russia. Temporarily capturing southeast Estonia, Russian Prince Yaroslav in 1030 founded Tartu—the first Estonian city.

Toward the close of Estonia's Viking era, German merchants arrived to exploit Estonian trade. Catholic missionaries also came from Denmark, trying unsuccessfully to convert the pagan Estonians to Christianity. Both Denmark and the Germans saw the value of conquering small but strategic Estonia.

Conquest commenced in 1202, when Estonia was invaded by the Knights of the Sword—a German religious army formed by Bishop Albert of Riga. Estonian resistance was so great that in 1219 Denmark had to come to the invaders' rescue. Landing troops at Tallinn, where they built a fort, Danish King Valdemar II attacked northern Estonia while the Knights battled in the south. But the valiant Estonians in 1223 repulsed both invasions, driving out the German Knights and confining the Danes to the fortress of Tallinn.

Poorly armed and politically divided, Estonia could not consolidate its victory. Again the Danes and Germans attacked, completely conquering the country by 1227. Denmark seized control of northern Estonia, while the Knights became masters of the south. Thus Estonia lost its independence, which was not regained for seven hundred years.

The Danes and Germans converted Estonia to

Russian Prince Yaroslav the Wise, who in 1030 founded Tartu—the first Estonian city. Sovfoto

Estonian wooden fort being stormed by the German "Knights of the Sword," who commenced conquering Estonia in 1202. Photo by Artur Kalm

Estonia's first hero, Lembitu, who united his countrymen to fight both the Russians and the Knights of the Sword. He died in battle against the Knights in 1217. *Photo by Artur Kalm*

Still in use today is Tallinn's town hall, built in the fourteenth century by the Teutonic Knights who were enslaving the Estonians. *Sovfoto*

Roman Catholicism and conducted lucrative trade with Russia. So important was this commerce that the Estonian cities of Tallinn and Parnu became members of the wealthy Hanseatic League. Meanwhile the Knights of the Sword were absorbed by an even stronger German religious army—the Teutonic Knights.

The Estonians did not submit passively to foreign rule. A revolt in 1343 almost overthrew the Danish overlords, who were saved only by military assistance from the Teutonic Knights. To avoid further trouble Denmark in 1346 sold its Estonian lands to the Knights, who thus gained control of all Estonia.

During the next two hundred years, the

Knights ruled the country with an iron hand. They were the landowning nobility and forced the Estonians to be their serfs. The system was vicious, for the local landlord was also the local judge, brutally punishing serfs who resisted Teutonic oppression. When many Estonians tried to escape to foreign countries, a law of 1421 converted the serfs into slaves forbidden to emigrate.

Early in the sixteenth century the Protestant Reformation triumphed in Estonia when the nobles adopted Luther's teachings. Their Estonian slaves had no choice except to obey orders to practice Protestantism. Hence Estonia became predominantly Lutheran and has worshipped in this faith ever since. The first book published in the Estonian language was a Lutheran catechism of 1535.

New foreign conquerors arrived during the long Livonian War that started in 1558, when the Russian armies of Tsar Ivan the Terrible invaded and subdued most of Estonia. The Bishop of Osel hurriedly sold his huge island to Denmark. The disheartened Teutonic Knights disbanded, selling south Estonia to the King of Poland. Unwilling to accept either Russian or Polish rule, Tallinn townsmen and nobles of the Estonian north requested and received protection from Sweden. Combined Swedish-Polish forces finally defeated the Russian army, which withdrew to its homeland in 1582.

Sweden took control of northern Estonia with its cities of Narva and Tallinn. South Estonia and the city of Tartu were annexed to the Polish kingdom. In both north and south the nobility remained mostly German, the former Teutonic Knights now becoming the so-called Baltic barons. In the meantime, half the Estonian nation had perished—helpless victims of the foreign armies fighting the Livonian War.

A new war started in 1619, when Sweden invaded south Estonia, driving out the Poles by 1625. Now Estonia was reunited under Swedish rule, which continued for eighty-five years. Sympathizing with the Estonians, the Swedes introduced many reforms. Swedish King Gustavus Adolphus II forbade landlords to be judges and established a special court to hear peasant grievances. To promote culture, he founded Estonia's first university in 1632 at Tartu. His successors returned Osel to Estonia in 1645 by purchasing the island from Denmark.

Toward the close of the seventeenth century, schools were opened for peasant children. The workload was reduced for serfs on the king's "crown lands," which covered about half of Estonia's countryside. Following the royal example, the Baltic barons treated their serfs less harshly. This pleasant era is described by Estonian historians as "the good Swedish times."

Mild Swedish rule was ended by the Great Northern War, in which Russia, Poland, and Denmark joined forces against Sweden. For Estonia the war began in 1700 at the Battle of Narva, where a mere 8,000 Swedish troops captured a Russian army of 40,000 men. After this military lesson from the Swedes, Tsar Peter the Great formed a new Russian army better trained and better equipped. Again invading Estonia, Peter conquered the entire country by 1710. The peace treaty of 1721 awarded Estonia to Russia.

Angry at Sweden for reducing landlord privileges, the Baltic barons had conspired to aid Russian victory in Estonia. When Russia won, the tsar rewarded the barons by giving them ownership of the crown lands, complete authority over the serfs,

Swedish King Gustavus Adolphus, who in 1625 became ruler of all Estonia. He tried to protect Estonian serfs from mistreatment by their German landlords. *NYPL*

Estonia's oldest university, founded in 1632 at Tartu by King Gustavus Adolphus. *Sovfoto*

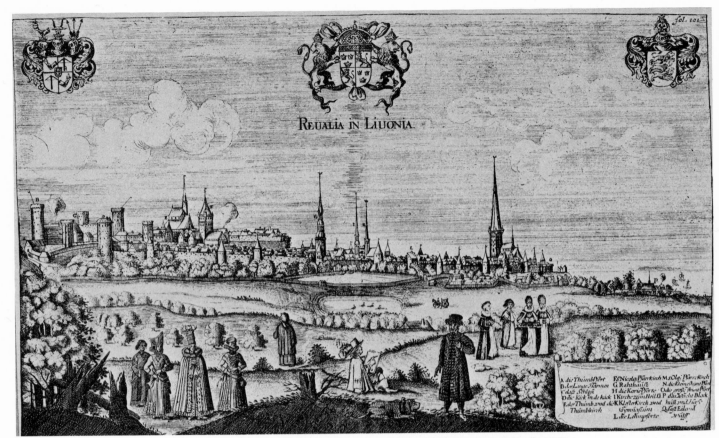

Tallinn in the seventeenth century, when Estonia was under humane Swedish rule. *NYPL*

Swedish King Charles XII leading his 8,000 troops to victory over a 40,000-man Russian army in 1700 at the blizzardy Battle of Narva. *LC*

Estonian peasant serfs of the eighteenth century, when their country had fallen under Russian rule. *LC*

House and barn of an Estonian peasant family in the nineteenth ◄ century, when the freed serfs became tenant farmers of their German landlords. *Sovfoto*

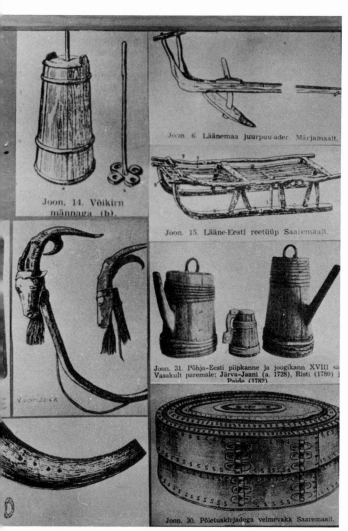

Wooden implements used by Estonian peasants of the eighteenth century. *Photo by Artur Kalm*

Gingerbread mansion of a Baltic Baron. *LC*

Estonia's nineteenth-century oppressors—the German "Baltic Barons" who were both the landlords and the big businessmen. Tsarist Russia let them rule the Estonians. *LC*

and control of Estonia's police, courts, and local government. Estonia thus gained home rule—not for Estonians but for the German nobles. So harsh was baronial rule that the serfs rebelled several times during the late eighteenth century only to be suppressed by the Russian army and local police.

Despite their tyranny, the barons brought some benefits to Estonia. Anxious to preserve Teutonic culture, they protected Estonians from the Russification so common in other regions of the Tsarist Empire. Estonian peasants learned highly intensive farming from their German landlords. When industry was started by the barons, Estonian workers acquired German manufacturing techniques.

Industrialization finally convinced the Baltic barons that serfdom had to be abolished. Being bound to the soil, serfs could not move from country to city to man the growing industries. Impoverished serfs were also a poor market for factory-made goods. So the barons petitioned the tsar, who freed the Estonian serfs by decrees of 1816 and 1819.

Liberation of the serfs gave Estonia an advantage over most of the Russian empire, where serfdom was not abolished until 1861. Estonian industry expanded and was more efficient than

Russian manufacturing. The freed serfs became tenant farmers or factory laborers, earning more money than before. By 1860 Estonian peasants were permitted to buy plots of land from the nobles. Much land changed hands, and at the dawn of the twentieth century the peasants owned two-fifths of all Estonian farmland. After election reforms of the 1880s, the Estonians won control of many local governments from the Baltic barons.

All these reforms inspired great cultural creativity during the late nineteenth and early twentieth centuries. The massive epic poem *Son of Kalev* by F. R. Kreutswald recalled forgotten glories of Estonian history. A realistic school of writers appealed to national pride, while the "Young Estonia" authors perfected the written language. By intensive research, scholars compiled and published 130,000 native folk songs, 115,000 children's jingles, and 160,000 peasant superstitions.

The cultural revival intensified Estonian longing for liberty. During the Crimean War of the 1850s, in which Russia fought Britain and France, high hopes were aroused by the Anglo-French naval blockade of Tallinn. But the peace treaty left Estonia under tsarist rule. Estonians willingly took part in the Russian Revolution of 1905, only to be again suppressed.

The opportunity for independence finally arose from Russian defeat in World War I (1914–18).

After the tsar abdicated in March 1917, the Russian Provisional Government granted autonomy to the Estonians, who wisely began forming their own army. Then in November came the Russian Bolshevik Revolution, led by a treacherous Lenin who said Russia's minorities could secede. Estonia immediately seceded and was immediately invaded by Lenin's Red Army.

After the German army drove out the Red Russians, Estonia declared its independence on February 24, 1918. In the Soviet-German peace treaty of Brest-Litovsk (March 3, 1918) and a supplementary agreement during August, Russia waived all claims to Estonia. Then Germany staked its claim: Estonia and Latvia should unite in a "Baltic Duchy" ruled by the German emperor.

But in the autumn of 1918 Germany surrendered to the Western Allies, so the German army had to leave Estonia. As the Germans departed, the Soviet Russians again invaded. Aided by a British naval squadron and Finnish, Danish, and Swedish volunteers, the 80,000-man Estonian army commanded by the able General Johan Laidoner expelled the Red Army by early 1919. Next, Estonian troops helped Latvia defeat both the So-

Carl Jakobson in the late nineteenth century founded the magazine *Sakala*, which proclaimed Estonians to be equal to the Baltic Barons. He believed Estonia's salvation might come from cooperation with Russian liberals. *ECG*

An illustration for the Estonian epic poem "Kalevipoeg" ("Son of Kalev") written by Dr. Friedrich Kreutzwald (1803–82) to arouse interest in native folklore. It was one of the greatest works published during the Estonian renaissance of the nineteenth century. *Photo by Artur Kalm*

Mass song festivals, with thousands of choristers singing native songs, aroused love of country during the Estonian renaissance. *Sovfoto*

Cavalry of the Estonian army, which was formed in 1917 to fight for independence from Russia. *NYPL*

General Johan Laidoner *(second from left)* commanding the Estonian army which in 1919 repulsed all invasions by the Soviet Russians. *UPI*

viet Russians and German General Von der Goltz, who tried to seize Latvia by fighting Russia.

During 1919 a White Russian army based in Estonia conducted two unsuccessful campaigns to capture Leningrad. To avoid further complications, Estonia disarmed the Whites, who, like the Red Russians, disapproved of Estonian independence. The power of another troublesome group, the Baltic barons, was broken by dividing their estates among the Estonian peasantry. Finally the Treaty of Tartu (February 2, 1920) established peace with Soviet Russia, which agreed to Estonian freedom.

Though free from Red Russians, White Russians, and Baltic barons, the new Estonian nation was vexed by many problems. Before World War I, Tsarist Russia had been Estonia's main market, buying two-thirds of her annual manufactures. Soviet Russia had neither the money nor desire to continue such heavy trade. Some large Estonian factories had to close. Trade was reoriented toward Britain and Germany, and farm products replaced industrial goods as Estonia's main export.

A constitution of 1920 made Estonia a republic with a strong parliament, weak premier, and no president. Because sixteen political parties competed for power, the premiers were chosen by short-lived political coalitions. During 1919–33

In 1919 the Estonian army even had this tiny air force, at least useful for scouting. *LC*

The British naval squadron that in 1919 helped Estonia by guarding its coast from Soviet marine invasion. *LC*

A Soviet Russian destroyer, captured by the British naval squadron in the Finnish Gulf and turned over to Estonian command. *LC*

General Von der Goltz, whose German troops tried to conquer Latvia after World War I. He was defeated by combined operations of the Estonian and Latvian armies. *UPI*

When Estonia declared its independence in February 1918, these three leaders headed its newly formed government. *From left to right: J. Vilms, K. Konik, and Konstantin Päts. Photo by Artur Kalm*

Headquarters of the free Estonian government was this stately "Castle of the Domhill," in Tallinn. *Photo by Artur Kalm*

President Konstantin Päts (*front row, center*) and his 1936 cabinet, which successfully instigated constitutional reform. The officer in uniform is General Laidoner, Army Commander in Chief. *LC*

there were twenty cabinets, each averaging only eight months in office. In 1933 a veterans' party named the "Old Combatants" (VAPS) convinced the electorate to adopt a new constitution with an almost dictatorial presidency. Konstantin Päts, Estonia's first premier of 1918, became president and ruled as mild dictator until 1938, when he began sharing power with parliament.

Over these years Estonia sought international security by concluding a 1923 alliance with Latvia and a 1932 nonaggression pact with Russia.

Both treaties were of little use in 1939, when the secret protocol of the Nazi-Soviet Pact awarded Estonia to the USSR. During the autumn of 1939, Russia demanded air and naval bases in Estonia, which dared not refuse. No less than 25,000 Soviet troops entered the tiny country, whose own army numbered only 16,000.

In June 1940 Russia ordered Estonia to form a pro-Soviet government and admit more Red Army troops. Estonia sadly submitted. Elections supervised by Soviet tanks produced a cabinet of left-

Honoring Estonian independence, President Päts lights the "holy flame" at Tallinn's "Liberty Memorial" on September 28, 1939— the day Soviet pressure forced him to permit the establishment of Russian military and naval bases on Estonian soil. *UPI*

Parade of "happy" Estonians in August 1940 welcoming Estonia's annexation by the USSR. Their bitterness shows in their faces. *Sovfoto*

An old-fashioned Soviet warship entering Tallinn harbor in the fall of 1939 to establish a Russian naval base. *UPI*

wing Socialists, who let Estonia be annexed by the USSR. Soviet police then executed 1,900 anti-Communist Estonians, and exiled 58,000 others to prison camps or other forced labor in Russia. Among the deportees were President Päts and Commander in Chief Laidoner, both of whom died in Soviet prisons.

When Hitler's Wehrmacht invaded the USSR in June 1941, Estonian guerrillas immediately aided the German advance by sabotaging Red Army communications. Soon Nazi troops occupied Estonia; they remained till 1944. Both voluntarily and by conscription, several thousand Estonian soldiers joined the German army to fight hated

The last premier of free Estonia, Professor Jüri Uluots, who resigned in June 1940 when Soviet troops seized all Estonian cities. *LC*

Waving his cap to a Tallinn crowd is Andrei Zhdanov, the USSR Politburo member who arrived in June 1940 to communize Estonia. *LC*

Far left: Deported to Russian imprisonment, never to return, was General Johan Laidoner, Commander in Chief of Estonia's army. *LC. Left:* Also deported in 1940 to prison death in Russia was Estonia's Evangelical Lutheran Bishop. *Photo by Artur Kalm*

Russia's puppets, the Estonian Communist government of 1940. The wall portraits (*from left to right*) are Stalin, Engels, Marx, and Lenin. *LC*

The Nazi-Soviet War: German troops occupying Estonia in August 1941. *Photo by Artur Kalm*

Tallinn in 1941, after being partly destroyed by the retreating Russians, who abandoned the ruins to the German Wehrmacht. *UPI*

German troops examining the ruins of Narva, which they had just captured. *Photo by Artur Kalm*

To save this army truck and wagon train from German capture, the retreating Russians ran it over a steep cliff. In the foreground are corpses of Red Army horses. *UPI*

Estonian Communist quisling Nikolai Karotamm (*center*) greeting Russian tank troops when the Soviet army reconquered Estonia in 1944. *Sovfoto*

Russian tankists talking with Estonians just after Soviet recapture of Tallinn. *Sovfoto*

War damage in an Estonian city recaptured by the Russians. *Photo by Artur Kalm*

Phony festivities were staged in 1944 when Estonia was forcibly reannexed by the USSR. Even this old locomotive joined the show. This picture is Stalin; the slogan chants: "Brotherly greetings to the people of Estonia from the peoples of the USSR!" *LC*

"Happy" Estonians parading a giant copy of their new "Stalin Constitution," which deprived Estonia of any autonomy. *LC*

Russia. Estonia's home guard helped the Germans by patrolling the Estonian countryside.

But the Nazi occupation was not popular. Instead of returning to Estonian owners the lands and factories nationalized by the USSR, Germany seized these properties as enemy booty. Estonia's economy was bled white to support the Nazi army, which opposed any attempt for Estonian independence. But as the lesser of two evils, the Nazis were more humane than the Soviets.

In 1944, when the German army had to retreat from Estonia, 65,000 Estonians fled to Sweden and Germany rather than suffer again under Russian rule. Others became the "Brethren of the Woods," harassing Soviet officials by guerrilla raids as late as 1954. But the Brethren could not prevent Communization of Estonia.

Again Estonia had to trade almost entirely with Russia. The shale, cement, fertilizer, textile, fishing, and electric-power industries expanded enormously to supply the greedy USSR. Grain and flax acreages were reduced so that peasants could concentrate on livestock products for Leningrad.

Thousands of Estonians risked their lives in small boats to sail away from Russian reconquest. Most refugee craft headed for Sweden, but this frail ship went all the way to Miami, Florida. *UPI*

A group of the "Brethren of the Woods"—Estonian guerrillas who sabotaged the Soviet occupation from 1944 to 1954. They operated in the forests, and were protected by the peasants. *ECG*

After World War II, the Estonian Soviet Republic was forced to cede some borderland to the Russian Soviet Republic. In this lost territory was the famed Pechory Monastery. *ECG*

Estonian refugees parading in New York City. The banner thanks the United States for never officially recognizing the Soviet annexation of Estonia. *Photo by Artur Kalm*

Back in Estonia, the puppet parliament meets under the watchful eye of Russia's Lenin. *Sovfoto*

At least 60,000 peasants were deported to Russian prison camps for resisting farm collectivization. Countless clergymen were arrested, leaving half the Lutheran churches without ministers. Iron Communists purged even the original puppet leaders in order to replace them with left-wing Socialists.

Estonia's prewar population was 88 percent Estonian. Today the proportion has fallen to 75 percent because of Estonian deportations and heavy Russian immigration. Still Estonia survives, and by Soviet standards even prospers. And hope is never lost for future Estonian freedom.

Latvia

THOUGH SMALL in area and population, Latvia is among East Europe's most capable nations. With just pride, the tall blond Latvians boast of their worldwide achievements. When completed in the fourteenth century, Saint Peter's Church in the Latvian capital city of Riga lofted the highest wooden spire in the world. During the same creative period, the Duchy of Courland, in southwest Latvia, was a great naval power, founding overseas colonies in both Africa and the West Indies. Early in the present century, Riga was the world's largest seaport for export of timber. By the late 1930s a Riga factory invented and manufactured the "Minox," the first miniature camera in the world.

Today Latvia is forced to be one of the fifteen Soviet republics within the USSR. In per capita rank among these republics, Latvia is first in hospital facilities, national income, and industrial production. As Latvians say, they have learned to prosper under alien rule.

These great successes have been achieved by a very small country. Latvia has a territory of only 25,000 square miles, about the same as that of West Virginia.

Bounded on the north by Estonia, on the east by Russia, on the south by Lithuania, and to the west by the Baltic Sea and the Gulf of Riga, Latvia resembles a sylvan glen opening out to the amber beaches of the pine-wreathed coast. Much of the country lies in the lowlands of the Western Dvina (Daugava in Latvian) River, which rises in northern Russia, then flows northwest across Latvia into the Gulf of Riga.

North and south of the Dvina are picturesque wooded hills, which in northern Latvia are so beautiful that they are called the "Livonian Switzerland." Both in the valleys and amid the hills are countless swamps and three thousand lakes. Everywhere there are small and big forests; they cover one-third of the country.

Resources are sparse. There are no minerals except limestone and other building materials. Peat is dug from the swamps and burned as low-grade fuel. All high-grade fuels like coal, oil, and gas must be imported from the western USSR. Since iron ore is missing, the one small steel mill simply resmelts metal scrap. Because the forests were overcut in the past, lumbering has declined in an effort to save the remaining trees. Once an exporter of timber, Latvia now imports her wood.

Nor does nature favor agriculture. The soil is poor and often stony. Though northerly crops such as rye, flax, sugar beets, and potatoes are grown, Latvia does not feed itself and must import Russian grain to survive.

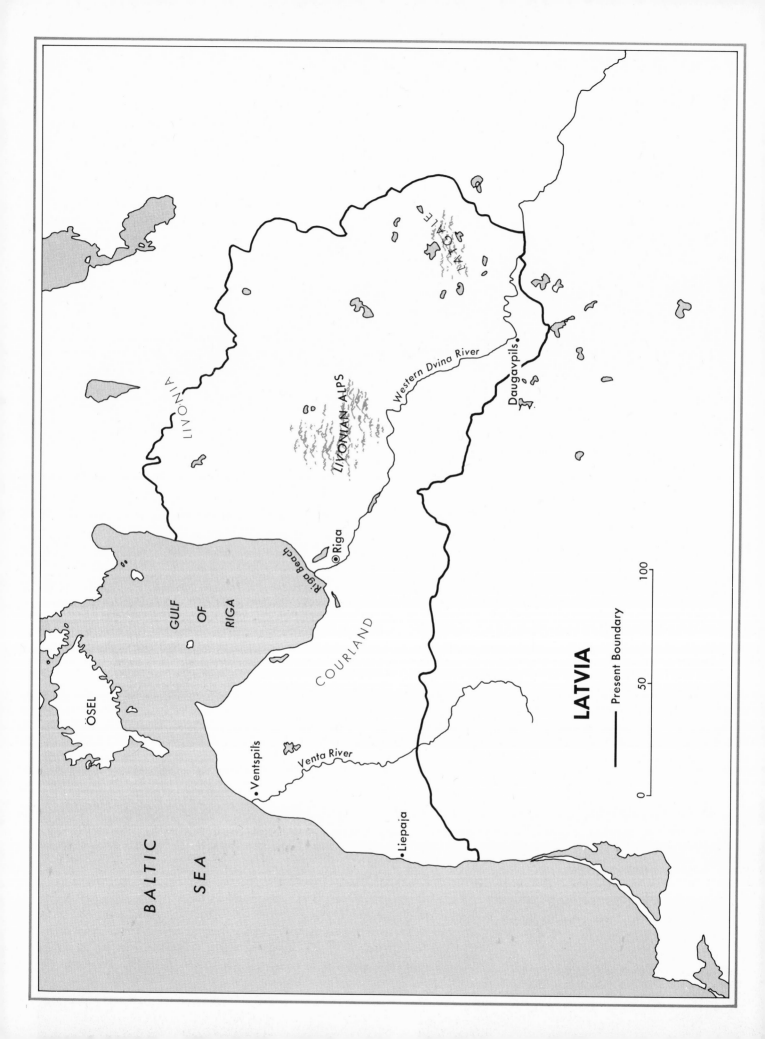

BALTIC

SEA

ÖSEL

GULF

OF

RIGA

Riga Beach

⊙Riga

LIVONIA

LIVONIAN ALPS

Western Dvina River

LATGALE

Daugavpils.

COURLAND

•Ventspils

Venta River

•Liepaja

LATVIA

—— Present Boundary

0   50   100

L A T V I A

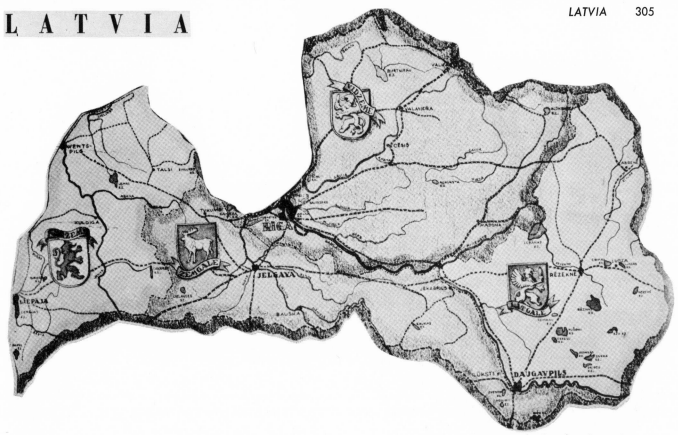

Strong lions and stately deer graced pre-Communist Latvian emblems, as on this map displaying the state seals of each major region.

Saint Peter's church in Riga once lofted the tallest wooden tower in the world. Soviet bombardment destroyed this historic spire during a battle of World War II. *LC*

Latvia has the best hospital network of any Soviet republic. This sunny sanitarium overlooks a Baltic beach. *Sovfoto*

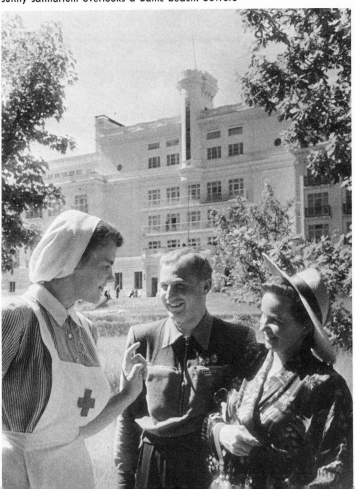

The secret of Latvia's success is its hardworking and highly educated people. Latvia's school system is one of the best in the Soviet Union. As early as the 1930s, Latvia had a higher percentage of young people in college than any other European nation.

Since most raw materials for industry must be imported, Latvian manufacturing concentrates on high-quality products easy to sell abroad. Today the country is a major supplier of radios, telephones, electric motors, and electric trains to the other parts of the USSR. Also well developed are sea-connected industries such as fishing, fish canning, and the construction of ultramodern trawlers. Two-thirds of the Latvian people live in cities, and manufacturing accounts for a vast 80 percent of all economic output.

The other 20 percent comes from the farms, which overcome the disadvantage of poor soil by concentrating on cattle, hogs, and chickens. Latvia has long been a major exporter of butter, fresh meat, bacon, and eggs, with large amounts of these delicacies now being shipped to stores of the nearby big Russian city of Leningrad. Though most Latvian industry is urban, everywhere throughout the countryside are local slaughterhouses and creameries.

For many centuries the Latvian lands have been conquered and reconquered by Germans, Swedes, Poles, and Russians. Often Latvia was divided, with different areas under different rule. History has thus created three distinct Latvian regions: North of the Dvina River and bordering the Gulf of Riga is Livonia (Vidzeme in Latvian), whose chief city is Riga. Located on the Dvina River nine miles from Riga Gulf, Riga is a city of spires and towers overlooking quaint, narrow medieval streets. With its population of 733,000, Riga is the largest Latvian city and the greatest cultural center of the three Baltic states. The many factories of Riga produce 70 percent of all Latvian industrial output. Flower gardens are everywhere in the city, and nearby is lush Riga beach, which in summer attracts vacationers from all regions of the USSR.

Also north of the Dvina River but bordering Russia is Latgale, where many Russians live among the Latvians. The largest city is Daugavpils (formerly Dvinsk), a Dvina River port and center of the lumber industry.

South of the Dvina with a seacoast on the Baltic is Courland (Kurland—Kurzeme and Zemgale in Latvian). Liepaja (formerly Libau) with a population of 100,000 is the biggest city, a huge Baltic port, and a major base of the Soviet navy. Also busy is the port town of Ventspils (formerly Windau), a center of oil export and the woodworking industry. The harbors of both cities are open all year long, in contrast to Riga which is icebound at the height of winter.

The railways of Latvia portray the country's importance to the USSR. Riga has a direct rail connection to the lower Volga valley, Ventspils to Moscow, and Liepaja to the northern Ukraine.

Low hills, crowned by meadows and woods, dominate much of the Latvian countryside. *American Latvian Association*

Strip farming near a peasant village.

Latvia's main mineral is peat, which is dug, dried, then burned as fuel. This peat quarry dates from the pre-Communist period. *UPI*

A farmhouse almost buried in a sea of grain.

A new school in Riga. Latvian grade and high school education lasts one year longer than in most other Soviet republics. *Sovfoto*

Headquarters of the brilliant Latvian Academy of Sciences. *Sovfoto*

Dark brown cattle—a special Latvian breed.

THE LATVIAN NATION

	Pre-World War II	Present
Area (square miles)	24,800	24,700
Population	1,950,000	2,365,000

In percent of total population

	Pre-World War II	Present
Rate of literacy	100%	100%
Urban populace	35%	65%

Major Nationalities

	Pre-World War II	Present
Latvians	77%	66%
Russians	12%	27%
Jews	4%	1.5%
Germans	3%	almost 0

Main Religions

	Pre-World War II	Present
Protestant (Lutheran)	56%	50%
Catholic	24%	20%
Orthodox	9%	20%
Jewish	4%	1%

THE LATVIAN ECONOMY

	Unit of Measurement	Pre-World War II	Present
Industrial Production			
Electricity	(kilowatt-hours)	250,000,000	2,600,000,000
Steel	(metric tons)	28,000	520,000
Cement	" "	125,000	814,000
Cotton cloth	(meters)	20,600,000	61,100,000
Machine tools		—	36,000
Agricultural Production			
Grain	(metric tons)	1,370,000	1,050,000
Potatoes	" "	2,100,000	2,100,000
Sugar beets	" "	338,000	378,000
Number of Livestock			
Cattle		1,200,000	1,100,000
Swine		800,000	800,000
Communications			
Length of railways	(miles)	2,000	1,700
Length of highways	"	22,000	15,000

Telephones and phone switchboards are major Latvian manufactures. *Sovfoto*

Fishing is big business along Latvia's Baltic coast. Here smoked smelts are packed for shipment. *Sovfoto*

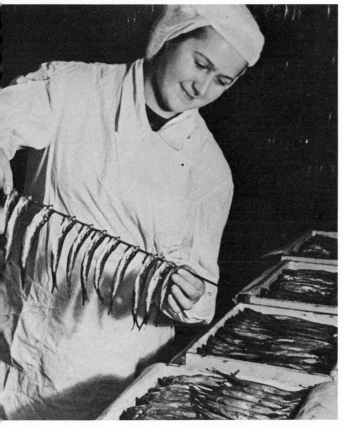

Prize pigs like these produce Latvia's tasty bacon and ham. *Sovfoto*

Latvia's capital city of Riga, when it was a medieval fortress.

Much Soviet foreign trade flows through these three Latvian harbors. Latvia has lost its independence simply because it is so useful.

Despite their location in northeast Europe, the Latvians are not Scandinavians, Germans, or Slavs. Instead they are Balts, closely related to the neighboring Lithuanians. A small but ancient people, the Latvians have inhabited their Baltic homeland since at least 1500 B.C. At first they called themselves "Aestians," but then adopted the name of "Laeti" (Clearers of the Forest). Gradually Laeti changed into the word Latvians. They were Indo-Europeans who absorbed another local nationality —the Finnish Livs.

There was no Latvian kingdom. The early Latvians lived in tribes headed by princes. For protection they often lived in wooden forts, which looked much like the stockades built by American pioneers.

The old section of modern Riga still retains medieval charm. In the background is the Dvina River.

The city of Riga contains more industry than all the rest of Latvia. Above is Riga's main power station, whose giant smokestacks dwarf its old office tower. *Sovfoto*

Riga's Baltic beach, the largest in Latvia, lures tourists from all areas of the USSR. *Sovfoto*

A typical Riga park with close-cropped lawns, ornamental trees, and big banks of flowers. *Sovfoto*

Blue sea, green forest, and golden sand make the Riga seaside one of the most beautiful beaches in the world. *Sovfoto*

The busy Baltic port of Liepaja (formerly Libau), which also maintains a big naval base. *Sovfoto*

A fisherman family, father and son, mend their nets along the Courland coast. *Sovfoto*

A winter caravan of freight ships winds through water cleared by an icebreaker in the frozen Gulf of Riga. *Sovfoto*

Latvian railroad cars built in Riga, which supplies electric trains to all Soviet subways and railways. *Sovfoto*

Latvian medieval wooden fort. *American Latvian Association*

In the early Middle Ages the Latvian and Lithuanian tribes *(within black border)* were harassed by both Scandinavians and Slavs. *American Latvian Association*

Latvia was in relative isolation until the ninth century A.D., when Scandinavian Vikings began sailing their boats up the Dvina River to trade with Russia. In this era began the Russo-Latvian wars that were to continue for centuries. No less than 160 Latvian forts had to be built along the relatively short Russian frontier.

Late in the twelfth century, German merchants began settling on the Baltic coast. With them came German and Danish missionaries who tried and failed to convert the pagan Latvians to Christianity.

Bishop Albert of Bremen then launched a German crusade into Latvia. Creating a religious army called the "Knights of the Sword," Albert landed at Riga in 1201, founded a city there, and was ordained the regional bishop. His knights

A commander of the Livonian Knights (Knights of the Sword)—the German religious army that conquered and Christianized Latvia during the thirteenth century. *American Latvian Association*

Treaty of surrender of a Latvian tribe to the Livonian Knights in the year 1230. *American Latvian Association*

A thirteenth-century church built by the German invaders. *American Latvian Association*

Latvian cargo boats arriving at a medieval German port. *NYPL*

Whipping and tongue-clipping were common punishments for Latvian serfs who disobeyed German feudal lords.

began conquering and Christianizing Latvia, which the Pope proclaimed a church-state named "Terra Mariana" (Land of the Virgin Mary). By 1237 the Knights of the Sword merged with an even more powerful German religious army: the Teutonic Knights.

Already weakened by Russian attacks, the Latvians could not repulse the Germans. By the close of the thirteenth century the Knights controlled all of Latvia, Riga had joined Germany's Hanseatic League, and Terra Mariana was an autonomous principality of the Holy Roman Empire.

German rule was harsh. The Knights carved Latvia into estates, forcing the Latvians to be their helpless serfs. So powerful did the knight-landlords become that even the Bishop of Riga lost control of them.

But neighboring nations began challenging the Knights. Starting in the fifteenth century, Latvia became a battleground for several hundred years of war. Russian attacks were so strong and long that by 1562 the Teutonic Knights disbanded, and the church-state of Terra Mariana was partitioned by Poland and Sweden.

Polish rule created a religious dilemma. Before disbanding, most of the Teutonic Knights—and their serfs—had become Lutheran. The Poles

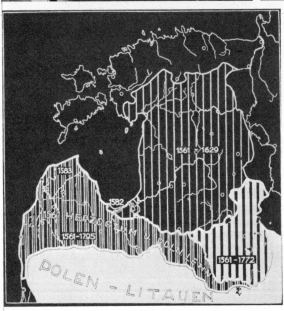

Top left: This sturdy tower was built by the Teutonic Knights during the fourteenth century. *American Latvian Association*

Center: Two views of Riga castle in 1515, when it was the headquarters of the Teutonic Knights. *American Latvian Association*

Top right: The first book printed in the Latvian language—a Catholic catechism. *American Latvian Association*

Left: Map showing the Polish occupation of Latvia from the sixteenth to eighteenth centuries.

hoped to restore Roman Catholicism but were too busy fighting Orthodox Russia. So Latvia remained mostly Lutheran, with large Catholic and Orthodox minorities. But the Polish religious effort produced in 1585 the first book printed in the Latvian language—a Catholic catechism.

Poland won the Livonian War (1558–82) against Russia, but lost the Polish-Swedish War (1620–29), which destroyed half of Latvia's popu-

lation. Sweden annexed Livonia. It became a Swedish granary for almost a hundred years.

Swedish rule was both progressive and mild. In 1675 the Swedish king seized most Livonian estates, dispossessing the German landlords who had thrived under Polish rule. As serfs of the Swedish crown, the Latvians of Livonia fared much better than before. But the dispossessed Germans, or so-called Baltic barons, intrigued to regain their estates by conspiring with Sweden's enemies.

Meanwhile Courland prospered under Polish rule and became a tiny great power. As an autonomous German duchy within the Polish Empire, Courland developed a huge shipbuilding industry that built one of the world's largest navies. Overseas colonies were established at Tobago in the

Gustavus Adolphus, Sweden's greatest king, who started Swedish rule over Livonia in 1629. *PIAS*

This ornamental partition in Riga's Dome Cathedral is a vivid reminder that Courland once possessed an African colony. *Sovfoto*

West Indies and Gambia in Africa. "Too small to be a kingdom, and too big to be a duchy," Courland often stayed neutral in Poland's foreign wars.

Mild Swedish, Polish, and Cour rule vanished in the eighteenth century when Russia finally achieved its eight-hundred-year dream of Baltic coast conquest. Commencing the Great Northern War in 1700 against Sweden, Tsar Peter the Great conquered Livonia in 1710. Russian Empress Catherine the Great seized Latgale in the First Partition of Poland (1772). Courland remained free until 1795, when it too was gobbled up by Russia.

At first Latvia suffered greatly under Russian rule. The Baltic barons took back the Livonian estates, whose serfs lost all rights previously granted by Sweden. The huts, livestock, and even personal belongings of the serfs were now the property of the landlord, who could dispose of them as he saw fit. Latvian local government was dominated by the barons, who reigned in the tradition of their ancestral Teutonic Knights.

But the nineteenth century brought progress and reform. Finally realizing that serfs were inefficient farm laborers, the barons asked Tsar Alexander I to abolish Latvian serfdom. The liberal tsar complied, freeing the serfs in both Courland (1817) and Livonia (1819).

At first most former serfs remained on the

Abolition of serfdom in the nineteenth century caused great growth of Latvian art and culture. This painting combines colorful symbols from peasant folklore. *American Latvian Association*

Latvia treasures its historic monuments, like this Dome Cathedral window picturing the ▶ cathedral builders. *Sovfoto*

Mass choral festivals are held every year, with huge choirs singing patriotic songs.

Gay folk dancing at a song festival. *Sovfoto*

estates as tenant farmers, since they were liberated without land. But by 1861 they were permitted to buy land and to migrate to the cities. In the same year Latgale's serfs were freed with land. At long last, many Latvian peasants began to prosper. Others found more profitable employment in the booming city industries, which arose after construction of the giant railways linking Latvia with inland Russia.

National culture revived almost like magic. Latvian newspapers and political groups began challenging the governmental power of the Baltic barons. Latvian banks, cooperatives, and businessmen ended German monopoly of industry and trade. Huge song festivals with thousands of voices aroused patriotic emotions. Many Latvians aided the 1905 Russian Revolution, which the Baltic barons opposed.

By the start of World War I (1914–18), Latvia was ready for independence. But freedom was not won easily. In 1915 the German army conquered Courland and Riga, with the Dvina River becoming the fighting front between the Russian and German troops. Latvian rifle regiments of the

Krisjanis Barons—greatest historian on Latvian folklore.

Russian police searching Riga pedestrians during the 1905 Revolution. *Sovfoto*

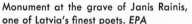

Monument at the grave of Janis Rainis, one of Latvia's finest poets. *EPA*

Signing of the 1918 Treaty of Brest-Litovsk, which transferred Latvia from Russia to Germany. *UPI*

Russian army held this front, saving Livonia and Latgale from German conquest until 1918.

After Tsar Nicholas II abdicated early in 1917, he was succeeded by the Russian Provisional Government. Then, by late 1917, Lenin's Bolsheviks overthrew the Russian Provisional Government and concluded an armistice with Germany. The Soviet-German peace treaty of Brest-Litovsk (March 3, 1918) surrendered all Latvia to Germany.

By autumn Germany itself surrendered to the Western Allies, who ordered all German troops to leave Latvia, which on November 18, 1918, declared its independence.

For the next two years the newborn state had to fight for sheer survival. Russia's Red Army ravaged the countryside, trying to create a Latvian Soviet Republic. Led first by General Rudiger Von der Goltz and later by Colonel Avalov Bermondt, German troops tried to conquer Courland. Finally both the Germans and Russians were routed by combined operations of the Estonian, Latvian, and

General Rudiger von der Goltz organized a German army that tried and failed to conquer newly independent Latvia. *LC*

Even barefoot peasants volunteered for the Latvian army, which by 1920 defeated the Germans in the west and Russians in the east.

Polish armies, aided by the British navy. The German troops were sent home, and a Russo-Latvian peace treaty was signed in 1920.

The new nation then began the painful task of peaceful reconstruction. A quarter of the Latvian population had been killed by war, and most industry lay in ruins. The unfriendly USSR refused to revive the former heavy Russo-Latvian trade or to ship goods through Latvian ports.

But Latvian ingenuity overcame all economic obstacles. New industries were built to replace the old. New markets for foreign trade were developed in Britain and Germany. The estates of the Baltic barons were broken up and divided among the Latvian peasants. Only a few years after its war of independence, Latvia was again prosperous.

Political stability was not so easy. More than twenty political parties competed for parliamentary power. All governmental cabinets had to be coalitions, and they were short lived. After the rise and

Latvia's first cabinet, headed by Premier Karlis Ulmanis *(center of front row)*. Before World War I, Ulmanis went to college in the United States at the University of Nebraska. *American Latvian Association.*

Premier Ulmanis inspecting troops at the front during the liberation war of 1919/20. *PIAS*

The Latvian cabinet of 1934, again headed by Ulmanis (*second from left in front row*), who was given almost dictatorial powers.

During Latvian independence these Riga market-halls were the largest in Europe. *American Latvian Association*

USSR Premier Molotov in August 1939 signing the Nazi-Soviet Pact, which assigned Latvia to Russia's sphere of influence. Second from left stands Stalin, showing no emotion. *UPI*

Unwilling to risk suicidal war against giant Russia, Latvia in the fall of 1939 granted bases to Soviet troops. These Latvian women weep as they read this sad news. *UPI*

fall of eighteen cabinets in fourteen years, the old independence leader Karlis Ulmanis in 1934 became a benevolent dictator to bring order out of chaos.

During this period Latvia sought security abroad by concluding a defensive alliance with Estonia in 1923, a friendship treaty with Lithuania in 1934, and nonaggression pacts with the USSR in 1932 and with Nazi Germany in June 1939.

These nonaggression agreements proved worthless when the infamous Nazi-Soviet Pact of August 23, 1939, allotted Latvia to Russia's sphere of influence. In the fall of 1939, the USSR demanded and obtained air and naval bases around Liepaja and Ventspils, plus a Latvian-Soviet military alliance. Hitler immediately ordered most Germans to leave Latvia and resettle in the Third Reich.

In June 1940, Russia accused Latvia of violating the Soviet-Latvian alliance and demanded a more friendly Latvian government. More Soviet troops poured into Latvia, 2,500 Russian tanks occupying Riga alone. Sadly, Latvia submitted to Soviet military occupation.

A "spontaneous" pro-Communist demonstration during the 1940 rigged elections in Soviet-occupied Latvia. These elections turned Latvia into a Soviet republic of the USSR. The slogan on the banner reads: "Long live Stalin!" *Sovfoto*

To escape German capture in 1941, Soviet police fled in panic, leaving unburied the victims of their last-minute executions. This Latvian woman searches for a relative among corpses in a police courtyard. *American Latvian Association*

An "election" after Latvia became a USSR republic. Behind the voters are Stalin's portrait and a Soviet flag. *Sovfoto*

A rigged election produced a rigged parliament that helped the USSR annex Latvia in August 1940. Soviet police arrested and executed 1,300 Latvian leaders. Another 35,000 Latvians were deported to USSR prison camps in 1940/41, the most distinguished deportee being President Ulmanis, who later died in a Soviet prison. All Latvian land, most industry, and many buildings became the property of the Soviet state.

When Hitler's Wehrmacht invaded Russia during June 1941, most Latvians welcomed the German troops who conquered Latvia within a month. A few Latvians even volunteered for service in the German army.

But the Nazis soon outwore their welcome.

The Latvian cabinet on the eve of World War II. All cabinet ministers with one exception (Alfreds Berzins, *second from left in front row*) were killed by the Russian police or died in Soviet prison camps.

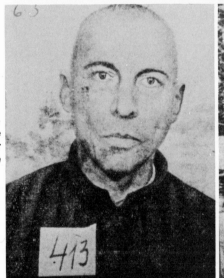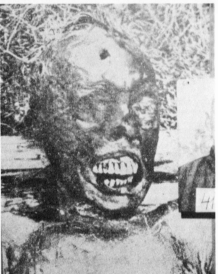

The chief of the Latvian national guard, before and after Soviet torture. These Russian police photos were found after the German invasion. *American Latvian Association*

Russia's Red Army returned in 1944, driving out the Germans. Here Soviet troops bridge a Latvian stream. *Sovfoto*

A war-damaged theatre in Daugavpils just after Russian recapture. Over the door hangs a German sign: "Movies for soldiers only." *Sovfoto*

Latvian guerrillas who fought the Nazi occupation forces. Other guerrillas harassed the returning Russians. *Sovfoto*

Latvian life is grim under the present Soviet occupation. A well-fed Soviet officer pays no attention to the poor Latvian woman trundling firewood along a Riga street. *UPI*

Instead of returning industry to Latvian ownership, Germany seized it as war booty. Some Baltic barons returned and tried to regain their estates. Nazi slaughter of 95,000 Latvian Jews horrified Latvia, which had been benevolent toward all racial and religious minorities. A small Latvian underground formed to harass the German overlords.

Yet when Russia's Red Army reconquered Latvia in 1944, 120,000 Latvians fled with the retreating German troops, never to return. Bad as Nazi tyranny had been, it was milder than Russian rule.

The second Soviet occupation was worse than the first. Another 120,000 Latvians were shipped off in cattle cars to USSR prison camps. About half of the deportees were hardworking peasants who resisted Communist collectivization of their tiny farms. As the Latvian prisoners left, Russians immigrated to replace them. Prewar Latvia's population was 77 percent Latvian and 12 percent Russian. Today the percentages are 66 and 27.

Although the Communists greatly expanded Latvian industry, fishing and shipping, the grain, flax, and potato harvests have actually declined. Real wages are only 50 percent of those before the war. National culture is discouraged, and four-fifths of the churches have been forced to close. Riga's beautiful Lutheran cathedral has been converted into a commercial concert hall.

Still the Latvians resist. Anti-Soviet guerrillas fought in the forests until 1954. Top Latvian Communist officials were purged by USSR leader Khrushchev for opposing Russification of Latvia's industry, officialdom, and schools. Every year the Soviet press criticizes Latvian intellectuals and youth for excessive nationalism. As under the Baltic barons, Tsarist Russia, and the Teutonic Knights, Latvia still survives as a nation.

Riga's Dome Cathedral has been converted into a Communist concert hall. This interior view shows that all religious ornaments have been removed. *Sovfoto*

Stark symbol of Soviet occupation—a Russian sentry guarding a Riga bridge. Says the sign: "Movement of pedestrians across the bridge only ON THE RIGHT SIDE." *UPI*

BALTIC

SEA

Memel•

•Kaunus

Vilnius

Niemen River

Dnieper River

Moscow•

Kiev•

LITHUANIA

——— Present Boundary

- - - - Boundary of 1400

0   100   200

Scale of Miles

BLACK   SEA

Lithuania

The Communist state seal of present-day Lithuania, which is forced to be a Soviet Republic of the USSR. In both Lithuanian and Russian, the slogan reads: "Proletarians of all countries, unite!" *Sovfoto*

OF THE THREE Baltic states, only Lithuania has ruled a vast empire. In the age of chivalry the Lithuanian domain reached almost to Moscow and extended from the Baltic to the Black Sea. The powerful Lithuanian army freed countless Belorussians and Ukrainians from the Mongol yoke. A Lithuanian leader commanded the East European army that in a single battle destroyed forever the power of Germany's Teutonic Knights. Wisely and well did the Lithuanian grand dukes govern their huge empire, tolerating and even encouraging all races and religions. Poland's greatest royal dynasty was Lithuanian.

Today Lithuania is forced to be a Soviet republic of the USSR. Yet anti-Soviet guerrillas still roam the forests, occasionally killing a cruel Communist local official. No less than 300,000 Soviet troops are stationed in Lithuania to keep the country quiet.

Who are these mighty Lithuanian warriors? They are Indo-European Balts, closely akin to the neighboring Latvians. Tall, blond, and husky, they are both brave and skillful in battle. Another of their claims to fame is their language—the most ancient in Europe, even older than Latin or Greek. Scholars of Indo-European linguistics classify Lithuanian as the key to history of most other European languages. So close is Lithuanian to India's Sanskrit that a Lithuanian peasant can understand simple Sanskrit speech.

All this greatness has evolved from a very small country, whose area today is only 25,200 square miles—about the same size as West Virginia. Bounded on the north by Latvia, on the east by Russia, on the south by Russia and Poland, and to the west by the Baltic Sea, Lithuania consists mainly of the valley of the Niemen (Nemunas) River. Rising in Russia, this waterway flows northwest across southern Lithuania into the Baltic Sea. Central Lithuania is a fertile lowland growing grain and sugar beets. This plain is enclosed by wooded hills in the west along the seacoast, and to the east along the Russian frontier. Almost a tenth of the country is marshland, and there are three thousand picturesque lakes. The badly depleted forests still cover one-fifth of Lithuania's territory. Half the country is suitable for farming—a higher proportion than in either Estonia or Latvia.

Peat is the main mineral, providing one-third of Lithuanian fuel. Clay, sand, and limestone are quarried for building material. But the most exotic resource is amber, dredged from the beaches of the pine-shrouded coast. Lithuania has almost a world monopoly in amber, whose sale in former centuries often saved the state treasury from bankruptcy.

With weapons like these maces, the medieval Lithuanians defeated the mighty Teutonic Knights. This folk dance also shows the costumes of Lithuania's medieval warriors. *Sovfoto*

The stately Niemen River. Most of Lithuania lies within its broad valley. *Sovfoto*

The lush Lithuanian countryside—a blend of lakes, woods, and fertile fields. *Sovfoto*

Combing the beach for precious amber washed ashore by heavy waves. *Sovfoto*

Even the Communist government dares not destroy the roadside shrines of devoutly Catholic Lithuania. *Sovfoto*

Once mainly agricultural, Lithuania today has a large industry. This huge power plant, built in the 1960s, symbolizes Lithuanian industrial strength. *Sovfoto*

Lithuania is famous for fine livestock, like these robust sheep. *Sovfoto*

Lithuania's population of 3,100,000 is the largest of the three Baltic states. In the past, most Lithuanians were peasants, raising livestock and cultivating rye, oats, wheat, potatoes, sugar beets, and flax. Industry was small, and devoted mainly to food processing. Because of the short coastline, fishing and shipping were little developed for a seaside nation.

Soviet rule has wrought great changes in Lithuanian economic life. Today more than half the population live and work in cities. Food processing is still the largest industry, specializing in butter, bacon, sugar, and canned fish. But Lithuania has also developed precision-machine building; they manufacture machine tools, farm equipment, radios, electric motors, and turbines. Fishing and the construction of fishing trawlers have become major occupations. Lithuanian food, fish, and machines are exported to all corners of the USSR.

Agriculture has been revamped. Grain, potato, and flax acreage has been reduced so that more land can be used for pasture. Though cattle and hogs were always more important than field crops, Communism is converting Lithuania into one vast meat and dairy farm. In the past Lithuania grew enough grain to feed itself. Now grain must be imported from other regions of the USSR.

Three cities have played key roles in Lithuanian history. In the southeast on a tributary of the Niemen River is Vilnius (formerly Vilna, Wilno), founded in the fourteenth century and proud of its university dating from 1578. With a

Beautiful modern Vilnius, the largest city in Lithuania. *EPA*

Vilnius University today holds its annual festival "baptizing" the ▶
incoming freshmen. *Sovfoto*

How a class looked in Vilnius University, when it was first founded
in the sixteenth century. The lecturer (*on the right, with uplifted
arms*) is the university's first rector. *PIAS*

THE LITHUANIAN NATION

	Pre-World War II	Present
Area (square miles)	23,000	25,200
Population	3,200,000	3,129,000

In percent of total population

Rate of literacy	95%	100%
Urban populace	23%	50%

Major Nationalities

Lithuanians	81%	78%
Russians	2%	12%
Poles	3%	8%
Jews	7%	
Germans	4%	2%
Latvians	3%	

Main Religion

Catholic	86%	90%

THE LITHUANIAN ECONOMY

	Unit of Measurement	Pre-World War II	Post-World War II	Present
Industrial Production				
Electricity	(kilowatt-hours)	81,000,000	34,600,000	6,025,000,000
Steel	(metric tons)	—	—	6,000
Cement	" "	—	—	852,000
Cotton cloth	(meters)	2,400,000	100,000	24,500,000
Machine tools	(pieces)	—	—	18,900
Agricultural Production				
Grain	(metric tons)	1,800,000	1,172,400	1,800,000
Potatoes	" "	2,700,000	3,121,800	3,000,000
Sugar beets	" "	255,000	349,300	776,000
Flax	" "	30,000	10,000	12,000
Number of Livestock				
Cattle		1,200,000	456,700	1,700,000
Swine		1,200,000	518,900	1,700,000
Communications				
Length of railways	(miles)	1,250	1,320	1,240
Length of highways	"	23,500	25,400	21,000

Kaunas, Lithuania's largest industrial city, as it looked before World War II at the height of Lithuanian independence. *UPI*

◄ Today's medical college at Kaunas—a city where every tenth resident is a student. *Sovfoto*

The busy docks of Klaipeda (formerly Memel), Lithuania's sole seaport. *Sovfoto*

population of 335,000, Vilnius is the largest city and capital of Lithuania. Besides operating a diversified industry, the city is a junction for five mainline railways.

On the Niemen River in south central Lithuania is Kaunas (formerly Kovno), a city containing 300,000 people and half of the country's industry. The local factories produce furniture, textiles, and machines, and package meat. When Poland occupied Vilnius in the period between World Wars I and II, Kaunas served as the Lithuanian capital.

On the coast north of the Niemen estuary is Klaipeda (formerly Memel), Lithuania's sole Baltic port. Klaipeda has a population of 150,000 and is the country's chief shipbuilding center and main fishing harbor. It is also the largest submarine base on the Baltic for the Soviet naval fleet.

Large fishing trawlers like this refrigerator ship are built in Klaipeda shipyards. Note that the ship's name is painted in Russian Cyrillic letters instead of the Lithuanian Latin alphabet. *Sovfoto*

This Catholic church altar, made of trees, is a reminder that ancient Lithuanians held their pagan religious rites amid forests. *Sovfoto*

Klaipeda built this huge floating dock, which was then towed halfway around the world to a USSR Pacific port. *Sovfoto*

Ancient Aestian (Lithuanian) wooden fort. *NYPL*

the Greeks and Romans carved into costly jewels. The primitive Aestians were astounded by the high prices paid for amber, which they simply picked up from the coastal beaches.

At first there was no Lithuanian state. The Aestians lived in tribes ruled by princes. Tradition says that by the fifth century A.D., several tribes had formed a loose federation headed by a pagan high priest. This trend toward unity was later to be Lithuania's salvation.

Unlike Estonia and Latvia, Lithuania had little contact with the Scandinavian Vikings, who by the ninth century were crossing the east Baltic coast to trade with Russia. The Vikings traveled

As early as 1500 B.C., the Lithuanians were living in their present homeland, which was then completely covered by forests. They called themselves "Aestians" (the Honorables), and were pagan nature worshipers. Merchants from the Mediterranean visited them to buy amber, which

Left: Lithuanian warriors of the ninth century, armed with spear, mace, bow and arrow, and wooden shields. *NYPL.* An officer (*center*) and soldiers of the Teutonic Knights, the German religious army that tried and failed to conquer Lithuania during the thirteenth and fourteenth centuries. These military monks emblazoned crosses on their cloaks and shields. *NYPL*

Coronation ceremony in 1253 of Mindaugas, Lithuania's first king, who by uniting the Lithuanians saved his country from the Teutonic Knights. *NYPL*

land and river routes farther north, leaving the Lithuanian forests relatively undisturbed.

The first real threat to Lithuanian independence came early in the twelfth century, when Russia's Kiev kingdom launched an invasion. Lithuania's princes not only repelled the Russians, but counterattacked. By the close of the century Lithuania had conquered and annexed the west Belorussian city of Grodno.

The Kiev kingdom soon ceased to be a threat, falling apart into feudal states which by the mid-thirteenth century had been overwhelmed by the Mongol Horde. But a new and greater danger arose in the west from two German religious armies: the Teutonic Knights and the Knights of the Sword. To the south of Lithuania lay East Prussia, which the Teutonic Knights completely conquered, an-

nihilating the original Prussians who were kinsmen of the Lithuanians. North of Lithuania was Latvia, defeated and occupied by the Knights of the Sword, whose army was soon absorbed by the Teutonic Knights. Early in the thirteenth century the Knights invaded Lithuania from north and south, trying desperately to conquer the pagan forestland that wedged between their Christian territories.

The Lithuanian tribes saved themselves by uniting under a great military leader, Prince Mindaugas (Mindovg), who defeated the Knights in the west and the Mongols in the east. Hoping to end the Knights' Christian crusades against the pagan Lithuanians, Mindaugas in 1251 became a Catholic and with papal blessing was crowned King of Lithuania. But the greedy Knights still attacked, and in 1262 Mindaugas angrily renounced his Christian faith. He was assassinated a year later by a jealous relative who resented the strong-arm tactics used for Lithuanian unification.

But Lithuania remained united and in the late thirteenth century repulsed invasions from Russia, Poland, and the Teutonic Knights. Victories over Russia brought all west Belorussia under Lithuanian rule.

Then came the reign of Grand Duke Gediminas (Gedimin, 1316–41), who proudly called himself "King of Lithuania and Many Ruthenians [Russians]." A great warrior, he conquered and annexed east Belorussia and the western Ukraine. Tired of ruling from a tent, Gediminas enlarged the

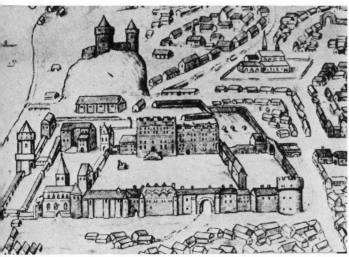

Medieval Vilnius, when it was first built into a city by Gediminas (1316–41), "King of Lithuania and Many Ruthenians." And the same section of Vilnius as it looks today. *Sovfoto*

Lithuanian Grand Duke Algirdas (1345–77) proudly knocking at the gates of Moscow, which his armies captured twice. *NYPL*

Muscovites *(right)* humbly offering tribute to Grand Duke Algirdas. In the background are the Kremlin walls. *NYPL*

old village of Vilnius into his capital city. Gediminas governed his empire with tolerance and skill. Though a pagan, he welcomed Catholic missionaries and allowed Vilnius to build an Orthodox church. Both pagan and Christian priests were made a special class with special privileges. German merchants and artisans were settled in Lithuanian towns to develop crafts and trade. Each province was controlled by a royal governor, who removed local power from the hands of the nobles. Old Slavonic was the written language of the court, and Lithuanians and East Slavs intermarried freely.

Upon his death Gediminas was succeeded by his sons Algirdas and Kestutis (co-rulers 1345–77), who were equally capable. Their armies successfully battled the Teutonic Knights, Poles, Hungarians, and Mongol Tatars, once almost capturing Moscow. More Russian cities were annexed, and the Lithuanian Empire expanded to the shore of the Black Sea. To protect their empire, Algirdas and Kestutis built a chain of strong forts along the far-flung frontiers.

During the reign of Algirdas's son, Grand Duke Jagiello (Jogaila, 1382–1434), Lithuania achieved its greatest glory. Bessarabia and much of Romania were conquered and annexed. The entire Ukraine was under Jagiello's control. The Lithua-

Polish Queen Jadwiga, whose marriage to Lithuanian Grand Duke Jagiello in 1386 united the Polish and Lithuanian thrones. *PIAS*

King Jagiello converting the pagan Lithuanians to Catholic Christianity, as he had promised to do when marrying Polish Queen Jadwiga. *NYPL*

Ruins of a castle near Vilnius built by Grand Duke Vytautas, a great warrior who governed Lithuania after his cousin King Jagiello moved to Poland. *Sovfoto*

At the Battle of Tannenberg (1410) in East Prussia, the combined armies of Vytautas and Jagiello routed the Teutonic Knights, who were never again a menace. Here Vytautas gazes scornfully at the corpse of the Grand Master of the Teutonic Knights, who was killed in the fighting. *NYPL*

nian domain extended eastward as far as Tula—a Russian city directly south of Moscow. Lithuania governed a vast empire in which only one-tenth of the population was Lithuanian.

Anxious to appease Lithuania and seeking a king, Poland offered its throne to Jagiello. Poland's terms were that Jagiello had to marry the Polish child-queen Jadwiga, become a Roman Catholic, and convert pagan Lithuania to Catholicism. Jagiello accepted the terms, marrying Jadwiga in 1386. Thus began the able Jagiellon dynasty, which

was to rule Poland for almost two hundred years. The marriage also united Poland and Lithuania into a federation, though both maintained separate armies, treasuries, and local administrations until the sixteenth century.

Jagiello moved to Poland, leaving Lithuania under the governorship of his cousin Duke Vytau-

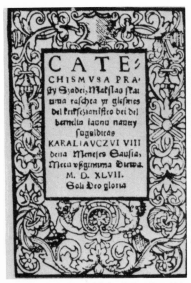

The first book published in the Lithuanian language—a Lutheran catechism of 1547. *NYPL*

Polish-Lithuanian King Stephen Bathory who founded the University of Vilnius in 1578. *PIAS*

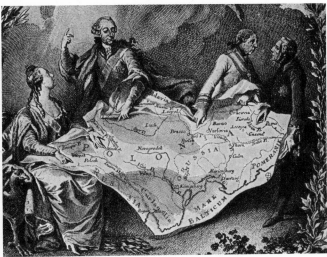

Russian Empress Catherine the Great and Prussian King Frederick the Great (with Austrian help) in the late 1700s divide up Poland-Lithuania, with Russia annexing all Lithuanian territories. This cartoon was drawn in the eighteenth century.

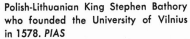

Lithuanian peasants of the late seventeenth century, with their hand tools, wooden dishes, and homemade musical instruments. *NYPL*

tas (Vitovt, Witold). The two cousins invaded East Prussia with a combined Lithuanian-Polish army, which also included Russians, Czechs, and even Tatars. Using Tatar tactics, this multinational army in 1410 completely crushed the Teutonic Knights at the Battle of Tannenberg. Though the Knights continued to exist, never again were they a threat to Poland-Lithuania.

Union with Poland both helped and harmed Lithuania. From Poland, Lithuania received Chris-tianity and a high level of culture. Lithuania's nobles became Polonized, adopting the Polish language and customs. But the Jagiellon kings spent most of their time in Poland, neglecting Lithuania. Under Polish influence, Lithuania in 1501 hurt its peasants by making them serfs. In 1569 the Union of Lublin created a joint Polish-Lithuanian assembly of nobles, in which Poles outnumbered Lithuanians three to one. This assembly undermined the power of the Polish kings, who could not provide Poland-Lithuania with a strong central government.

As central authority declined, so did the Polish-Lithuanian empire. The Ukrainians, who had once welcomed Lithuanian rule as better than Tatar, started endless anti-Polish rebellions. Turkey seized the Black Sea coast. And Russia began reconquering lands it had lost to Lithuania.

Still the Lithuanian Empire remained large until Poland lost a Russo-Polish war, and by the Treaty of Andrussovo (1667) surrendered the eastern Ukraine to Moscow. Then the eighteenth century ended both Lithuanian Empire and independence. In the First Partition of Poland (1772), Russian Empress Catherine the Great took eastern Belorussia. The Second Partition (1793) gave Russia central Belorussia and the western Ukraine. By the Third Partition (1795), Lithuania proper became a Russian province.

General Jokūbas Jasinskis in 1794 commanding the unsuccessful Lithuanian revolt against Russia. His troops briefly freed Vilnius from tsarist control. *NYPL*

Jasinskis's irregular cavalry preparing to ambush the Russian enemy. *NYPL*

Napoleon's Grand Army in 1812 invaded Russia from Vilnius, and retreated along the same route. Here is the retreat, with some French soldiers so cold that they wrapped themselves in sacred vestments looted from Lithuanian churches. *NYPL*

Lithuanian hopes for independence rose in 1812 when Napoleon's Grand Army invaded Russia. The invasion was launched from Vilnius, which promptly formed a Lithuanian Provisional Government. But Napoleon was defeated, Russia reconquered Lithuania, and the provisional government disbanded.

In 1830 Lithuania revolted unsuccessfully against tsarist rule. Russian revenge was severe. Vilnius University and most Lithuanian schools were forced to close. Russian became the official language, and Lithuanian national costumes were forbidden. Even the name "Lithuania" was abolished, and the country became Russia's "Northwest Territory."

After Lithuania's serfs were freed, the Lithuanians in 1863 again rebelled unsuccessfully against Russia. So tsarist police began to watch Lithuania's Catholic church schools and forbade any literature to be published in the Lithuanian Latin alphabet. But the Catholic clergy kept Lithuanian culture alive despite police surveillance. Exiles in Germany published Lithuanian nationalistic books and newspapers, which were easily smuggled into the Lithuanian homeland.

During the Russian Revolution of 1905, Lithuania demanded political autonomy. No autonomy was granted, but the Latin alphabet was restored.

World War I finally gave Lithuania an opportunity for independence. During 1915–18 Lithuania was occupied by the German army, which encouraged anti-Russian sentiment. On February

Left: Bishop Motiejus Valancius (1801–75) was the first to publish Lithuanian nationalistic literature in East Prussia, then smuggle it into Russian-occupied Lithuania. *Right:* Simanas Daukantas (1793–1864), the first Lithuanian historian to write his works in the Lithuanian language. *NYPL*

Left: Dr. Janas Basanavicius (1851–1927), who in 1883 in exile founded the political magazine *Dawn,* which was secretly circulated in Lithuania and aroused great patriotic emotion. *Right:* Dr. Vincas Kudirka (1858–99), author of the national anthem: "Lithuania Our Country!" *NYPL*

Clergymen were in the forefront of the Lithuanian revolutionary movement. Here is Reverend Antanas Mackevicius, one of the leaders of the 1863 rebellion. *NYPL*

Russian General Mikhail Muraviev, who crushed the 1863 revolt, personally supervising the hanging of Lithuanian rebels. *NYPL*

German troops invading Lithuania during World War I. For fresh milk they have seized a peasant's cow. *Photoworld*

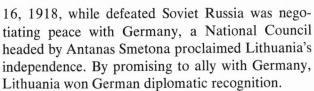

Antanas Smetona (and wife), leader of the independence movement which freed Lithuania in 1918. He was the country's first president, 1919–22, and regained the presidency in 1926. *UPI*

16, 1918, while defeated Soviet Russia was negotiating peace with Germany, a National Council headed by Antanas Smetona proclaimed Lithuania's independence. By promising to ally with Germany, Lithuania won German diplomatic recognition.

Under German pressure Lithuania proclaimed itself a kingdom and invited German Duke Wilhelm Urach to be the king. Then, on November 11, 1918, Germany ended World War I by surrendering to the Western Allies. Lithuania hurriedly changed into a republic and rejected the unfortunate duke, who had already started studying the Lithuanian language.

For the next two years Lithuania had to defend its independence from invasions by Russia's Red Army, the Polish Legion, White Russians, and German troops. Both the Germans and Russians were forced to withdraw, and in July 1920 Russia signed the Treaty of Moscow recognizing Lithuanian independence.

But the Lithuanians could not defeat the Poles, who in October 1920 seized and annexed Vilnius—Lithuania's historic capital. Poland claimed that the city was mostly Polish in population. Lithuania did not fight to regain Vilnius, but maintained a diplomatic state of war against Poland until 1938.

Meanwhile, the Western Allies had internationalized Memel and placed it under their own protection. Memel had been founded in 1200 by the Teutonic Knights and was still inhabited mainly by Germans. Imitating the Poles, Lithuania in 1923 seized Memel by force. A year later the Conference of Allied Ambassadors recognized Lithuania's right to rule this port city.

Despite such international crises, independent Lithuania prospered. The large estates, which had held 40 percent of the farmland, were broken up and divided among the peasants. Most of these estates were owned by Polish or Polonized Lithuanian gentry, who had already fled from Lithuania to Poland. The small peasant farms specialized in cattle and hogs, and livestock products comprised three-fifths of Lithuanian exports. Since Soviet Russia refused to trade heavily, Britain and Germany became Lithuania's main trading partners.

In 1926 Lithuania concluded a nonaggression pact with Communist Russia and permitted Communist demonstrations in Lithuanian cities. The worried Lithuanian army overthrew Lithuania's left-wing cabinet and installed the old independence leader Smetona as dictator-president.

Vilnius in 1920 was seized and annexed by Poland, whose army was commanded by Marshal Josef Pilsudski, shown here *(seated and facing camera)* surrounded by his staff. *UPI*

With a band gaily playing, Lithuanian troops march into Memel (now Klaipeda) in 1923 and annex this seaport to Lithuania. From 1918 till 1923, Memel had been under international Allied control. *UPI*

Memel, as this seaport looked in early 1939, when Hitler demanded it for Germany. *UPI*

Smetona twice modified the constitution to give himself more presidential power. Though a benevolent dictator, he did not hesitate to crush Nazi organizations formed by Lithuania's Germans.

A parade of Lithuanian troops. The tiny Lithuanian army (25,000 men) could not hope to withstand Hitler's mighty Wehrmacht. *UPI*

The German navy steams into Memel harbor, 1939. (Lithuania's one naval ship had already fled.) *UPI*

Free Lithuania's entire navy: one patrol boat. *UPI*

Changing of street signs in German-occupied Memel. Down comes "President Smetona Street." Up goes "Adolf Hitler Street." *UPI*

German troops in March 1939 occupying Memel, which Lithuania had to yield to Hitler. *UPI*

On the eve of World War II, Lithuania again was in international danger. In 1938 Poland forced Lithuania to resume normal diplomatic relations, which had been suspended since 1920. Hitler seized Memel early in 1939, promising to guarantee Lithuania's remaining frontiers.

A happy Hitler tours his new possession, Memel. *UPI*

Lithuanian troops in 1939 fall occupying Vilnius—Stalin's temporary gift to Lithuania after Russia seized east Poland. Less than a year later, Stalin annexed Lithuania (and Vilnius) to the USSR. *UPI*

When Hitler attacked Russia in June 1941, his army overran Lithuania in just a few days. Before the Soviet police ran away, they shot their Lithuanian political prisoners. Here Lithuanian women are searching for relatives among the corpses.

Hitler's guarantee proved worthless in the fall of 1939, when a secret Soviet-German agreement placed Lithuania in Russia's sphere of influence. In October the USSR demanded and obtained a Soviet-Lithuanian alliance that permitted Russian military bases on Lithuanian soil. About 25,000 Soviet troops entered Lithuania, whose whole army numbered 25,000. To soften Lithuanian resentment, the USSR returned Vilnius to Lithuania.

In June 1940, falsely claiming that Smetona had violated the alliance, Moscow ordered Lithuania to admit more Russian troops and to form a pro-Soviet government. Lithuania sadly submitted. Elections under the guns of Soviet troops created a socialist parliament, which requested Russian annexation. By August, Lithuania was a Soviet Republic of the USSR.

The Communists nationalized all Lithuanian land, all industry, and many buildings. No less than 34,000 Lithuanians were deported to USSR prison camps. To save the Lithuanian Germans,

The Nazi occupation lasted until 1944, then back came the revengeful Russians. Here is Vilnius, just after Russian reconquest. *Sovfoto*

Battle debris in Vilnius, after the Russians had ousted the Germans. *Sovfoto*

Two Lithuanian youngsters, searching vainly for their family home in war-devastated Vilnius. *Sovfoto*

A Lithuanian woman kisses the hand of her dead husband, slain by the Soviet police.

Soviet Lithuania's Communist government—Moscow's puppets. But even these local Reds sometimes oppose Russification. *Sovfoto*

Almost all Lithuanian farms have been forced to collectivize. Here combines are reaping what appears to be a poor (short-stemmed) crop, which often occurs on the hated collectives. *Sovfoto*

Hitler arranged for their emigration to the Third Reich. Lithuanian President Smetona also fled to Germany, thus escaping Soviet execution.

Somehow Lithuania maintained an armed underground during Soviet occupation. When Hitler invaded the USSR in 1941, the underground fought the Russians, freeing Vilnius and Kaunas before the German army arrived. A Provisional Government declared Lithuania again to be an independent nation.

But the German troops, who occupied Lithu-

ania till 1944, soon stopped the independence movement. Lithuania was governed like a captured enemy province. Instead of returning the nationalized land to peasant ownership, the Germans seized it as war booty. As many as 100,000 Lithuanians were sent to Germany as slave labor. Almost all of Lithuania's 200,000 Jews were exterminated. To avoid conscription into the German army, many Lithuanian men fled into the forests to become anti-German guerrillas. Yet when Russia's Red Army reconquered Lithuania in 1944,

Under Communism, Lithuania's industry is no longer its own. This power station has to supply electricity to four neighboring Soviet republics. *Sovfoto*

70,000 Lithuanians fled with the retreating German troops.

The second Soviet occupation was worse than the first. Again there were mass deportations to USSR prison camps. Of the 200,000 deportees, half were peasants resisting farm collectivization. So many priests were arrested, that only half of the Catholic churches remain open for worship. The living standard has fallen to 50 percent of what it was before the war.

Lithuania is today a Soviet armed camp. It has hidden military airfields built with underground hangars. Rocket bases line the coast, occasionally firing practice shots over the Baltic Sea. Huge concrete pens have been constructed in Memel to house submarines safely.

Lithuania has not accepted Communism meekly. The guerrilla underground is still in the forests, now harassing the Russians. Soviet newspapers complain constantly about excessive nationalism among Lithuanian intellectuals, peasants, young people, and clergymen. Many Lithuanian Communists have been purged for resisting Russification.

As soon as the opportunity arises, the brave Lithuanians will probably revolt again.

Symbol of Soviet occupation: giant statue of Lenin dominating Vilnius's "Lenin Square." *Sovfoto*

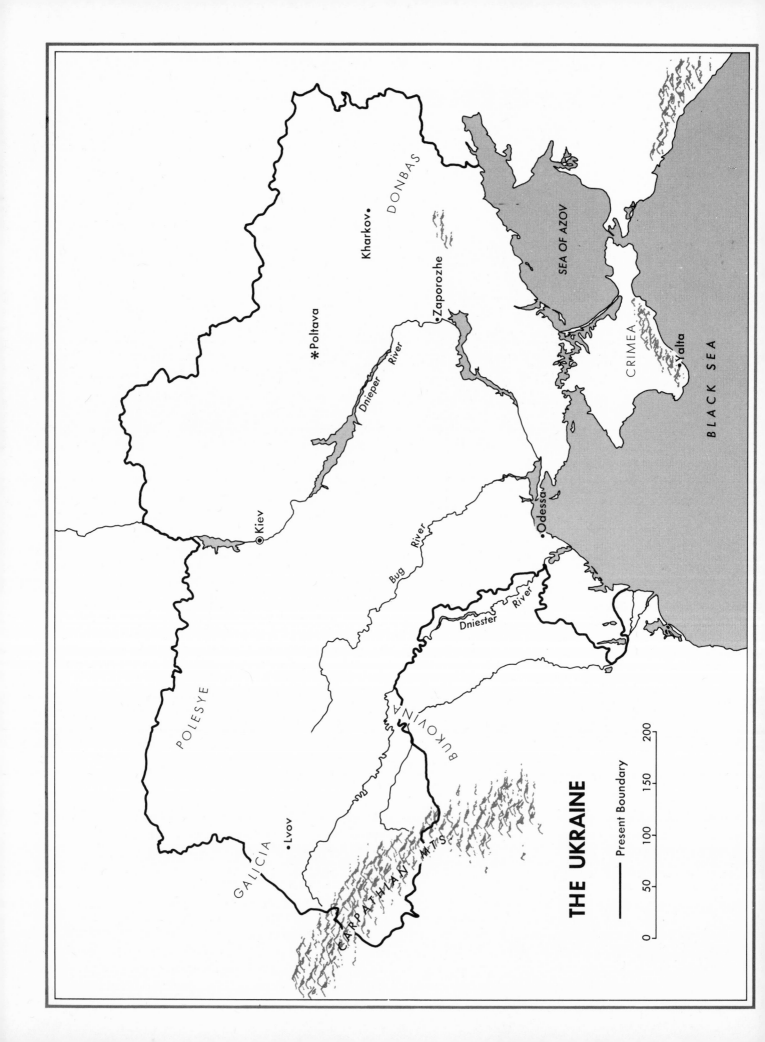

THE UKRAINE

— Present Boundary

0 50 100 150 200

BLACK SEA

SEA OF AZOV

CRIMEA

Yalta

Odessa

DONBAS

Kharkov

Zaporozhe

*Poltava

Dnieper River

Kiev

Bug River

Dniester River

POLESYE

BUKOVINA

GALICIA

Lvov

CARPATHIAN MTS.

The Ukraine

"BORDERLAND" IS THE precise meaning of the word Ukraine, which in medieval centuries was truly a frontier country for endless wars between Moscow and East European powers. Lithuania, Poland, Russia, Turkey, and the Tatars all battled to control the fertile Ukrainian steppes, whose fiery Cossacks harassed every foreign conqueror. Russia finally won, so today the Ukraine is a Soviet Republic of the USSR. But the tall, husky, brunette Ukrainians resent Russian rule and constantly organize patriotic groups striving for national autonomy or independence.

If the Ukraine were free today, it would be one of the world's richest countries. Ukrainian industry is so big that only the United States, Russia, and Japan are more productive. Per capita output of coal and steel in the Ukraine is higher than in the USA. Ukrainian farms harvest more grain than Canada, which is one of the world's greatest granaries. The once underdeveloped "borderland" of East Europe has become an economic giant, dwarfing the East European nations that formerly ruled it.

Achievement of such greatness requires considerable territory, and the Ukrainian lands cover 240,000 square miles—an area almost as large as the state of Texas. This sizable territory is very strategically located. To the north and east is the USSR, and on the west lie Poland, Czechoslovakia, Hungary, Romania, and Soviet Bessarabia. In the south are the Black and Azov seas, whose cosmopolitan ports link the Ukraine with the entire world. Thus the Ukraine is a major gateway for Russian trade with both East Europe and countries far overseas. Of all the Soviet republics, the Ukraine has the densest railway network. From Odessa, the largest Ukrainian seaport and second greatest port in the USSR, Soviet ships make regular runs halfway around the world to the Siberian Pacific coast.

Land transport is aided by the Ukrainian terrain, which is mostly one vast plain. The only mountains are the Carpathians in the far west and the Crimean in the far south. Otherwise the Ukraine resembles in climate, appearance, and natural vegetation the great plains of Montana.

The Ukrainian plain, or so-called steppeland, divides into three distinct zones: in the northwest and north is the heavily wooded Polesye with its many meadows, streams, and swamps. Because there is little good farmland, the peasants mainly raise livestock.

South of the Polesye is the wooded steppe, stretching in a great belt from west to east across the central Ukraine. The few trees grow mostly along streams, and the open fields are rich black earth. The sugar beets of the wooded steppe provide three-fifths of the sugar for the entire USSR.

Rich fertile soil covers the vast Ukrainian steppes. This fine crop is as high as the farm woman's waist. *Photoworld*

This huge grain elevator, the largest in the USSR, faces the Black Sea at the Ukrainian port of Nikolayev. *Sovfoto*

The Black Sea, which links the Ukraine to all the world's oceans. These sailboats are practicing for international races. *Sovfoto*

Down to the docks goes this giant stairway at Odessa, the Ukraine's greatest port on the Black Sea. *Sovfoto*

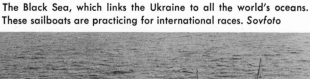

Most Soviet vegetable oil for cooking comes from sunflowers, and most USSR sunflowers grow like fields of gold on the Ukrainian wooded steppe.

Almost the entire south Ukraine is the treeless steppe, whose few trees must be planted and do not reproduce themselves. One can see for miles over this sea of land, often viewing brilliant sun-shine on one horizon while a thunderstorm darkens the opposite sky. Here the soil is rich black, chestnut, or chocolate earth. The treeless steppe is one of the greatest Soviet granaries and grows one-fifth of all USSR grain.

All three steppes raise much livestock, which in the wooded and treeless steppes feeds on waste

Busy docks at Odessa, second largest seaport in the entire USSR.
Sovfoto

Fishing boats from the Crimea unloading their catch at Odessa.
Sovfoto

A farm village in the Ukrainian wooded steppe. In the background is the city of Poltava. *EPA*

A tractor team cultivating sugar beet sprouts in the Vinnitsa region. The Ukraine is one of the world's top producers of beet sugar. *Sovfoto*

Collective-farm women harvesting grain on the Ukrainian tree-less steppe. Most collective-farm work is performed by women, because of male casualties in war and the migration of peasant boys into cities. *Sovfoto*

From grapes like these come the tasty Ukrainian wines. *Sovfoto*

Ruthenian shepherds just after milking their sheep. *Sovfoto*

products from farm fields. One-fourth of USSR cattle and over half of Soviet hogs are raised on Ukrainian farmsteads.

The two mountain areas are more famous for minerals than products of the fields. In the Crimean Mountains are deposits of rich iron ore. Carpathian mines yield salt, building materials, some oil, and enormous amounts of natural gas. Pipelines carry Carpathian gas to Lithuania, Latvia, the mid-Ukraine, and even to Moscow. One third of all USSR natural gas comes from the Ukraine.

Yet the greatest mineral wealth is on the steppes rather than in the mountains. The Donets basin (Donbas) of the eastern Ukraine is one of the largest coal-mining regions in the USSR. In the central Ukraine is the Dnieper River, flowing from the north down to the Black Sea. The so-called Dnieper bend contains the biggest iron

The rare metal, titanium, will be processed by this huge plant being built on the Crimean peninsula. *UPI*

A fishing enthusiast preparing his bait on the bank of the Dnieper —the Ukraine's largest river. *Sovfoto*

The old section of Kharkov, the greatest industrial city in the Ukraine. *UPI*

Kharkov's high-rise apartments for Soviet bureaucrats. *UPI*

mines of the Soviet Union. Huge steel mills operate night and day in both Ukrainian areas. The Ukraine mines one-third of USSR coal and smelts two-fifths of Soviet steel.

On the basis of its coal and steel, the Ukraine has developed a vast machinery industry specializing in heavy equipment that consumes much metal. Thus the main manufactures are tanks, tractors, turbines, trucks, mining and metallurgical machinery, railway freight cars, locomotives, and ships. The largest machinery center is Kharkov, a city of 1,223,000 people located near the Donbas. When the German army captured Kharkov during World War II, Hitler joyfully boasted that Russia was finished.

There is also a large light industry, refining sugar and salt, canning fruit, and making tasty wine. The largest center of light industry is Kiev, the Ukrainian capital city with a population of 1,-632,000. Founded twelve hundred years ago, Kiev is called the "Mother of Russian cities" and has been a storm center of Ukrainian history.

Because of the tremendous industry, more than half of the 47,000,000 people in the Ukraine live in cities. Of the total population, three-fourths are Ukrainian and one-sixth are Russian. The countryside is almost solidly Ukrainian, while the Russians reside in the cities and operate the industries. Also in the towns and ports are many small minorities, especially Poles and Jews.

THE UKRAINIAN NATION

	Pre- World War II	Post- World War II	Present
Area			
(square miles)	214,600	223,000	240,000
Population	42,300,000	40,600,000	47,136,000

In percent of total population

	Pre- World War II	Post- World War II	Present
Rate of literacy	90%	90%	100%
Urban populace	34%	34%	55%
Major Nationalities			
Ukrainians	80%	75%	76%
Russians	9%	9%	18%
Jews	5%	2%	2%
Main Religions			
Orthodox	70%	70% }	90%
Uniate	20%	20% }	
Jewish	5%	2%	2%

THE UKRAINIAN ECONOMY

	Unit of Measurement	Pre- World War II	Post- World War II	Present
Industrial Production				
Coal	(metric tons)	69,000,000	23,000,000	200,400,000
Steel	" "	8,900,000	2,400,000	44,200,000
Refined sugar	" "	1,580,000	530,000	6,360,000
Agricultural Production				
Grain	" "	26,400,000	13,000,000	27,900,000
Potatoes	" "	20,700,000	10,000,000	22,500,000
Sugar beets	" "	13,000,000	6,000,000	57,300,000
Sunflower seed	" "	950,000	500,000	2,700,000
Number of Livestock				
Cattle		11,000,000	6,000,000	20,200,000
Swine		9,200,000	5,000,000	14,500,000
Communications				
Length of railways	(miles)	12,500	8,000	13,600

Ukrainian peasant women are famous for their colorful embroidery. Here pillow cases are being decorated with gay designs. *Sovfoto*

Kiev, the Ukrainian capital, is a museum city of churches, cathedrals, and monumental buildings. Below is one of Kiev's stately palaces. *UPI*

A textile mill in Kiev, which is the largest center for Ukrainian light industry. *UPI*

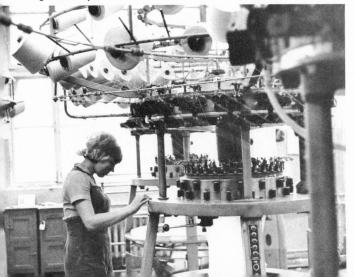

A grand old church in Kiev. *UPI*

In both antiquity and the early Middle Ages the Ukrainian treeless steppe was the natural highway into Europe for fierce nomadic tribes of Asian horsemen. A tribe would conquer the steppeland, control it for one or more centuries, then either migrate into Europe or be slaughtered by new invasions of the stronger nomads. Thus the ancient Ukraine was successively ruled by many invaders: the Iranian Scythians (700–200 B.C.), Iranian Sarmatians (200 B.C.–A.D. 200), Germanic Goths (A.D. 200–370), Turkic Huns (370–558), Mongol-Turkic Avars (558–650), and the Khazars (650–737), who were Turkic but adopted the Jewish religion. Since the sixth century B.C. the Greeks occupied many Black Sea ports which later became part of the Roman Empire.

Amid all these conquests and reconquests, the East Slavs moved quietly into the Ukraine from the Carpathians as early as the fifth century B.C. Being farmers and large in number, they survived

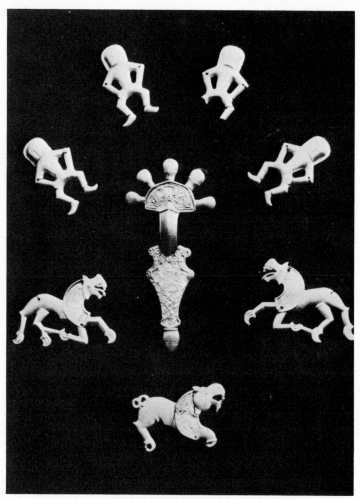

Silver ornaments of the Eastern Slavs of the sixth and seventh centuries A.D. *Sovfoto*

Prince Oleg (879–913), founder of the medieval Kiev state, besieging Byzantium, which saved itself by making trade concessions. *NYPL*

Grand Prince Sviatoslav (962–72) of Kiev capturing a Bulgarian city. He ruled all Ukrainian lands from the Danube River to the Volga. *NYPL*

Kievan soldiers of the tenth century. *NYPL*

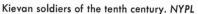

and outlived the relatively small nomadic tribes who successively ruled them.

By the ninth century A.D. the Scandinavian Vikings crossed the Baltic Sea, went the short distance inland to the headwaters of the Dnieper River, and sailed downriver into the Ukraine, uniting the East Slavs into a powerful state. Kiev was the capital, and the state called itself "Kievan Rus" (Kievan Russia). At the time there was no Ukrainian nationality, the Russians and Ukrainians being the same people.

From the ninth to the eleventh century Kievan Rus was the center of Russian culture and power. But the Kiev princes began dividing their domains among their relatives, so centralized au-

Monument in Kiev to Saint Vladimir, the prince who in 988 made Orthodox Christianity the official religion for the previously pagan Kiev state. Today's Communist regime dares not disturb this giant statue, which overlooks the Dnieper River where Vladimir baptized the people of Kiev. *Sovfoto*

Kiev's majestic cathedral of Saint Sofia, built in 1038 by Prince Yaroslav the Wise, who also issued the first Kievan code of laws. Three of his daughters became queens—of Norway, Hungary, and France. *Sovfoto*

Kiev's last great medieval ruler was Prince Vladimir Monomakh (1113–25), whose testament advised his sons to govern with mercy and justice. Here he is sending one of his sons to administer a provincial city. *NYPL*

Slavs battling the dread Mongols (*right*), who conquered Kiev in 1240 and wiped out the Kievan state. Most buildings in Kiev were destroyed, and for miles around the steppe was littered with skulls and bones. *NYPL*

thority degenerated into feudalism. Constant attacks by new Asian nomads drove many East Slavs north, where they found protection in the forests, becoming the "Great Russian" and "Belorussian" nationalities.

The Slavs remaining in the Ukraine were conquered by the Mongols in the thirteenth century. Many sought safety in Polish Galicia, not returning until Mongol power waned. After the Mongols came other alien rulers, with whom the steppe Slavs sometimes intermarried. Thus the Ukrainians became a distinct nationality with a language, appearance, and customs different from the Russians.

By the fourteenth century Lithuania wrested control of the western and central Ukraine from the Mongols, whose own empire was now disintegrating. The Ukrainians at first welcomed Lithuanian rule as delivery from the Mongol yoke. And the Lithuanians were not too harsh, showing respect for Ukrainian culture.

But in 1569 Lithuania united completely with Poland, whose oppressive nobility soon dominated all Lithuanian territories. The rich Ukrainian farmlands were divided into Polish-owned estates, and attempts were made to Polonize the Ukrainian culture. Polish priests tried to Catholicize the Ukrainians, who had adopted Orthodox Christianity back in the era of Kievan Rus. Some Ukrainians became Catholic. Others adopted Uniatism, which uses the Orthodox service but accepts papal rule. Most remained Orthodox, the main Ukrainian religion today.

Poland was not strong enough to stop the terrible raids into the Ukraine by the Crimean Tatars —the descendants of the Mongol Horde. Slaughtering the Ukrainians and carrying off slaves, the Tatars sometimes drove as far north as the Polesye forest. To protect themselves the Ukrainian peasants armed, banded together, and lived a half-military, half-agricultural life. They proudly named themselves "Cossacks" (Kozaks—"Free Warriors"). By the sixteenth century the Cossacks formed a regular army, the Zaporozhian Sich, living on heavily fortified islands of the Dnieper River. Members of the Sich did not marry, and elected their leaders who were called "hetmen." Soon the Cossacks were fighting the Poles, Tatars, and Turks.

A Cossack rebellion in the mid-seventeenth century freed the central Ukraine from Polish oppression. But the Ukrainians, fearing Polish reconquest, placed themselves under Russian protection

Under Lithuanian rule from the fourteenth century, and Polish rule from the sixteenth, the oppressed Ukrainians still managed to preserve their native culture. Above is Prince Vasyl-Kostiantyn Ostrozky, who in the 1570s founded a Ukrainian school and printing press. Illustration is from a Ukrainian book published in 1607. The book title was intriguing: *Medicine for Sleepy Minds. NYPL*

In the seventeenth century, Metropolitan Petro Mohyla founded the Kiev Academy, which became the cultural center for the entire Ukraine. *NYPL*

At the Kiev Academy, which trained many Ukrainian nationalist leaders. *NYPL*

in 1654. Russia promised that the Ukraine would be autonomous under the local rule of the Cossack hetman.

This promise soon proved worthless. The autocratic Russian tsars had no intention of tolerating an autonomous democratic Ukraine. Taking shrewd advantage of incompetent hetmen and jealousy among Cossack officers, Moscow steadily reduced Ukrainian national rights. In a desperate attempt to save the Ukraine, Hetman Ivan Mazeppa in 1708/09 allied his Cossacks with the Swedish army invading Russia. But Mazeppa could muster few troops to aid the Swedes, whose strength was already declining. At the Battle of Poltava in the

Far left:
Bohdan Khmelnytsky in 1648 led a massive Cossack revolution that freed much of the Ukraine from Polish misrule. Fearing Polish reconquest, he placed his free Ukraine in 1654 under Tsarist Russian protection. *NYPL*

Left:
Monument to Bohdan Khmelnytsky in Kiev. Ukrainians consider him one of their greatest heroes. *Sovfoto*

This peaceful-looking hill was once the fortified stronghold of Khmelnytsky, when he was warring against Poles and Tatars. *Sovfoto*

Left:
Swedish King Charles XII led his army into the Ukraine in 1708 to seek Cossack support in his war against Russia. *NYPL*

Right:
Cossack Hetman Ivan Mazeppa allied with Charles XII to free the Ukraine from Russian tyranny, but was unable to muster many troops.

Russian Tsar Peter the Great, who in 1709 defeated the combined Swedish-Cossack forces at the Battle of Poltava. Afterward he put the Cossacks under Russian commanders. *NYPL*

Taras Shevchenko (1814–61), the greatest Ukrainian poet, was exiled for ten years to the Urals for participating in an antitsarist secret society. His writings were an eloquent appeal for Ukrainian freedom.

The giant Shevchenko monument in Poltava. *Sovfoto*

While Tsarist Russia repressed Ukrainian culture, Austria did the opposite in its province of Galicia (western Ukraine). Above is Lvov University where nineteenth-century Austria encouraged Ukrainian studies. *Sovfoto*

northern Ukraine, Tsar Peter the Great routed the combined Swedish-Ukrainian forces. Mazeppa fled to Turkey, and Peter subdued the Ukrainian countryside. The office of hetman was abolished, and Russian colonels took command of the Cossack regiments.

Russian Empress Catherine the Great (1762–96) added more Ukrainian territory to the Tsarist Empire. By victories over the Tatars and Turks, she conquered the entire Ukrainian coastline along the Black Sea. By her three partitions of Poland, Russia annexed most of the Ukrainian lands west of the Dnieper River. But while Catherine united most of the Ukraine, she was an oppressive ruler. Ukrainian free peasants were converted into serfs, and the Russian army destroyed forever the Zaporozhian Sich. Meanwhile, the Polish partitions left Ukrainian Galicia and Bucovina under Austrian control.

During the nineteenth and early twentieth centuries, Ukrainian history was simply a part of the history of Austro-Hungary and Russia. Tsarist rule was cruel. Russian became the official language, and at times the Ukrainian tongue could not be used in printed works. Buildings could not even be designed in Ukrainian architectual style.

In contrast, starting around 1850, Austria began encouraging the Ukrainian desire for independence. Ukrainian cultural studies were revived at Lvov University in Galicia. Tons of Ukrainian nationalist literature were printed in Austrian terri-

World War I: Tsar Nicholas II touring the Ukrainian front. In the front seat (*wearing the belt of bullets*) is a Cossack guard. *Photoworld*

German troops advancing through the ruins of a Ukrainian town, after capturing it during World War I. *Photoworld*

Ukrainian civilians searching for valuables in the ashes of their home destroyed in World War I by a Russo-German battle. *Photoworld*

tories and smuggled into the Russian Ukraine. Knowing that most Ukrainians suffered under Russian tyranny, Austria believed that this propaganda would weaken the Tsarist Empire.

World War I (1914–17) and the Russian Civil War (1918–20) brought only misery to the Ukrainians. In the first of these wars Galicia became a battleground between the Russian and Austro-German armies. Within Russia itself the tsar was overthrown in March 1917 and was succeeded by a weak Provisional Government. A Ukrainian assembly immediately convened in Kiev, demanding Ukrainian autonomy which Russia refused to grant. After Lenin's Bolsheviks had overthrown the Russian Provisional Government, the Ukrainian assembly on January 22, 1918, declared the Ukraine to be an independent nation.

Then came the Russian Civil War, during which five Ukrainian governments competed at times for power. Two were nationalist; one, Communist; another, national Communist; and the fifth, anarchist. At first the German army occupied the Ukraine, but had to withdraw after Germany lost World War I. Red and White Russian forces battled across the Ukrainian steppes. The French occupied the Black Sea coast, hoping to convert the Ukraine into their zone of influence. Then Poland invaded the Ukraine in 1920, only to be driven out by Russia's Red Army.

At the war's end most of the Ukraine was forced to become the Ukrainian Soviet Republic. Galicia passed under Polish rule, and the Carpathian Ukraine (Ruthenia) was awarded by the

Ukrainians excitedly parading in 1918 to celebrate the Ukraine's declaration of independence. *UPI*

Simon Petlyura (*left*) headed the free Ukrainian army which ousted Skoropadski, but was defeated in 1919 by the White Russians. *UPI*

Kaiser Wilhelm II of Germany (*left*) talking with General Pavel Skoropadski—the puppet hetman installed by the Germans when they occupied the Ukraine in early 1918. After German troops withdrew in the fall of 1918, Skoropadski was overthrown by Ukrainian nationalists. *UPI*

General Anton Denikin led the White Russian conquest of the Ukraine in 1919. Within a year, his forces were routed by the Russian Reds. *UPI*

Soldiers of the Ukrainian independence army, which during 1918–20 battled the White Russians, Red Russians, and Poles. In 1920 these fighters for freedom were finally overwhelmed by Lenin's Red Army. *UPI*

As soon as Soviet Russia controlled the Ukraine, Communists began preaching Marxism to Ukrainian youths.
Here Soviet President Mikhail Kalinin propagandizes Ukrainian peasant children. *Photoworld*

With great loss of peasant lives (5,000,000), the Ukrainian countryside was collectivized at gunpoint in the early 1930s. These resentful city girls were ordered into a collective-farm village to help reap the harvest. *UPI*

Communal livestock are often poorly fed, like these bony horses in a Ukrainian collectivized village. *EPA*

In the fall of 1939 the USSR annexed the western Ukraine, which had been under Polish rule since World War I. Soviet-controlled elections, like this one in Lvov, went through the motions of approving this forcible annexation. *Sovfoto*

Western Allies to Czechoslovakia. In 1922 the Soviet Ukraine was formally annexed into the USSR.

Communist control helped develop the Ukraine by eliminating illiteracy and greatly expanding industry. The Ukrainian language could be used freely, and again buildings could be built in Ukrainian architectual style. But the Ukrainians still longed for independence. Members of a secret Ukrainian military organization were discovered in the early 1930s in the ministerial offices of the Soviet Ukrainian government. Gunpoint collectivization of agriculture in the same period caused several million deaths among Ukrainian peasants, and the survivors bitterly hated communism. When Hitler invaded the Ukraine in 1941, many Ukrainians welcomed the German conquerors.

But the Germans continued the hated collective farms, exiled many Ukrainians to slave labor in the Reich, and treated Ukrainians as an inferior race. Soon the Ukrainians formed guerrilla bands

After the smoke of battle cleared: Ukrainian peasants come out of hiding to meet their German conquerors. *Photoworld*

Instead of liberating the Ukrainians, Hitler enslaved them. Here Ukrainian peasants till the fields under the watchful eye of a German guard. *UPI*

July 1941: Hitler's army invading the Ukrainian steppeland. By the end of the year, the entire Ukraine was under Nazi occupation. *UPI*

Ukrainian peasants huddle on the sidelines while Nazi and Soviet troops fight through their village homes. *UPI*

A German antiaircraft gun protects a Ukrainian farm from Soviet air raids, while the peasants bring in the harvest. *UPI*

Nazi troops battling into a Ukrainian village. *UPI*

Ukrainian guerrillas like these harassed the German occupation of 1941/42, then tried to sabotage the Russian reconquest of 1943. They wanted to rid the Ukraine of all alien rulers. *Sovfoto*

German troops trying to locate guerrilla snipers in a Ukrainian peasant village. *UPI*

Ukrainian guerrillas often attacked German vehicles moving along the roads. These Nazi soldiers are trying to defend their motor convoy. *UPI*

Trucks and military cars abandoned by the retreating Germans as Russia's Red Army reconquered the Ukraine in 1943. *Sovfoto*

During World War II, the Nazis brought many Ukrainians into Germany as slave labor. Freed by German defeat, most Ukrainians in Germany refused to return to the USSR, then emigrated to various Western countries. This mother and daughter are living happily today in the United States. *UPI*

which at first harassed the Germans and then fought the Russians, who reconquered the Ukraine during 1943/44.

At the end of the Nazi-Soviet War, Russia tried to flatter the Soviet Ukraine by giving it Galicia, Ruthenia, and Bucovina. Thanks to Stalin's insistence, the Ukrainian Soviet Republic also received a seat in the United Nations. Yet the Ukrainian Soviet government, Communist party, and agricultural officialdom were purged right down to the village level to crush Ukrainian nationalism. Two million Ukrainians were accused of collaborating with the Germans and were deported to other regions of the USSR.

Under Soviet rule some Ukrainians, such as Nikita Khrushchev (former USSR premier), Nikolai Podgorny (USSR president), and Marshal Andrei Grechko (minister of defense), have risen high in the USSR hierarchy. But nationalist guerrillas roamed the Ukrainian forests until the late 1950s, and many Ukrainian writers were purged in the 1960s for criticizing Russian rule. Though they have been taught the Russian language, most steppe peasants refuse to speak it and converse only in Ukrainian. The Ukraine is a powder keg that Moscow finds hard to control.

The Ukraine again under Soviet rule, after World War II: a Kiev parade carrying portraits of Marx, Lenin, and Stalin. *Sovfoto*

Some Russified Ukrainians have risen to high rank in the central government of the USSR. One was Nikita Khrushchev—Soviet dictator from 1957 to 1964. *UPI*

The USSR high command of 1971 (*from left to right*): Defense Minister Andrei Grechko, Communist party Secretary-General Leonid Brezhnev, Premier Aleksei Kosygin, and President Nikolai Podgorny. Grechko and Podgorny are Ukrainians. Brezhnev is a Russian born and raised in the Ukraine. *UPI*

A banner symbolizing Soviet occupation: "Toilers of the hero-city of Kiev! By new labor successes celebrate the 100th anniversary of the birth of Vladimir Ilich Lenin!" On the right stands his giant statue. *Sovfoto*

Selected Bibliography

Areawide

BROWN, J. F. *The New Eastern Europe*. New York: Praeger, 1966.

KASER, MICHAEL. *Comecon*. London: Oxford University Press, 1965.

LONDON, KURT, ed. *Eastern Europe in Transition*. Baltimore: Johns Hopkins University Press, 1966.

SETON-WATSON, HUGH. *The East European Revolution*. New York: Praeger, 1950.

————. *Eastern Europe between the Wars*. New York: Praeger, 1946.

Baltic States

MANNING, CLARENCE A. *The Forgotten Republics*. New York: Philosophical Library, 1952.

PAGE, STANLEY W. *The Formation of the Baltic States*. Cambridge: Harvard University Press, 1959.

TARULIS, ALBERTAS. *Soviet Policy toward the Baltic States*. South Bend: Notre Dame University Press, 1959.

Albania

AMERY, JULIAN. *Sons of the Eagle*. New York: Macmillan, 1949.

GEGAJ, ATHANAS, and KRASNIQI, REXHEP. *Albania*. New York: Free Albania Committee, 1964.

HAMM, HARRY. *Albania: China's Beachhead in Europe*. New York: Praeger, 1963.

NOLI, FAN S. *George Castrioti Scanderbeg*. New York: International Universities Press, 1947.

PANO, NICHOLAS C. *The People's Republic of Albania*. Baltimore: Johns Hopkins University Press, 1968.

SKENDI, STAVRO, ed. *Albania*. New York: Praeger, 1957.

Bulgaria

BLACK, CYRIL EDWIN. *The Establishment of Constitutional Government in Bulgaria*. Princeton: Princeton University Press, 1944.

Bulgaria. New York: Bulgarian National Committee, 1964.

DELLIN, L. A. D., ed. *Bulgaria*. New York: Praeger, 1957.

MACDERMOTT, MERCIA. *A History of Bulgaria, 1393–1885*. London: Allen and Unwin, 1962.

NEWMAN, BERNARD. *Bulgarian Background*. London: Robert Hale, 1961.

ROTHSCHILD, JOSEPH. *The Communist Party of Bulgaria*. New York: Columbia University Press, 1959.

Czechoslovakia

BUSEK, VRATISLAV, and SPULBER, NICHOLAS, eds. *Czechoslovakia*. New York: Praeger, 1957.

Czech Black Book, The. New York: Praeger, 1969.

Czechoslovakia. New York: Assembly of Captive European Nations, 1964.

KORBEL, JOSEF. *The Communist Subversion of Czechoslovakia, 1938–1948*. Princeton: Princeton University Press, 1959.

SCHWARTZ, HARRY. *Prague's 200 Days*. New York: Praeger, 1969.

THOMSON, SAMUEL HARRISON. *Czechoslovakia in European History*. Princeton: Princeton University Press, 1953.

East Germany

BRANT, STEFAN. *The East German Uprising*. New York: Praeger, 1957.

DAVISON, W. PHILLIPS. *The Berlin Blockade*. Princeton: Princeton University Press, 1958.

DORNBERG, JOHN. *The Other Germany*. Garden City: Doubleday, 1968.

GROTHE, PETER. *To Win the Minds of Men: The Story of the Communist Propaganda in East Germany*. Palo Alto: Pacific Books, 1958.

LEONHARD, WOLFGANG. *Child of the Revolution*. Chicago: Regnery, 1958.

NETTL, J. P. *The Eastern Zone and Soviet Policy in Germany, 1945–1950*. New York: Oxford University Press, 1951.

Estonia

Estonia, Independent and a Soviet Colony. New York: Committee for a Free Estonia, 1961.

KAREDA, ENDEL. *Estonia, the Forgotten Nation*. Toronto: Estonian Central Council in Canada, 1961.

KUTT, ALEXANDER, and VAHTER, LEONHARD. *Estonia*. New York: Committee for a Free Estonia, 1964.

NODEL, EMANUEL. *Estonia: Nation on the Anvil*. New York: Bookman Associates, 1963.

RAUD, VILLIBALD. *Estonia, A Reference Book*. New York: Nordic Press, 1953.

UUSTALU, EVALD. *The History of the Estonian Republic*. London: Boreas, 1952.

Hungary

HELMREICH, ERNST C., ed. *Hungary*. New York: Praeger, 1957.

KOVACS, IMRE. *Facts about Hungary*. New York: The

Hungarian Committee, 1966.

LENGYEL, EMIL. *1,000 Years of Hungary.* New York: John Day, 1958.

MACARTNEY, C. A. *Hungary, A Short History.* Chicago: Aldine, 1962.

NAGY, FERENC. *Struggle behind the Iron Curtain.* New York: Macmillan, 1948.

ZINNER, PAUL E. *Revolution in Hungary.* New York: Columbia University Press, 1962.

Latvia

BERZINS, ALFREDS. *The Unpunished Crime.* New York: Robert Speller, 1963.

BILMANIS, ALFRED. *A History of Latvia.* Princeton: Princeton University Press, 1951.

———. *Latvia as an Independent State.* Washington: Latvian Legation, 1947.

Latvia. Washington: American Latvian Association, 1968.

RUTKIS, J., ed. *Latvia, Country and People.* Stockholm: Latvian National Foundation, 1967.

SPEKKE, ARNOLDS. *History of Latvia.* Stockholm: Goppers, 1957.

Lithuania

BUDRECKIS, ALGIRDAS. *The Lithuanian National Revolt of 1941.* Boston: Lithuanian Encyclopedia Press, 1968.

GERUTIS, A. *Lithuania 700 Years.* New York: Manyland Books, 1969.

JURGELA, K. R. *History of the Lithuanian Nation.* New York: Lithuanian Cultural Institute, 1948.

SENN, A. E. *The Emergence of Modern Lithuania.* New York: Columbia University Press, 1959.

VAITIEKUNAS, VYTAUTAS. *Lithuania.* New York: The Committee for a Free Lithuania, 1965.

VARDYS, V. STANLEY, ed. *Lithuania under the Soviets.* New York: Praeger, 1965.

Poland

Cambridge History of Poland. New York: Macmillan, 1941.

COATES, W. P., and COATES, Z. K. *Six Centuries of Russo-Polish Relations.* London: Lawrence and Wishart, 1948.

HALECKI, OSKAR, ed. *Poland.* New York: Praeger, 1957.

MORRISON, JAMES F. *The Polish People's Republic.* Baltimore: Johns Hopkins University Press, 1968.

SYROP, KONRAD. *Spring in October: The Story of the Polish Revolution of 1956.* New York: Praeger, 1958.

ZAWODNY, J. K. *Death in the Forest.* South Bend: Notre Dame University Press, 1962.

Romania

CRETZIANU, ALEXANDRE, ed. *Captive Rumania.* New York: Praeger, 1956.

FISCHER-GALATI, STEPHEN, ed. *Romania.* New York: Praeger, 1957.

———. *Twentieth Century Rumania.* New York: Columbia University Press, 1970.

FLOYD, DAVID. *Rumania: Russia's Dissident Ally.* New York: Praeger, 1965.

IONESCU, GHITA. *Communism in Rumania.* London: Oxford University Press, 1964.

SETON-WATSON, ROBERT W. *A History of the Roumanians.* Cambridge: Cambridge University Press, 1934.

The Ukraine

ALLEN, W. E. D. *The Ukraine: A History.* New York: Cambridge University Press, 1941.

ARMSTRONG, JOHN A. *Ukrainian Nationalism, 1939–1945.* New York: Columbia University Press, 1963.

RESHETAR, JOHN S. *The Ukrainian Revolution, 1917–1920.* Princeton: Princeton University Press, 1952.

SULLIVANT, ROBERT S. *Soviet Politics and the Ukraine.* New York: Columbia University Press, 1963.

VERNADSKY, G. *Bogdan, Hetman of Ukraine.* New Haven: Yale University Press, 1940.

———. *Kievan Russia.* New Haven: Yale University Press, 1948.

Yugoslavia

BASS, ROBERT, and MARBURY, ELIZABETH. *The Soviet-Yugoslav Controversy, 1948–1958.* New York: Prospect Books, 1959.

BYRNES, ROBERT F., ed. *Yugoslavia.* New York: Praeger, 1957.

CLISSOLD, STEPHEN, ed. *A Short History of Yugoslavia: From Early Times to 1966.* Cambridge: Cambridge University Press, 1966.

DEDIJER, VLADIMIR. *Tito.* New York: Simon and Schuster, 1953.

DJILAS, MILOVAN. *Conversations with Stalin.* New York: Harcourt, Brace and World, 1962.

TOMASIC, D. A. *National Communism and Soviet Strategy.* Washington: Public Affairs Press, 1957.

Index

Italic figures refer to illustrations.